# THE PSYCHOTHERAPIST'S GUIDE TO HUMAN MEMORY

# THE
# PSYCHOTHERAPIST'S
# GUIDE TO
# HUMAN MEMORY

## JANET L. JONES
*Fort Lewis College*

A Member of the Perseus Books Group

Copyright © 1999 by Basic Books,
A Member of the Perseus Books Group

A CIP catalog record for this book is available from the Library of Congress.
ISBN: 0-465-08517-2

99  00  01  02  ❖/RRD  10  9  8  7  6  5  4  3  2  1

*The palest ink is better than the sharpest memory.*
—**Chinese proverb**

# Contents

| | | |
|---|---|---|
| 1 | Memory and Self | 1 |
| 2 | Remembrance Then and Now | 11 |
| 3 | Memories from the Cradle | 27 |
| 4 | Accuracy and Confidence | 45 |
| 5 | Construction and Distortion | 61 |
| 6 | Memory and Mood | 79 |
| 7 | Memories for Trauma | 97 |
| 8 | Implicit Recollection | 117 |
| 9 | Hemispheric Differences in Memory | 135 |
| 10 | False Memories | 155 |
| 11 | Enhancing Retrieval | 177 |
| 12 | Bridging the Canyon | 203 |

| | |
|---|---|
| For Further Reading | 227 |
| Notes | 229 |
| Glossary | 255 |
| References | 263 |
| Acknowledgments | 283 |
| About the Author | 285 |
| Index | 287 |

# CHAPTER 1

# Memory and Self

*At the edge of every experience is the refracted light of recollection, snagged there like an image in a beveled mirror.*

**—Carol Shields**

Imagine a day in your life without memory. The first deficits that probably come to mind include failing to recall people's names, losing important objects like your keys or car, or forgetting to carry out routine tasks. Yet a day without memory would also mean that you would not recognize family, friends, and coworkers even if you knew their names, you would not know how to drive the car even if you could find it, and you would not be able to carry out daily tasks even if you remembered to try. Most of us take memory so much for granted that we do not realize its importance. Without it, the knowledge we use in every part of our lives would be bankrupt, leaving us incapable of even the simplest activities. We would not recall where we live or work, who our children or spouses are, what occupation we hold, or what dreams and aspirations we had cherished in the past or hoped for in the future. Without memory, we would not even know who we are.

The beveled mirror of memory distills every experience and emotion, and it builds the beliefs and expectations that cause us to behave in certain ways. It blends these snagged images into our very personalities, fusing inborn character traits with the richness of an individual's environmental past.

Even the life events we record in letters, tapes, and photographs are filtered by reminiscence before they reach page or film, and are then constructed anew when we read, hear, or view them later. Memory sustains relationships of all kinds—relationships with friends, enemies, strangers, coworkers, siblings, sales clerks; relationships among parents and children, teachers and students, physicians and patients, therapists and clients, people and pets, even between human beings and technological machines.

As the engine of personal identity, memory stores our knowledge of self, offers a conscious awareness of being, allows us to present ourselves in an unending variety of ways, imagines different egos, and alters self-concept as needed. It forms a stable personality but simultaneously permits us to change with experience. It also governs creativity, just as Mnemosyne (NEM-uh-zyne), the Greek goddess of memory, rules her nine daughters known as the Muses. And with memory we come closest to mastering time: In many ways, remembrance is our strongest link—indeed, our *only* link—to past, present, and future.

But despite her impressive achievements, Mnemosyne offers no guarantees and relinquishes little control. She usually operates without our conscious guidance to produce results that are as often negative as they are positive, and like an arrogant architect, she designs the mental temple that she thinks we should have rather than the one we really want. Further, the dual nature of her capacity to create and comprehend is riddled with Olympian potholes. Memory comprehends its own creation of self in an inward spiral that encourages egocentrism and thwarts objectivity. To understand oneself through memory requires skill. We explore our distant and recent pasts in the context of an overwhelming present and an uncertain future, reminiscing confidently about our lives and explaining ourselves according to those recollections. Memory seems simple, but like an errant hammer that lands on the thumb as often as it strikes the nail, it can be a difficult tool to use.

Memory and self have attracted attention in recent years, even if the relationship between them remains underemphasized. However, the concepts are by no means new: Ancient scholars contemplated them at length, publishing their ideas in a number of well-known treatises. Two thousand years later, the British philosopher John Locke argued that memory and self are identical, and John Stuart Mill referred to them as "two sides of the same fact."[1] The very foundation of Sigmund Freud's psychoanalytic theory, and its phenomenal influence on all of twentieth-century culture, rests on the connection between memory and self. In fact, memory is a core component of any psychotherapy that relies on clients' recollections and understandings of life events. Current psychologists have even suggested that memory plays an abnormally heightened role in issues of self, either through unique processes of autobiographical remembrance or through greater familiarity with the self as an optimally enriched structure of knowledge.[2]

Despite scholarly scrutiny, the concepts of memory and self remain loosely defined. "Memory" can refer to a broad range of cognitive activities: solving a problem, making decisions, perceiving the external world, using language, recognizing similarities, forming analogies, creating new ideas or inventions, remembering names, thinking, knowing how to ride a bike, understanding why the French Revolution occurred, constructing narrative stories of one's life, recalling what we ate for breakfast, feeling the emotion of a past event . . . the list could go on and on. Even psychologists who have devoted their entire careers to the study of human memory debate the limits of its scope. And "self," a term usually preceded by the modifier "elusive," is even more amorphous. We talk of real selves, possible selves, me-selves, I-selves, and inner selves; self-concept, self-image, self-esteem, self-identity, self-schemas, self-beliefs, self-discrepancies, self-guides; and then of course there is the ubiquitous "I" with whom each of us lives. Perhaps memory and self are merely theoretical constructs or, to extend a recent metaphor, "convenient chapter headings" that help us to organize internal confusion.[3]

Regardless of the fuzziness that surrounds these concepts, psychological scholars, scientists, and practitioners agree that memory and self are crucial features of the mental landscape. Given the central position of memory in creating a self and comprehending it—the very focus of most psychological therapy—one might assume that the empirical study of human memory would be a primary requirement of every psychotherapist's training. But, in fact, it is not.

The 250,000 registered mental health care providers in the United States include doctors of medicine specializing in psychiatry, doctors of philosophy specializing in clinical or counseling psychology, and therapists with master's degrees in counseling psychology or social work.[4] In addition, there are untold numbers of providers who have no formal education or certification. None of these psychological practitioners—licensed, unlicensed, educated, or uneducated—are required to demonstrate empirical knowledge of human memory. And, although many therapists apply *theories* of reminiscence to their work with troubled clients, few apply known facts about the normal processes of remembering and forgetting.

Practitioners whose knowledge of human memory is weak cannot offer the best of psychology to clients at risk, especially when attempting to recover potential recollections of distant events. During the 1990s, a number of cases appeared in which some therapists' slippery grasp of mnemonic fundamentals increased the mental anguish that their clients experienced. More often than not, unlicensed psychotherapists with no formal education in psychology have been blamed for this state of affairs. But pointing the finger at others is always an easier solution than looking deep inside oneself and one's discipline for abandoned responsibility. Although the number of unlicensed and uneducated therapists practicing professional psychology in the United States is disturbing, it should be of even greater concern to us that practitioners with strong credentials seldom understand the normal functions of human memory as creator and comprehender of self.

In 1992, Michael Yapko, a clinical psychologist and marriage/family therapist, conducted a survey of nearly one thousand psychotherapists who held medical, doctoral, or master's degrees in psychology or related fields.[5] The typical survey respondent was forty-four years old, worked in a private clinical practice, and had been providing psychotherapy professionally for an average of eleven years. The survey results demonstrate a shocking degree of dangerous misinformation concerning the basic facts of human memory. To give readers a full account of these results, I quote some of the statements used in Yapko's survey and provide the percentage of respondents who agreed that each statement was true.

- "The mind is like a computer, accurately recording events as they actually occurred." 33 percent agreed

- "Events that we know occurred but can't remember are repressed memories—i.e., memories that are psychologically defended against." 59 percent agreed

- "If someone doesn't remember much about his or her childhood, it is most likely because it was somehow traumatic." 49 percent agreed

- "One's level of certainty about a memory is strongly positively cor-related with that memory's accuracy." 24 percent agreed

- "I believe that early memories, even from the first year of life, are accurately stored and retrievable." 41 percent agreed

- "Hypnosis enables people to accurately remember things they oth-erwise could not." 75 percent agreed

- "Therapists can have greater faith in details of a traumatic event when obtained hypnotically than otherwise." 47 percent agreed

- "Hypnosis can be used to recover memories of actual events as far back as birth." 54 percent agreed

- "Hypnotically obtained memories are more accurate than simply just remembering." 43 percent agreed[6]

All of these statements are known to be false. Some of the empirical facts they disclaim have been common knowledge within experimental psychology for more than sixty years. In every instance, no evidence exists to support the statement, while a great deal of evidence exists to refute it.

Yapko's results are not the only indications that there is a perplexing knowledge gap in the minds of many psychotherapists. A more recent survey, conducted in 1995 by Debra Poole and her colleagues, shows widespread use of highly suggestive techniques of memory therapy among licensed psychotherapists with doctoral degrees in clinical psychology.[7] For example, 41 percent relied on dream interpretation to recover accurate memories of life events, 40 percent used family photographs and journaling to boost clients' recall, and 32 percent used hypnosis to enhance recall despite its well-known inability to do so. In addition, these clinical psychologists demonstrated a sharp lack of agreement as to the appropriateness of such techniques for producing useful recollections. Thus, 27 percent of the survey respondents disapproved of journaling techniques and dream interpretation for the purpose of recovering accurate memories, and 30 percent disapproved of the use of hypnosis in memory recovery. These techniques are useful in certain settings for specific reasons, of course, but not for the express purpose of improving the accuracy of a client's recollections. In fact, each of the three techniques mentioned here is known to increase suggestibility, reduce recall accuracy, and boost confidence in incorrect memories.

Based on their results, Poole and her colleagues argue that there is "an urgent need to investigate the safety of memory-focused therapy."[8] They estimate that hundreds of thousands of clients are receiving such treatment from licensed clinical psychologists each year. This estimate does not address the larger combined number of clients who are seen by licensed counseling psychologists, psychiatrists, and social workers, or by unlicensed providers.

Why do highly educated, well-qualified practitioners lack the knowledge of memory needed to provide the best therapy for their clients? I would argue that there are a number of interconnected reasons, some based in the discipline of psychology itself and others in our culture at large. We live in an anti-intellectual society that derides legitimate expertise while it glorifies the words that drop from the ignorant lips of our grotesquely paid celebrities. Thus, Americans listen enraptured when Roseanne Barr says that she has recovered memories from infancy, but we change channels on the rare occasions that a qualified scholar of infant memory is invited to present the facts. Attention spans decrease as daily workloads increase: We find ourselves able to listen for ten seconds but no more, just long enough to hear a misleading sound bite of inaccurate news. Few of us bother to delve into a topic deeply enough to gain a genuine understanding of its complexities and contradictions, apparently forgetting Pope's maxim that "a little learning is a dangerous thing."[9] Increasing reliance on technology exacerbates the problem: In their zeal to surf the net, many Americans fail to grasp the distinction between educated knowledge and expensive computers. We are tempted to spend five minutes purchasing the computer instead of five years gaining the knowledge that will allow us to effectively use the information pouring from the computer. In addition, our cultural misunderstanding of postmodern philosophy, fueled by inaccurate political rhetoric, has led us to suspect that in the contemporary world there are no truths, there are no facts; therefore, Roseanne's pronouncements about infant memory and the qualified scholar's are equally valid. Such falsehoods lead people to believe that knowledge is mere folly.

Those who know little of a subject tend to assume there is little to be known. This assumption proceeds in circular fashion to the destructive myth—so popular in American society—that the functioning of the human mind and brain is a dark mystery that even specialists do not comprehend.

Applied to human memory, this myth appears all too frequently even in intellectual literature. For example, one professor of history argues that "there is very little that is certain about [memory]. Despite the enormous amount of ongoing research, our knowledge . . . remains rudimentary."[10] More likely, it is this historian's knowledge of memory that remains rudimentary, just as my grasp of recent scholarship in history is weak. People who truly believe that little is known about the human mind and brain should be consigned to ten years' hard reading in a library of cognitive science containing volumes of pertinent intelligence from neurology, philosophy, linguistics, anthropology, computer science, and cognitive psychology.

Of course, uncertainties do exist. That we know a lot about memory does not mean we know everything. After all, we study an object—the human brain—that is believed to be the singularly most complex entity in the universe. Nonetheless, many of the principles by which memory operates are strongly supported and well known among specialists in relevant disciplines. They are waiting to be shared with practitioners who use remembrance, either directly or indirectly, as a psychotherapeutic tool.

Within the discipline of psychology reside further reasons for the qualified practitioner's perplexity about how people remember. Given the interdependence between memory and self, it is a travesty of psychological expertise that not even one course in the empirical study of human memory is required in master's, medical, or doctoral degree programs for budding mental health professionals. Most universities offer such courses on a regular basis, but only the students in areas of experimental psychology are encouraged to take them. Moreover, the typical course in human memory is so deeply immersed in the arcane practices of the laboratory as to impoverish the educations of both experimental and clinical students. People who wish to practice real therapy with real clients are unlikely to become intrigued by a subtopic of psychology that appears to be abstruse.

These disciplinary factors are intensified by their context: The traditional split between clinical and experimental psychology, ever widening since the discipline was founded, has become a gaping chasm that rivals the Grand Canyon. Each side assumes that the other has nothing to offer. Meanwhile, we lament a growing sense of fragmentation within the discipline, as if we are only suddenly aware of the cliffside strata that have marked psychology's evolution.

Not surprisingly, most individuals prefer to sidestep the quagmires of mistrust that psychological fragmentation has created. Instead of crossing enemy lines into the experimental bailiwick to enroll in an unrequired memory course, responsible practitioners may seek informal methods of bolstering their knowledge. Indeed, monographs, textbooks, and journal articles are available on the topic by the tens of thousands. But here we enter yet another area of difficulty: The specialized literature, while rich in content, is so replete with convoluted syntax and esoteric argot as to be nearly incomprehensible to the uninitiated reader. Textbooks tend to be tedious and long-winded, written for an audience very different from that of the professional psychotherapist. Although the clinical literature contains a few articles applying empirical principles of memory to therapeutic settings and situations,[11] they usually do so in a didactic manner that instructs more than it informs. Such instruction, while useful, prevents therapists from gaining general information about remembrance that they can tailor to an assortment of their own clients' needs, with all the specificity that each unique individual requires. And until now, no basic guide to the empirical knowledge of human memory has been composed expressly for psychological practitioners.

So, although some help is available for the resourceful therapist, those who wish to enlarge their general grasp of human remembrance quickly seem to be foiled at every turn. Therefore, this book is designed to achieve three primary goals: First, it serves as a concise introduction to the basic principles of remembering and forgetting that are likely to be especially important in therapeutic settings. Second, it acts as a compass to guide readers through the jungle of existing memory literature without getting lost. Third, it uses the topic of memory as a prime example of the need for mutual collaboration between clinical and experimental forms of psychology. Throughout the book I have tried to explain mnemonic principles in clear language that accurately conveys the empirical research but eliminates most of the technical jargon that saturates experimental psychology. Most of the research results I present have undergone extensive replication using both laboratory and naturalistic methods of inquiry. Preliminary findings, speculative interpretations, and unsupported theories are included only occasionally and are carefully identified. This book certainly does not attempt to tell therapists how to do their work; instead, I have tried to present knowledge in a very general way so that practitioners can fashion their own applications to specific clients and problems.

Following a brief historical overview of memory science and scholarship, eight subsequent chapters address memories from infancy; confidence and accuracy in recollection; memory construction and distortion; the effects of emotion, mood, and trauma on reminiscence; implicit recollection; hemispheric differences in remembering; and the creation of illusory memories. Using knowledge from these chapters as a platform, I then offer an array of proven techniques that can enhance memory retrieval, and I show why other procedures can be harmful. The book ends with a broader view of the relationship between clinical and experimental psychology as it pertains to the future study of human memory. At that point I consider the consequences—to all psychologists, to knowledge of the human mind and brain, to clients in desperate need of help, and to the discipline of psychology itself—of allowing the abyss between experimental and clinical territories to enlarge. Finally, I offer a few humble suggestions for change.

To serve its ambitions as a guide, the final pages of this book contain extensive source documentation in the form of notes, an alphabetical list of references, a glossary of terms, a list of suggestions for further reading, a list of common journals that publish basic memory research, and a detailed index. Endnotes are identified with superscript numbers throughout the book, to rescue readers from the inevitable thicket of names and dates that APA-style citations impose. I hope readers will use the endnotes to verify my claims, evaluate them critically, or learn more about a particular topic. All of the original sources can be acquired through a college library or bookstore. The glossary of terms is intended to help those individuals who elect to read original studies that are published in the specialized memory literature. These aids are offered in the sincere spirit of providing reference information that may be of constructive use.

This book is not limited to psychotherapists who specialize in topics of trauma or memory recovery. Because of its constant but dynamic interconnection with the human self, I hold a strong conviction that memory is an integral part of every psychotherapeutic experience. This means that the principles presented in this guide must be accessible to all psychological practitioners regardless of their specific orientations. In accord with that belief, I use the term "psychotherapist" to refer to anyone who provides psychological therapy. I ask readers to understand that writing for such a broad audience—comprised of individuals whose educational backgrounds, professional experiences, and psychological knowledge bases differ dramatically—is a dangerous undertaking. When expository choices had to be made, I erred on the side of simplicity, but at no point in this book do I wish to insult any reader's intelligence.

I hope this guide will provide useful information to all psychotherapists. It represents only one attempt to bridge a tiny span of the canyon that separates clinical and experimental camps, but perhaps it can serve as a catalyst, encouraging more psychologists from both sides to share their knowledge with each other. Our mutual effort will improve both the quality of care that psychological clients receive and the quality of knowledge that psychological researchers discover about the innermost workings of the human mind and brain.

# CHAPTER 2

# Remembrance Then and Now

*The mind fits the world and shapes it as a river fits and shapes its own banks.*

—**Annie Dillard**

Although people of many cultures have been fascinated with human memory for millennia, its prominence as a scholarly topic waxes and wanes with disciplinary paradigm shifts and cultural fluctuations. For example, the 1880s stand out as a time when memory was explored in a societal milieu that was as intrigued by amnesia, hysteria, and multiple personality as it was determined to create a new discipline of psychology based entirely on the scientific method. Almost exactly one century later, cognitive science, an interdisciplinary study of the human mind that employs a wider variety of methodologies, was developed partly to extend memory scholarship; this occurred just prior to the recovered memory movement's domination of American media. Looking over the centuries with a broader view, the forces of modernity—especially their emphasis on self, privacy, and individualism—also shaped the study of human memory and its application in clinical settings.

## MEMORY AMONG THE PHILOSOPHERS

Ancient scholars of both Eastern and Western traditions considered memory one of their primary topics. The Chinese believed that memory should be developed through experiential practice, as a spiritual way of overcoming

11

self-consciousness and therefore mastering the mind.[1] Thus, while Western tradition tends to separate action from knowledge, Eastern philosophy holds that action *is* knowledge. The Chinese emphasis on rote memorization emerged at a later time, largely in response to political needs.

That the ancients of Western tradition also held memory in high esteem is evidenced by their belief in gods and goddesses who governed learning, memory, and wisdom. The oldest known is probably Thoth, memory god of the Egyptians between 3000 and 4000 B.C.[2] Considered the ruler of Egypt before the arrival of mortal kings, Thoth invented writing, developed the calendar, healed with magic, and judged innocence or guilt according to personal standards of authenticity. Five millennia later, memory is still linked to language, time, healing, and truth. Mnemosyne, whom you have already met in chapter 1, was exalted in ancient Greece around 1000 B.C.[3] The daughter of heaven (Uranus) and Earth (Gaea), she ruled memory and inspiration through her offspring, the nine Muses. Minerva served as the Roman goddess of memory near the same time.[4]

Western dignitaries from 550 B.C. to A.D. 270 often mentioned memory in their writings,[5] but Plato and Aristotle were the first to attempt to explain how memory works.[6] Plato's doctrine of reminiscence presented the extreme nativist view that all knowledge exists in the immortal soul at birth, gained during previous lives of learning. Thus, he argued in *Meno* that "all inquiry and all learning is but recollection,"[7] exalting memory as the door to knowledge and spirituality. Instead of learning anew, we need only remember what our souls already know. Aristotle's doctrine of abstraction, on the other hand, devalued memory as merely a faculty of sense perception that is dependent on time. He postulated an active intellect that creates general concepts by abstracting imaged forms from sense impressions. These abstract concepts are then remembered by virtue of association, so that certain thoughts or events are recalled in connection with each other. The classic laws of association, originating with Aristotle and developing further under the British empiricists, are based on contiguity in space or time, simultaneity, and contrast.

In addition to conceiving the doctrines of reminiscence and abstraction, Plato and Aristotle proffered a bevy of questions about memory that remain the object of inquiry today: How is memory different in youth and old age? What happens to our knowledge of unattended events? Which method of mental organization yields the best retention and recall? How important is frequency of repetition? Do animals other than humans have memory and, if so, how does it work? What are the potential links between memory and intelligence? Do different emotions cause us to remember in different ways? And how is mental illness connected to memory? Some of these topics were rejuvenated by Augustine (A.D. 354–430), who extended the scholarship on emotion and memory, and by Aquinas (1225–1274), who sharpened Aristotle's ideas concerning the use of active intellect during abstraction.

Plato's and Aristotle's philosophical interest in remembrance was undoubtedly heightened by the Sophist emphasis on rhetoric. To enhance the persuasive nature of their oratory, elite youth of Greece were taught to organize, remember, and present their ideas according to memorization techniques such as the method of loci. The use of memory as a rhetorical aid persisted through Roman times, with mnemonics advocated by Cicero and Quintilian. During the medieval age, troubadours traveled from one village to the next relating to the illiterate masses the news of the day in rhyme and song. The best troubadours were renowned for their ability to memorize hundreds of new lines of poetry after listening to them only three times, and rhyme remained in use for most written documents until the fourteenth century.[8]

Skipping forward to the seventeenth century, the British philosopher John Locke was one of the first Westerners to consider in depth the connection between memory and personal identity. He argued that identity takes two forms: a forensic ("person") identity and a physical ("man") identity. Forensic identity was based on memory and responsibility, generated in light of social questions concerning the legal accountability of people who had no memory of their actions. Should a somnambulist, for example, be punished for a crime committed during the dissociated state? Locke said yes, on the grounds that forensic identity required full accountability for one's behavior regardless of whether it was recalled. He even went on to say that memory *is* identity, an equation that was contested in subsequent years to create a philosophical debate that continues today.[9]

## MEMORY IN EARLY PSYCHOLOGY

The study of memory remained the province of philosophers and orators until psychology was founded as a separate discipline in the late 1800s. At that time, three strands converged to alter the course of memory scholarship significantly. First, the early clinicians, including Sigmund Freud, Jean Charcot, and Pierre Janet, developed theories proposing that unconscious knowledge of past events was instrumental in the development of normal and pathological personalities.[10] Their success in treating patients with amnesia, hysteria, and dissociative states fascinated the lay public, spawning a host of literary narratives that dramatized disorders such as split personality and fugue. Second, Paul Broca's neurological autopsies of aphasics showed that mental faculties of language production are linked to an area near the Sylvian fissure in the left frontal lobe of the brain. Such precise localization implied that mental abilities of all kinds might be governed by specific areas of neuroanatomy, a suggestion that galvanized neurological research on patients with rare organic disorders. Third, within the new discipline of psychology, Hermann Ebbinghaus demonstrated in his research on normal forgetting that memory could be studied scientifically.

Ebbinghaus is considered the patriarch of empirical research on memory. Having written his dissertation on the unconscious mind just six years prior to the official founding of psychology by Wilhelm Wundt in 1879, Ebbinghaus inflicted upon himself the daily memorization of hundreds of meaningless syllables such as "zud." His intent was to study memory scientifically, just as Gustav Fechner had scrutinized the psychological perceptions of brightness and loudness using scientific techniques. In simplified terms, this entailed conducting a series of controlled experiments in which Ebbinghaus memorized nonsense syllables, then recorded those he was able to recall after various retention intervals had passed. Although I must admit that his research ranks among the most boring investigations of memory, it also occupies an honorable position among the signal inquiries that sculpted the face of experimental psychology.

Ebbinghaus's research program was a radical course of action: Even the scientistic Wundt had argued that faculties such as memory and language would never be amenable to scientific inquiry. But Ebbinghaus succeeded in controlling the variables of word meaning and timing of presentation, producing experimental results that showed the rate of forgetting over time as well as the amount of time saved in relearning forgotten nonsense syllables. These results allowed him to prove to the burgeoning but skeptical psychological community that memory could be studied scientifically. Indeed, his research—more in methodology than results—has influenced an entire century of memory scholarship.[11]

Cultural ingredients were also important to the advancement of memory scholarship during the late 1800s. This period is known for the moral chaos of *fin de siècle*, the concept of private self as a cornerstone of modernity, and the proliferation of science as an epistemological worldview and as a boon to the technology that would take over twentieth-century life. The philosopher Ian Hacking argues that factors of modernity were crucial in conceiving the idea that human memory is an objective body of knowledge to be explored, creating a Foucaultian *savoir*, or implicit paradigm, that provided "new kinds of truths-or-falsehoods, new kinds of facts, new objects of knowledge."[12] This tacit epistemological change altered the very questions that could be asked and the types of answers that would be considered, not only within the discipline but also in the whole of society. Issues that had previously been addressed at a moral level of value judgment were now ostensibly subject to scientific inquiry.

The soul, which Hacking characterizes as "the last bastion of thought free of scientific scrutiny"[13] in the nineteenth century, could now be understood. But that potential understanding was purchased at a high price: The soul would become a self, and the self would rely completely on memories. By substituting memory for soul, issues that were considered spiritual or moral in earlier times were taken over in the late 1800s by the psychiatric, neurological, and experimental sciences of memory. Hacking maintains that we live today with the legacy of this Faustian bargain, seeking to avoid the discomfort of making absolute moral judgments by leaning instead on scientific fact.

The disciplinary strands of the late 1800s are paradoxical in some ways. Although Freud, Broca, and Ebbinghaus were all studying memory at the same time, they were not converging on—or constructing together—the same body of theoretical and empirical knowledge about memory. In fact, there is no indication that the three ever attempted to collaborate with each other. As an eminent member of the official psychology, Ebbinghaus would have been loath to work with Freud, whose ideas were considered bizarre and unscientific by mainstream psychologists and therefore dangerous to the public acceptance of psychology as a science. Furthermore, experimental psychologists (Ph.D.s) of the time came from vastly different backgrounds than did neurologists and psychiatrists (M.D.s) whose work was considered a form of medical treatment that was in no way linked to the academic discipline of "psychology." The early psychologists—Wundt, Ebbinghaus, Fechner, and Edward Titchener—strenuously avoided connections with Freudian psychoanalysis or the popular occult ("psychical") arts because they feared that such bonds would cast doubt on their definition of psychology as an empirical science.

This is not to say that there was no crossover whatsoever between researchers and practitioners. Ebbinghaus did, for example, apply his study of the effects of fatigue to the memories of school pupils, and one of Wundt's Ph.D. students, Emil Kraepelin, went on to classify mental illnesses and explore the psychopathology of memory. Nevertheless, such cross-fertilization was rare. Even the official founding of clinical psychology in 1896 by another Ph.D. student of Wundt's, Lightner Witmer, was trivialized by mainstream psychologists for decades.

Following Ebbinghaus's lead in quantifying memory through science, early psychologists invented the memory drum, pursuit rotor, and stylus maze to investigate learning in human subjects.[14] They supplemented these apparatus with word stimuli such as paired associates to accompany the omnipresent nonsense syllable. Results were encouraging: Research on human learning conducted during the early 1900s showed that recognition superseded recall, that meaning aids memory, that practice is more effective when distributed than massed, that forgetting is caused not only by decay but also by interference, and that items presented at the beginning and end of a list are remembered more accurately than items presented in the middle of a list.

## THE BEHAVIORIST INFLUENCE

Soon, however, behaviorism gained increasing acceptance in American psychology, with the study of internal mental processes losing favor to an obsession with external stimulus and response. The mind, to the behaviorist, was merely a black box containing faculties that psychology could not, and should not, explore. Studies of animal learning became prolific, with Edward Thorndike's cats emerging from their puzzle boxes, Ivan Pavlov's dogs salivating at the associated bell, John Watson's hungry rats running tight mazes, and B. F. Skinner's pigeons pecking at varied rates according to different schedules of reinforcement. As the study of memory regressed, serious problems began to emerge from the learning fray. The preponderance of experimental results was acquired through research on animals, not humans, and the research focused almost exclusively on acquisition of habits rather than storage or recall of cognitive knowledge. Even if one accepted these experimental results as worthy of attention, they were overrunning the discipline with no theories offered to make sense of their meaning. Furthermore, psychologists began to realize that this kind of animal learning was not what most people thought of when they referred to "memory." If anything, it is exactly this type of research that has pushed many people away from a deeper understanding of human remembrance.

By the late 1950s a mounting number of psychologists had chafed under these constraints long enough and were ready to force open new territory that would permit—even encourage—them to investigate the intricacies of the working mind: perception, language, memory, and thought, in every detail of all their magnificence. If the work exemplified by Freud, Broca, and Ebbinghaus created a river of memory research near the end of the nineteenth century, the cognitive revolution sparked by Noam Chomsky, George Miller, and Ulric Neisser around 1960 was the equivalent of an ocean.

## THE COGNITIVE REVOLUTION

The cognitive psychologists differed dramatically from the behaviorists when they outlined their plans for the study of mental processing. No longer would psychology be dependent on laboratory rats; no longer would human knowledge be sketched as little more than positive and negative reinforcement; no longer would the grandeur of memory be limited to a puny behaviorist definition of learning. Skinner's pecking pigeons gave way to Chomsky's psycholinguistics, the study of the psychology of human language in which the internal processes of the black box were primary in importance. Meanwhile, Miller augmented his studies of language with forays into the capacity of working memory, yielding his classic "magic number" seven as the number of information chunks that could be manipulated simultaneously in the conscious mind. Neisser was instrumental as the revolutionary who took a broader look at what cognitive psychology could become, describing his vision in a 1967 book that called lagging psychologists to the front: *Cognitive Psychology*.[15] But the killing blow to behaviorism was Chomsky's well-supported theory of childhood language acquisition, which made Skinner's meager explanation look like a kindergarten game.[16]

As investigations into the psychology of language skyrocketed, memory became an acceptable topic of study once again. That psychology was ready for a revolution is corroborated by the fact that within approximately ten years, from about 1960 to about 1970, the majority of behaviorists changed their allegiance and began to conduct research within the cognitive realm.[17]

Since then, cognitive research has monopolized the field of experimental psychology. Most graduate schools in psychology today have no behaviorist program,[18] and working behaviorists are few and far between. One even refers to his specialty as "ghettoized."[19] The small number of radical behaviorists who do continue their research today seem to spend more time defending their field's existence than contributing to the literature of human psychological functioning. Meanwhile, the cognitive attitude has seeped deeply into most other areas of psychology: social, developmental, physiological, clinical, counseling, and even comparative. The creation of newer areas such as health and sport psychologies is a direct result of the cognitive revolution as well.

Despite its errors, the behaviorist tradition may have helped to ground psychology as a socially accepted discipline in the United States from 1920 until 1960. It provided the public with an understanding of the practical applications of the new discipline, and it established some basic principles of human behavior that have supplied an important foundation for further work. In addition, there is no doubt that behaviorist principles function well in the treatment of certain mental disorders, such as phobia and autism, or that the tools of positive and negative reinforcement have improved parental child-rearing practices as well as adult motivation. At the same time, however, behaviorism pulled turn-of-the-century psychologists away from crucial topics of the human psyche, forcing the discipline into a straitjacket of rules and limitations. To this day a frightening proportion of the lay public speaks of our discipline as little more than rats in a maze, assuming that all "experimental psychology" is behaviorist and that all "real psychology" is psychotherapy. They are not aware that most experimental psychologists work with human subjects and have never touched a laboratory rat.

The cognitive revolution in psychology has now fueled nearly forty years of research and theory on human memory, molding a strong body of knowledge about how memory actually works. It has been aided by impressive technological advances, such as image scans that form pictures of the functioning human brain, and by the development of complex experimental paradigms that enable us to discover the operations of invisible mental processes. Members of the cognitive revolution have also learned from their mistakes. We now realize that early cognitive theories of memory, such as the Atkinson and Shiffrin model of a unitary process divided into three categories—perceptual memory, short-term memory, and long-term memory—were far too simplistic. The wholesale application of information processing theory to the human mind was misconceived as well; with its flowcharts of input, output, and intervening processes, it sometimes looks like merely a more complicated version of the behaviorist's black box. The metaphor of the computer was overused and underdefined during the early years of cognitive psychology, implying incorrectly that humans were nothing more than machines. This implication deterred researchers who might otherwise have broadened their scope to include such topics as intuition, emotion, innovation, and creativity.

One of the strongest complaints came from Neisser himself, who argued in 1976 that cognitive psychology had become narrow and unproductive, yielding a litany of tedious results that had little bearing on everyday life.[20] In 1982 he extended that argument to studies of human memory, which were root-bound in controlled laboratory settings and recondite tasks.[21] Cognitive psychology, in the opinion of this leading cognitive psychologist, had offered nothing more than a "thundering silence" on important issues of everyday memory and, worse yet, had provided in twenty years of research only simple generalizations that were "familiar to the average middle-class third grader in America."[22] The important questions of memory—those asked by curious friends and intrigued acquaintances—were being ignored.

A few cognitive psychologists refuted Neisser's criticism, stating imperiously that psychology is not responsible for explaining memory to the general population. After all, they asked, "what other science . . . has established that its students should decide on the importance of questions by checking first with Aunt Martha?"[23] It is precisely this sort of arrogant attitude that has destroyed the public's faith in experimental psychology over the years. Fortunately, most of us took Neisser's warnings seriously, and several psychological leaders attacked the Aunt Martha rhetoric in a special issue of *American Psychologist*.[24] During the 1980s and 1990s, the science of memory has expanded from its narrow beginnings to include topics of everyday importance such as autobiographical memory, flashbulb memory, childhood amnesia, memory for names, foreign language learning, prospective memory for upcoming events and appointments, source amnesia, absentmindedness, involuntary memory, retention of school lessons, memory under stress, exceptional memory, narrative memory in literature and drama, eidetic imagery (better known as "photographic" memory), script memorization by actors, and a host of amnesias that alter forever the lives of a swelling number of brain injury victims in industrialized countries. As Endel Tulving, one of the most renowned memory scholars today, pointed out with respect to this burgeoning interest in naturalistic recollection, "There is room for many different kinds of facts and ideas about memory and for many approaches."[25]

## COGNITIVE SCIENCE

The widening scope of memory scholarship was also aided by the development of cognitive science during the mid–1980s. The term "cognitive science" is often misunderstood, being used inaccurately at times as a synonym for "artificial intelligence," "information processing," "experimental psychology," and "cognitive psychology." Those of us who call ourselves "cognitive scientists" suffer the amorphous definition gladly, taking comfort in the fact that at least it is less ambiguous than "cognitive psychologist" (often misinterpreted as signifying a psychotherapist who offers cognitive treatment) or "experimental psychologist" (including virtually every psychological specialization, even clinical, as long as the individual in question conducts some form of scientific research, which need not even be experimental). Moreover, neither of these terms carries the connotation of interdisciplinary work that is the hallmark of cognitive science. The field includes scholars from anthropology, neurology, philosophy, computer science, linguistics, and cognitive psychology who work together to broaden disciplinary perspectives, share knowledge across disciplines, and increase the number of acceptable methodologies far beyond the strict scientific experiment.[26]

Cognitive science has already yielded impressive insight into the human mind and brain, especially in the area of neurobiology of memory. That the field is likely to continue to blossom is suggested by the number of departments of cognitive science and neuroscience at undergraduate and graduate institutions in which psychologists now work apart from their colleagues in traditional psychology departments but closely with members of these other disciplines. Our common bond is, quite simply, a deep desire to understand the human mind and brain, regardless of the categorical cubbyholes in which our disciplines attempt to contain us.

In addition to the development of cognitive science, which opened the floodgates of memory research, we also have gained greater knowledge about memory in recent years because of the push toward applied knowledge. Alzheimer's disease, which attacks a growing number of Americans as greater proportions of the population live to an older age, has compelled researchers in many areas to learn more about memory so that this tragic illness can someday be treated or even cured. The possibility that traumatic memories affect people's lives long after the trauma occurred, whether consciously or unconsciously, has caused memory scholars to look much more carefully at the effects of stress on retention and recall of past events. The increase in amnesia victims, due to technological advances that permit us to save the lives of brain-injured people who in past years would have died from their accidents, is another important reason for the drive in memory research toward practical solutions as well as pure knowledge.

## MEMORY TERMINOLOGY TODAY

With the historical background in mind, we can begin to consider some of the knowledge about human memory that has been constructed during four decades of cognitive research and scholarship. But first we need to address the daunting vocabulary that infiltrates the memory literature, so that you can become familiar with common terms prior to their use in subsequent chapters. All of them are contained in the glossary at the end of this book if you need to refresh your memory of their meanings. By explaining the basic terminology, rather than translating it into common parlance, I hope to give psychotherapists a better opportunity to continue learning more about memory after reading this book.

Although their usage is subsiding in favor of more precise terms, two of the most common phrases appearing in the literature are short-term memory and long-term memory. I introduce them primarily to explain their inherent ambiguities. The term "short-term memory" alone is responsible for a great deal of confusion among researchers, practitioners, and the lay public. Most people assume it refers to our memories of events that occurred in the past day or so. Psychological practitioners extend the definition to cover events up to a week old.[27] However, in the jargon of cognitive research, short-term memory is reserved for one's conscious awareness of thoughts or events occurring in the immediate present. For example, the words you are reading right now are entering your short-term memory, and it is there that you have conscious knowledge of their existence. If you stop reading, you will probably be able to remember the last seven words or so because they are being held momentarily in your short-term memory. Once you continue reading without repeating those words to yourself, in just a few seconds they will either pass from short-term memory into long-term memory, where they may be stored verbatim or (more likely) as gist, or they will drop forgotten into the nebulous waters of the river Lethe. In the terminology of memory research, then, what you ate for breakfast this morning and what you saw out the window five minutes ago are not represented in short-term memory. They are either in long-term memory, or they are gone. The distinction will become important when we begin to consider empirical knowledge of human memory in subsequent chapters. Attempts to reconcile the confusing terminology have only resulted thus far in a proliferation of synonyms: "Short-term memory" (by its cognitive denotation) is now often called "working memory," "immediate memory," or "active memory."

The phrase "long-term memory" has been superseded by division into a number of more precise categories, but it, too, remains omnipresent in the published literature. It refers to all memories of facts, events, and procedures held in the mind. Some of these memories are available for recall or recognition; others are not. I do not mean to suggest, however, that all experienced events are stored in long-term memory; much of our daily lives is never held in memory but simply forgotten as soon as it occurs. Nor are we conscious of the representations stored in long-term memory; instead, they are held unconsciously until they are recalled into conscious awareness. Once pulled back into consciousness, they reside momentarily in short-term memory, while we think about them, then return to long-term memory for further retention.

## MULTIPLE MEMORY SYSTEMS

As you can see, the phrase "long-term memory" is so overgeneralized that it can refer to nearly everything about the entire prospect of the human mind. For this reason, and because we now know that different memory systems function in different neurological ways for various types of stored knowledge, long-term memory has been divided into a number of more specific categories. The trend toward multiple memory systems is propelled mostly by Tulving's convincing arguments that semantic, episodic, and procedural memories are subserved by disparate brain structures and functions, and, therefore, should not be lumped together into one all-purpose box. Semantic memory (sometimes called declarative memory) refers to one's knowledge of factual information, such as the date of the American Constitution's signing or the make of a particular car. It seems to be subserved primarily by the medial temporal lobe and diencephalon of the brain. Episodic memory is highly dependent on the frontal lobes and holds information concerning past events, such as the look on my husband's face when I told him I was thinking about writing another book. Tulving has defined the episodic system as governing memories of "the self's experiences in subjective space and time." The third type of memory, procedural, contains our knowledge of how to carry out skills that we have learned to do at some time in our lives—how to ride a bicycle, ice skate, or type, for example. It is mediated at least partly by the basal ganglia of the brain.[28]

Evidence that the three memory systems are separate is found in laboratory experiments and neuropsychological case studies. Tulving, for example, presents the case of an amnesic (K. C.) whose semantic memory is intact but whose episodic memory is seriously deficient. K. C. can recall accurately that he owned a particular car of a specific color and make, but he cannot recall a single instance in which he actually went somewhere in the car.[29] Similarly, many amnesics who have very poor semantic or episodic memories can still perform skills and procedures with alacrity.

The categories of semantic, episodic, and procedural memory are not mutually exclusive. In fact, they overlap to a great extent. For example, doing annual income taxes requires semantic memory for the type of information needed and procedural memory for the practice of filling out the tax form. Our knowledge of where and when we usually carry out the income tax procedure—at a brown desk in the middle bedroom, for instance—would be considered episodic. In addition, certain activities could fit as easily into one category as another: Finding the bathroom in a new friend's house might require semantic memory (you know where bathrooms are usually located in houses), episodic memory (you remember the friend telling you where the bathroom was on a previous occasion), or procedural memory (based on previous experience, you walk to the bathroom by following a path of left and right turns with little conscious awareness of exactly where the room will be).

Tulving argues that memory systems are further distinguished from one another by the form of conscious awareness that accompanies them. Episodic memory for specific events in certain times and places is characterized by a feeling of reexperiencing the original event. In other words, instead of merely knowing that some event occurred, we feel almost as if it is happening again, making "then" into a slightly altered form of "now." On the other hand, semantic memory is rarely accompanied by this type of awareness (called "autonoetic"), and procedural memory is usually not conscious at all. Thus, when we use a fact of knowledge, we do not reexperience our learning of it, and when we carry out some procedure from long ago, our bodies seem to respond automatically. Research continues on the links between differing types of awareness and distinct memory systems, as well as the neurological substrate for each.

Recollection can also be explicit or implicit. Explicit memories—whether semantic, episodic, or procedural—are characterized by awareness that we have the knowledge. On the other hand, implicit memories usually sneak up on us, providing tacit knowledge that seems rather surprising. As you might expect, semantic and episodic memories are often explicit, while procedural memories are frequently implicit. Of course, under certain conditions, this rough generalization also breaks down. In fact, one relatively recent trend in new memory research focuses on implicit recollection of semantic and episodic knowledge.

## AUTOBIOGRAPHICAL MEMORY

Autobiographical memory, or knowledge of one's life experiences and self-identity, is a critical part of our foray into empirical knowledge that can be applied productively to the clinical setting. Definitions of autobiographical memory are a source of perplexity and discontent in contemporary scholarship. The problem is both semantic and literal: We need a term that represents accurately the status of this memory system as it is genuinely constructed within the brain, but we also need more evidence that autobiographical memory actually is subserved by a separate structure or function of the brain. Some researchers believe that autobiographical memory is a subtype within the larger category of episodic memory, operating under similar principles within the same neurological structures. Others believe that the episodic and autobiographical systems are distinct from one another, but their reasons for this belief differ strongly. Some base their argument on methodological grounds, proposing that episodic and autobiographical memory differ only in their appearance, respectively, in laboratory experiments and naturalistic observation. Sometimes this argument is accompanied by the related notion that episodic memory studies rely on artificial stimuli while autobiographical memory research depends on everyday personal history that is highly meaningful to the individual. The other group of distinction proponents contends that autobiographical memory differs from episodic memory in its neurological structure, mental function, and memory content.

While no conclusive answer has yet been offered for this dilemma, I favor the last category of distinction proponents— those who believe that autobiographical memory is qualitatively different from episodic memory regardless of the methodology used to explore it. David Rubin, an experimental psychologist at Duke University, sets forth components of this sort of autobiographical memory that help to define it. These components include verbal narrative, imagery, emotion, and construction.[30] Thus, autobiographical memory is characterized as a recollection of life experiences formed into verbal narrative according to the discourse of one's culture. That verbal narrative is learned by telling stories about one's experience to family members and friends, and the narrative form itself becomes a part of the memory's structure as well as an important social technique of creating a sense of self. Perceptual imagery is usually strong in autobiographical memories, with the same kind of sensory reexperiencing that Tulving refers to as autonoetic awareness. We may see in our mind's eye a picture of the original event or hear a remembered but nonexistent voice speaking certain words. And, of course, such sensory imagery is not limited to sight and sound: Marcel Proust made an entire career of memory merely by tasting a madeleine.[31] Emotion is often linked with these sensory images, exacerbating the feeling of reexperience that occurs while thinking about the autobiographical memory. Finally, although all types of memory are known to be constructive, Rubin suggests that autobiographical memory is especially conducive to unintended on-the-spot creation.

Just as the categories of episodic, semantic, and procedural memories blend to represent a given situation, autobiographical reminiscence also transcends boundaries. Thus, you know semantic facts about your past that you do not necessarily relive in an episodic manner. But you can also dredge up remembrances of the same topic that do reenact a specific event. For example, you may recall from semantic memory the fact that your parents moved to a different state when you were a teenager; you may also retrieve episodic memories of loading the moving van or saying good-bye to close friends.

There are, of course, other types of memory that I have ignored, including prospective memory, generic event memory, perceptual memory, repisodic memory, and lexical memory, to name just a few. These are less likely to be of immediate value to therapists and, I believe, can be safely excluded from an introductory guide that makes no attempt to provide comprehensive coverage of the field. To capture the scope of human memory adequately and to provide practitioners with information that can be applied in therapeutic settings, I extract knowledge freely from all the categories discussed here. In the tradition of cognitive science, we will also consider research from an unfettered variety of methodologies and disciplines.

Memory holds a lofty position, not only within the realms of clinical and experimental psychology but also in contemporary life today. Those who doubt this assertion might think for a moment about the role of memory in literature, law, medicine, history, philosophy, and sociology. We are moving out of the modern age that ushered in the first wave of memory science during the late 1800s and into a postmodern era limned by a "loss of history, the dissolution of the centered self, the fading of individual style, and the predominance of pastiche."[32] The second wave of memory science—a veritable tsunami—heralds the late 1900s. The question of relativistic truths, the notion of self as personal historian, and the concept of memory as the key to identity—all of these issues color intellectual scholarship as it enters the twenty-first century. We suggest in countless ways that present experiences are perceived, understood, and remembered in the context of an individual's past and future. The story shapes the life as much as the life shapes the story.

# CHAPTER 3

# Memories from the Cradle

*If life has a base that it stands upon, if it is a bowl that one fills and fills and fills—*
*then my bowl without a doubt stands upon this memory. It is of lying half asleep, half*
*awake, in bed in the nursery at St. Ives. It is of hearing the waves breaking, one, two,*
*one, two, and sending a splash of water over the beach; and then breaking one, two,*
*one, two, behind a yellow blind. It is of hearing the blind draw its little acorn across*
*the floor as the wind blew the blind out. It is of lying and hearing this splash and*
*seeing this light, and feeling, it is almost impossible that I should be here; of feeling the*
*purest ecstasy I can conceive.*

—**Virginia Woolf**

A couple of years ago my students watched a therapist on a public television documentary explain a client's sudden recollection of being stuck inside her mother's fallopian tube.[1] This mnemonic epiphany solved the client's emotional problems, freeing her to live meaningfully without hunger for the daily food of psychotherapy. The therapist showed no sign of uncertainty or humor in her demeanor; she believed in this client's prenatal remembrance with stony conviction. My loquacious students sat dumbstruck, staring at each other agape as I rewound the video to play the scene again. After two replays, incredulity turned to dread. Earlier in the term they had snickered at Roseanne Barr's tale of memories from infancy and chuckled at the occasional birth canal reminiscence, but no one even smiled at *this*. Memories from the fallopian tube?

Unusual beliefs are pivotal in Freudian psychoanalysis and they can also play a substantial role in other forms of clinical treatment. Many practitioners analyze their clients' "memories" not for historical accuracy but for meaning. The significance of a belief, and its function in interpreting a client's behavior, may indeed be more important to the psychotherapist's goal than the ultimate truth or falsity of the belief itself. But this is exactly what made the video clip so frightening: Both client and therapist viewed the belief as a true memory—a veridical recollection of an actual experience, not a metaphorical rendering of underlying fears or fantasies. Neither of them was mining this "memory" for its therapeutic significance; instead, they embraced it at face value. The therapist was so confident of its authenticity that she appeared on national television to tell the story.

At no other time in American history would such accounts be accepted by any portion but a fringe minority of the populace. How ironic that during the 1990s, the very decade that has advanced scientific knowledge of human memory more than any other, so many Americans are willing to defy powerful evidence of infantile amnesia by believing in impossible memories. Even more disturbing, as we saw in chapter 1, 41 percent of formally educated psychotherapists believe that adults can retrieve accurate memories from the first year of life; 49 percent believe that difficulty in retrieving early memories signifies trauma. The American memory boom of the 1990s shows greater fascination with the recollection of events from early childhood and infancy—and in a much more literal sense—than even its European counterpart displayed during Freud's heyday.

## INFANTILE AMNESIA

As is true of any topic of ongoing scientific investigation, the field of infantile amnesia contains some intriguing controversies, a few perplexing mysteries, and several facts. One of those facts is that adults are not able to consciously recall autobiographical events that occurred prior to age two. There is no controversy or mystery here, and the flat assertion appears bold only to those who are not familiar with the ample research that unequivocally supports it. Hundreds of studies, dating back to the 1940s and forward to the 1990s, demonstrate this inability.[2] Almost all of them show that the average age at which one's first retrievable memory is stored is three and a half years. A few rare individuals are able to remember fragmented experiences from the age of two. In addition, most adults are unable to recall more than a few incomplete memories prior to age six.

Two terms, "infantile amnesia" and "childhood amnesia," are used interchangeably to refer to this common phenomenon. While accurate, the word "amnesia" is misleading in its implication of abnormality; in fact, it is utterly normal for an adult to have no memories of very early childhood or infancy. Most of us recall events from the late adolescent and early adulthood periods (roughly from age fifteen to thirty) more than events from any other time. This increase in remembering occurs across a wide variety of individuals from assorted cultures and with disparate backgrounds, and has been dubbed the "reminiscence bump" by cognitive scientists. There is no reason to suspect that the inability to recall early events is a symptom of childhood trauma; if it were, then virtually every adult on the planet has been traumatized in early years. Furthermore, we find no correlation whatsoever between the rate of early recall and the occurrence of known trauma during infancy or early childhood. In other words, people who were traumatized as young children are no more or less likely to recall events that occurred during their first six years than are people who experienced no trauma.

The fragmentary haziness of early recollections does make them difficult to assess, so researchers who study childhood amnesia are careful to corroborate subjects' experiential reports. Parents, older siblings, and friends are asked to verify subjects' stories, and historical events found in dated newspapers or personal letters are used. Eliciting early memories is also tricky because what seems important to an adult is often mundane to a child. Experimental psychologists who attempted to elicit early memories about the birth of a sibling, for instance, learned that most children view a sibling's birth as a rather trivial event, a commonplace that need not be remembered to begin with. Accordingly, one investigation showed that people who were younger than four years of age when a sibling was born recall nothing about the event.[3]

## FIRST MEMORIES

Everyone has a first memory, just as everyone took a first step and produced a first word, but confidence in one's knowledge of a first memory is not an appropriate test of its accuracy. For most of my life, my earliest memory was of a happy experience romping with our two Irish setters through a snow-filled forest beside a roadway where an old-fashioned red Jeep ("Lizzie") was parked. My godparents had that Jeep at their mountain cabin, where we often spent weekends. I dated the memory on the grounds that both dogs were gone by my third birthday. The memory was similar to Esther Salaman's description of childhood recollection: "Scenes lit up by sheets of summer lightning as one speeds in a train through the night."[4] It seemed to me like a visual flash, lighting up rapidly in the darkness of everything else I had forgotten, a bright moment on a dark background. It was also a comforting memory of cheerful times, one that I treasured not because it was first but because it was good. It provided all the social sustenance that early recollections should, allowing me to talk with my family about our former dogs, our fun times at the cabin, the songs we sang on the way, the old Jeep, people I loved, and the novelty of snow for a girl growing up in the desert. The "remember when?" game plays a pivotal role in most families and friendships, and ours was no exception.

Having cherished this first memory for better than two decades, long after the family itself had broken apart, I was not particularly amused one day to find an overexposed photograph among the black pages of an aged family album. There were the two dogs and the Jeep, there was the snowy forest, there was the old road to the cabin long since replaced by a modern freeway. I wasn't in the photograph at all. Worse yet, it had been taken before I was born. In fact, I held no true memory of the event itself; instead, I had unconsciously constructed a reminiscence by adding inferences, family stories, later experiences, and some wishful thinking to the memory of a photograph that I must have seen at some point during childhood. Such construction is typical of autobiographical memory throughout life, not just in the early years.

Early memories are also affected by the change in perspective that occurs between childhood and adult years. On my first visit to the neighborhood in which my husband grew up, he described his youthful bicycling adventures as we drove through the winding avenues near his former home. The brief journey from his house to a nearby lake, he explained, was highlighted by the perilous descent of what he and his boyhood buddies referred to as "Suicide Hill." Upon reaching the expected plunge, I braced for a plummeting nosedive of roller-coaster dimension, and sure enough, there it was: a gentle concavity in the pavement totaling about thirty yards from top to bottom. Most of us have experienced this change in memory's perspective, whether visiting a small grade school that once seemed cavernous or realizing that a tall, handsome parent is actually five feet six with narrow eyes. It occurs partly because we have changed in relative size to our surroundings, but also because Mnemosyne has gilded the experience little by little over time. As one psychologist has remarked, "With the passing of time, the good guys in our lives get a little better and the bad guys a little worse. The speed gets faster, the fish get bigger, the Depression gets tougher."[5]

Dating a memory is a much more tenuous process than we realize. Adult minds cannot collect the traces of an early childhood experience that occurred fifty years ago and determine precisely when the event transpired. For that matter, most of us have trouble remembering the specific year in which a given adult event occurred only a short time ago. Yet we are tempted to imagine that a first memory can be accurately dated even though early recollections themselves seldom contain external information that can reliably pinpoint their time of occurrence. Virginia Woolf's first memory is a good example of the dating problem. She slept in the same room at St. Ives every summer for several years, the waves breaking annually without end, the acorn of the blind drawn across the floor a million times. To determine whether that memory emanates from her second year of life or from her fourth or seventh is impossible without external corroboration.

Like the people who recall experiences in the birth canal, I believed resolutely in my first memory, and my husband is still unsettled about the demise of Suicide Hill. We did not purposely create our remembrances or tell them as falsehoods, just as the woman with fallopian memories did not lie when recounting her apparent recollections. To conclude from the evidence of memory construction that people make up stories with malicious intent and knowingly lie to others is to miss the point entirely. Memory—even the most confidently held memory of an important event that occurred during the prime of adult sensibility—is always affected by inference, expectation, and function, and it is altered unconsciously over the years by subsequent events that have their own inferences, expectations, and functions. As Proust once said, each moment is jostled by the next.[6]

The knowledge that adults cannot recall early events and that such amnesia is in no way a sign of trauma or abnormality is accepted widely among cognitive scientists, developmental psychologists, experimental psychologists, and neurologists. However, the mysteries and controversies of childhood amnesia have changed over the years as we have acquired more knowledge about the abilities of infants and the early genesis of the human brain. Such developments help us to understand why early memories are irretrievable in adulthood.

## NEUROLOGICAL DEVELOPMENT

Our understanding of neurological development has grown by leaps and bounds during the 1990s, dubbed by the U.S. Congress as the Decade of the Brain. Contrary to popular assumption, the newborn brain is far from being fully developed. In fact, 75 percent of the brain's volume and functional structure does not exist at birth; if it did, the infant's head would never fit through the birth canal. Instead, the newborn brain must mature over time with the help of input from the infant's environment. Faced with these facts, many people still cleave to their belief that the infant brain—like the infant hand—is complete but just not fully grown; in other words, that it has the capacity to do the same things an adult brain does but less of them. Nothing could be further from the truth.

To understand how neurological immaturity may affect memory, we need to consider the infant brain in some detail. I'll begin with a few reminders for those who may need a refresher course in basic neuro-babble. The building block of the human brain is the neuron, or nerve cell, which transmits electrical energy and chemicals across gaps between neurons that are called synapses. These synaptic connections create chains of neurons that communicate with one another to form ideas, perceptions, thoughts, feelings, and, yes, memories. Young cells that are destined by DNA to become neurons are known as neuroblasts and must develop full cell bodies (the rounded areas containing the nucleus of each cell), dendrites (the treelike branches that reach toward other neurons and accept synaptic transmissions), and axons (the long portion of each neuron that conveys an electrical charge toward the synapse and connecting dendrite of the next neuron). To speed the transmission of electrical impulses from one neuron to the next, the axons are eventually covered with a fatty sheath known as myelin. "Structures" of the human brain, like the hippocampus, diencephalon, and thalamus, are really just clusters of neurons with specific capacities and chemicals that have congregated in a rigidly organized architecture.

Many budding neuroblasts do exist at birth, but they are immature, unconnected, completely unmyelinated, and scattered willy-nilly throughout the brain. A newborn brain resembles the adult brain in about the same way that a germinating seed resembles a mature oak tree—in other words, not much. During the first year of life, neurons increase in number, their cell bodies become larger, dendrites branch out, axons grow in length and diameter, and chemical neurotransmitters begin to develop. The fatty myelin sheath forms around each axon, a process that does not even begin until after birth and is not finished until the child approaches adulthood. Functional capacities develop as physical structure allows, so that eventually a full-grown neuron will be capable of preserving its electrical polarity and operating under hormonal mediation to transmit impulses from one location to another. As individual neurons mature, they migrate to specific areas of the brain according to a combination of genetic coding and environmental experience. Upon arriving in the right territory, so to speak, they organize themselves into regimented groupings of lines and columns that would put the military to shame. Neurological growth does not occur in lockstep stages; certain regions of the brain develop more rapidly and at different times than others. Furthermore, it never ends; brand-new neural fibers have been observed in living brains that are over eighty years old.[7]

Although the brain does develop during gestation, much of the cell growth and migration, and almost all of the organization, connection, and myelination that I have described, occurs *after* the baby is born. It is completely absurd, therefore, to suggest that an egg residing in the fallopian tube, or a glob of undifferentiated neuroblasts lying in the womb, is capable of remembering events that would be retrieved decades later. Even the trembling slab of brain jello that exists at birth is woefully inadequate to the sophisticated task of creating, representing, and storing the simplest autobiographical memory. For that matter, at birth, even the ability to see a person or event is remarkably poor. The month-old infant has only 5 percent of the visual acuity of an adult, enough to see little more than a fuzzy blur.[8]

All of this rapid growth during the first year of life creates an infant brain that is quite malleable, or plastic, in its physical structure and function. Plasticity comprises a primary advantage of neurological immaturity at birth: It permits the infant brain to be tailored to its environment and to develop in remarkably innovative ways under unusual circumstances. For example, severe diseases sometimes require the removal of an entire hemisphere of the brain. If this rare operation is done during infancy, neurological plasticity allows the remaining hemisphere to generate all the functions and abilities of a normal brain. Early hemispherectomies cause no lingering deficit; outside of a medical lab, you and I wouldn't be able to tell the difference between a person with an intact brain and one in which an entire half had been removed. As you might expect, though, hemispherectomies done after infancy carry radical consequences in terms of cognitive deficit because the brain is no longer as plastic as it once was.

By two years of age, the brain's rampant growth culminates in the existence of far more neurons than it needs. In blatant denial to the claim that "more is better," the neurological process of pruning begins in many neural locations at this time. Neurons with few synaptic connections are pruned—killed—to allow greater organization and fuller resources to be devoted to the surviving cells. Under normal conditions of pruning, more human neurons die at age two than at any other age throughout life. Most people are surprised to learn this; we tend to imagine that all growth is good and forget that death sometimes has a positive purpose in life. We cannot conceive that part of a two-year-old's brain would be dying. Slides of stained brain tissue, viewed under a microscope, clearly show these processes of neural growth, organization, and pruning.

In general, most neurological development proceeds at a rapid pace during the first two years of life. Pruning occurs to aid growth and organization, and then development slows somewhat but continues until puberty.[9] At puberty, organized structures are established, and the plasticity that aided early growth is strongly reduced to encourage stabilization. Myelin accumulates around axons from infancy through adolescence. Patterns of neural connection, which are almost nonexistent at birth, continue to form as well. The fact that we continue to learn and change throughout life indicates that some neural plasticity is still available during adulthood and old age even though the brain's governing structures are finally in place.


## LOST MEMORIES

There is sufficient neurological evidence, then, to explain amnesia for events transpiring prior to age two. Until that time, the infant brain is simply not mature enough to form memories that can be sustained over a lifetime. However, the knowledge that adults and older children could not retrieve memories from their first years of life led psychologists to assume for many years that toddlers were equally amnesic. Recent discoveries suggest that this may not be the case. A number of studies now indicate that five-month-old babies recognize sounds that were presented prenatally[10] and recognize visual patterns, presented postnatally, after a two-week delay;[11] that six-month-old babies produce the same kicking motions needed to move a mobile attached to their feet when presented with it after a three-week delay;[12] and that nine-month-old babies reproduce novel acts after a twenty-four-hour delay.[13]

All studies must be evaluated critically, with a skeptical eye toward the many uncontrolled variables that could be responsible for results. The natural ingenuity of a typical toddler may cause her to carry out a procedure—kicking at a mobile or rolling a toy vehicle down a ramp—that was never observed, as well as one that was observed earlier but never remembered. Similarly, while motor responses and perceptual recognition clearly require a type of learning, they are not representative of what most psychologists or laypeople refer to when speaking of early "memories." After all, no one denies that infants learn. At the same time, we must not constrain our investigations too tightly. For example, a few scholars have argued that the recollection of an early event must be conscious, explicit, verbal, and autobiographical in order to count as an official childhood "memory." This definition is so restrictive as to rule out any prelinguistic reminiscence as well as knowledge of the past that may be stored in semantic memory.

With both caveats in mind, scientists working in the field have carved out an agreeable definition of the quest. Most researchers concur that the search for early memories should be limited to the declarative system, that is, semantic, episodic, or autobiographical memories signifying an ability to "know that." The "knowing how" of procedural memory, based on motor responses, reflexes, habit, perceptual recognition, immediate imitation, and simple association, is not what we are seeking in the infant or toddler. That some capacity for procedural memory exists from near birth is patently obvious. Therefore, studies demonstrating clever forms of procedural memory in infancy are given less attention than those showing that declarative memory is influencing a baby's behavior.

Psychologist Andrew Meltzoff has conducted the most compelling series of studies to demonstrate declarative memory in babies.[14] He designed a technique called "deferred imitation" in which babies observe an adult perform an unusual procedure (such as touching the forehead to a box in order to illuminate it) four times in only twenty seconds. Using this technique, Meltzoff showed that nine-month-old babies imitated the unusual procedures after a twenty-four-hour delay, and fourteen-month-olds after an eight-week delay. The babies in both studies had merely observed the unusual procedure but had never performed it. Babies of the same ages in respective control groups did not observe the procedure and, consequently, did not produce the novel acts on their own, indicating that some memory of the original observation must have been retained and retrieved. Meltzoff's results are particularly persuasive since the study relied not on procedural memory but on an element of declarative memory in which an act that had never been performed was represented abstractly. To support this interpretation, Meltzoff offers accounts of adult amnesics whose declarative memory deficits prevent them from carrying out deferred imitation, even though their memories for procedural acts and learned motor responses remain intact.

Recent research also demonstrates a lack of childhood amnesia among subjects slightly older than Meltzoff's. Preschoolers, for example, can accurately describe events that occurred when they were two years old even though their memories of those events are lost as they grow older.[15] A review of the recent literature on childhood amnesia attests to the fact that "children as young as two years can recall episodes for at least six months, [and] three-year-olds can produce spontaneous or elicited well-structured narratives of previous events."[16] These memories, the reviewers admit, are usually "incomplete and fragmentary," but their existence nevertheless indicates that toddlers remember more than we had expected given the childhood amnesia that marks adult memory. Several investigations also demonstrate that retention interval, the length of time between experiencing an event and recalling it, increases with age so that older children can retain their memories for a longer period of time than can younger children.[17]

## PSYCHOLOGICAL SHIFT

The current state of knowledge suggests, then, that a kind of psychological shift occurs around age three or four, a shift that simultaneously causes earlier memories to be forgotten and later memories to be held with greater tenacity. The ensuing question that has captivated the interest of cognitive scientists who conduct research in the area of infantile amnesia is: Why? What differences between early childhood and later childhood account for the psychological shift? What neurological or cognitive transformation occurs to prevent the teenager from remembering what the toddler knew?

Several potential answers exist. Differences in neurological development during the earliest years of life may account for part of the mystery. We know that different areas of the brain mature at different times, so the procedural memory system that underlies learning may be relatively mature during the early months of life in comparison to the lagging declarative memory system, which may be unable to represent, store, and/or retrieve experiences from infancy and early childhood. The onset of language use is another possibility; over many years, psychologists have suggested that early memories are irretrievable because they cannot be coded or represented linguistically. Yet another suggestion is that a cognitive sense of self must develop before a child has the organizational framework with which to store memories coherently and retrieve them on the basis of common cues.

## NEUROLOGICAL IMMATURITY

Applying our knowledge of neurogenesis to the maturation of the hippocampus and prefrontal cortex may provide deeper understanding of how memory systems are affected differentially by brain growth. The hippocampus is located in the medial (inner) temporal lobe, buried deep beneath the area of scalp that is just above and slightly behind the ears.[18] Case studies of amnesic patients have verified that the hippocampus plays a critical role in forming explicit memories of new events. The best known amnesic, H. M., lost his hippocampi during the pinnacle of American psychosurgery when his medial temporal lobes were sucked from his brain to treat severe epilepsy. Following the operation, H. M.'s epilepsy disappeared, as did his ability to form memories of new events. His short-term or working memory remained intact, so he was able to think consciously and had full awareness of the events around him while they were occurring. But a moment or two later, no memory of the event existed. Thus, H. M. met the same people or read the same magazine each time as if for the very first time. Like most amnesics who suffer hippocampal damage, H. M.'s procedural memory and, to an extent, his implicit memory remained functional.[19] This suggests that the hippocampus is the portion of the brain whose development we should investigate to test the theory that neurological immaturity of the declarative memory system causes childhood amnesia while procedural memory functions well enough to allow an infant to learn.

Hippocampal cells are among the earliest neuroblasts in the brain to be born but among the last to mature to full functional capacity. After migrating to the hippocampal region, the axons and dendrites of these young neurons grow very rapidly until about nine months of age, and pruning begins at about six months. By nine months the organizational architecture of the hippocampus is complete, even though neurons continue to enlarge and accrue myelin through sixteen years of age. Neural density also decreases steadily throughout life in this area after the more drastic early pruning has ceased. Organizational completion at nine months means that the architectural evolution of the hippocampus is quite rapid, establishing a fast pace of development that could easily prevent or alter the representation and storage of new events as memories.[20]

Another intriguing feature of the hippocampus that differs markedly from other parts of the brain is the fact that throughout adulthood it contains large quantities of a protein known to govern the structural and functional development of neurons.[21] This protein is found in other brain regions only during the early years of life and becomes virtually undetectible upon reaching adult age. Its continued secretion in the hippocampus may allow affected neurons to undergo continual remodeling—that is, to remain relatively plastic throughout life. Neuroscientists speculate that this increased plasticity could form the basis for lifelong declarative learning.[22]

Maturation of the prefrontal cortex is also relevant to questions of infantile amnesia. This area of the human brain is crucial for episodic memory and the autonoetic awareness that leads to the feeling of episodic reexperience. It is located at the front of the frontal lobes, just behind the forehead. K. C., the amnesic whose motorcycle accident caused head trauma including damage to the frontal lobes, is normal in intellectual function, vocabulary, semantic memory, recognition, and working memory, but he cannot dredge up memories of specific events that occurred in his recent or distant past.[23] In other words, although he knows about his past and can recall factual information about it, he has no episodic reexperiencing of specific events. K. C. is the same man who, in chapter 2, knew the make and color of a car he owned but could not recall a single instance of actually going anywhere in the car. In addition to case studies of amnesia, PET scans (images that display the functional operation of the brain) also indicate that the prefrontal cortex is most active during episodic memory tasks carried out by normal subjects.[24]

Prefrontal cortex matures even later than many other areas of the brain, not even starting to form synaptic connections until about one year of age. Prefrontal neurons then grow quickly in size and density until reaching their maximum at about two years of age, when pruning begins. PET scans attest that very little activity occurs in the prefrontal cortex until the age of twelve to eighteen months. An asymmetry in hemispheric function develops as well: about twenty-five PET studies to date have yielded consistent results showing that prefrontal cortex in the left hemisphere helps us encode episodic memories, whereas prefrontal cortex in the right hemisphere subserves the retrieval of those memories.[25] In all probability, during the first year or two of life, nascent prefrontal cortex is not able to function sufficiently to store or retrieve early autobiographical episodes.

To summarize the neurological transformation that might be responsible for a psychological shift in remembering that marks the end of childhood amnesia, both declarative and episodic memory may be poor during the first two years of life because of brain puerility. We have seen that the hippocampus, which forms new memories, cannot operate properly during the first nine months after birth, and it is not fully myelinated until age sixteen—about when the autobiographical "reminiscence bump" appears. Prefrontal cortex, which subserves episodic memory, is little more than a nonfunctional blob of unconnected neurons until one year of age, and during the second year of life it, too, experiences a fragile state of growth that precludes physiological function. Neurological studies suggest that the prefrontal cortex is probably of little value until age two.

Although we know that semantic and episodic systems are inoperable during infancy, more information about the genesis of procedural memory is needed. Procedural memory does not depend on either the hippocampus or the prefrontal cortex; instead, it is mediated at least in part by the cerebellum and basal ganglia.[26] Both of these areas are located deep in the paleomammalian layer of the brain that is thought to have appeared at a very early stage of human evolution.[27] In contrast, the prefrontal cortex needed for episodic memory probably evolved at a much later stage. If the ontological development of an individual brain indeed mimics the phylogenic hierarchy of Darwinian evolution, then it is likely that the procedural memory system matures earlier than the declarative memory system does. If so, it may therefore become functionally operational shortly after birth. At present we do not know whether this speculation will survive empirical tests.

To avoid potential misunderstanding, I should point out that although the hippocampus helps us form new memories and the left prefrontal cortex aids in the creation of episodic recollections, neither region stores memories at those locations. The long history of the search for the "engram," or memory trace, has resulted in widespread agreement among cognitive scientists and experimental psychologists that memories are stored throughout the entire associative cortex, without specific localization, probably in the form of distributed neurons that are connected in small networks. There is no reason to believe that the neural networks representing specific memories are located in either the hippocampus or the prefrontal cortex.

## LINGUISTIC IMMATURITY

A second possible explanation for the shift from early memory to adult amnesia has been proffered repeatedly by many psychologists over a long period of time. According to this hypothesis, language is the culprit.[28] Although the average child's production vocabulary blossoms at around eighteen months of age, children do not typically produce fluent, comprehensible discourse until age three or four—especially not in the form of linguistic narrative that is the common currency of autobiographical and episodic recollection in Anglo culture. Perhaps memories from early childhood cannot be retrieved in later (linguistic) years because they were not encoded or represented in a linguistic manner. Moreover, talking about our memories serves as a technique of organizing and remembering them; and it is true that frequent activation of a recollection—whether semantic, episodic, or autobiographical—strengthens its hold in the mind. The linguistic hypothesis works best to explain retrieval difficulties of early autobiographical memories, which are often assumed to be based entirely on verbal narrative, but it has also been extended to semantic knowledge.

Jean Piaget, the renowned developmental psychologist, was one proponent of the linguistic argument for infantile amnesia.[29] Clearly, language is a form of symbolic representation; if not the most effective, surely it is the most recurrent form of symbolic representation that we humans have at our disposal. If symbolic representation does not develop until the age of eighteen to twenty-four months, as Piaget theorized, then neither should language or memory. As evidence for his supposition, Piaget pointed to the fact that the conglomeration of abilities emerging at this age presages a common origin. Thus, only when a child becomes able to represent external events symbolically will she be able to remember those events in later life. To complicate matters, such representation is probably the platform for most cognitive functions, including language, memory, knowledge, and reasoning.

The linguistic analysis of infantile amnesia is tempting, but several flaws appear in the fabric upon closer inspection. First, the argument is based on the assumption that autobiographical memory is almost purely linguistic. Although it has been characterized in some circles as verbal narrative, our internal knowledge of past life experiences includes many sensory features. External cues to personal memory, for example, often take the form of visual scenes, sounds of nature or music, salient aromas and flavors, or raw emotions. To elicit a full autobiographical memory, these sensory cues must remain an integral part of the stored trace. The fact that we tend to share our memories by telling stories rather than painting pictures or composing music is no reason to assume that the memories themselves must be represented in the propositional code of language. Second, the linguistic analysis is flawed with respect to the difference in age between the average onset of fluent language production and the average onset of language comprehension. Virtually all children are capable of comprehending their native language long before they begin to produce it fluently. Comprehension alone should permit at least some linguistic encoding of early memories. The third problem appears through empirical studies showing that preschool children can indeed tell comprehensible and accurate stories of events that occurred prior to age three or four, even though they later lose those memories. This suggests that children can remember and share their knowledge of an event that occurred when their linguistic abilities were relatively primitive. And, finally, there is no evidence that nonlinguistic retrieval of early memories results in more accurate recollection. Empirical research has simply not borne out the popular assumption that visualization, artistic expression, movement, or tactile activities mediate the recollection of early event memories to any greater degree than they aid in the recollection of adult memories. All in all, while linguistic immaturity may play a role in adult inability to retrieve early childhood memories, it is not likely to account for the entire phenomenon of infantile amnesia.

## DEVELOPING A SENSE OF SELF

Psychologists Mark Howe and Mary Courage have provided a third potential answer to our question of psychological shift. They propose that the development of a cognitive sense of self around two years of age supplies an organizational framework that the child then employs to store and retrieve autobiographical memories. Social factors would encourage children to form this framework and use it, as when we pull family members closer together by sharing personal stories. Any memory fragments that are available during the first three years of life cannot be retained for long in the absence of this organizational framework of self.[30]

Howe and Courage note "the formidable challenge of tracing the origin and development of the intangible self in the inscrutable infant,"[31] but despite the difficulty of the task, they attempt to gather evidence for their proposal. Around two years of age, most children begin to recognize themselves in the mirror, to use the past tense so that they can describe previous events, to produce verbal narrative, and to use the self-referential pronouns "I" and "me." Two-year-olds rarely misuse these pronouns, even though they routinely hear themselves referred to by others as "you" and never as "me" or "I." The typical mistakes that children make when acquiring the past tense forms of irregular verbs (such as "I *sawed* the movie" or "He *swimmed* in the lake") are almost never accompanied by errors in their usage of personal pronouns. By comparison, blind children do not acquire correct pronoun use until age four or five, the same time that they begin to recognize their own voices on tape and start to talk of past events.

The notion of self-awareness as a harbinger of memory is also compatible with the results of PET scans showing little activity in the prefrontal cortex until twelve to eighteen months of age. This area helps to govern self-awareness as well as episodic memory. Howe and Courage turn the linguistic analysis on its head with their proposal that the emergence of a cognitive sense of self forms the demarcation line between normal amnesia for early childhood events and solid memory for later experiences. In their opinion, the linguistic ability to use personal pronouns correctly is caused by the emergence of a child's sense of self, and not vice versa.

The significance of a conscious sense of self in explaining childhood amnesia may also be related to the unfolding of autonoetic awareness, which characterizes episodic memory. There is no evidence that such awareness is present in the fleeting memories of events that occurred prior to age three or four, although the paucity of research is linked primarily to our inability to gauge levels of awareness in prelinguistic subjects. Nevertheless, it is possible that childhood amnesia is exacerbated by the lack of autonoetic awareness: If there was no "self" to personally experience an original event, there might be no way to reexperience it from a personal perspective in adult years.

As of this writing, cognitive scientists do not know which of the three hypotheses—neurological immaturity, linguistic performance, or sense of self—is responsible for childhood amnesia. It is very likely that all three play a role and that other important factors, yet undiscovered, lurk in the background. We do know without a doubt that memories of events occurring prior to age two are not available during adulthood, regardless of the perspicacity with which we try recall them. In addition, the vast majority of adults are unable to retrieve memories of events that occurred prior to age three or four, and autobiographical memories remain few and fragmentary until age six. This amnesia for early childhood events is perfectly normal; there is no reason to suspect that an individual who remembers nothing from his early years has been traumatized. As we will see in later chapters, efforts to encourage people to retrieve the irretrievable only result in the unconscious creation of faulty memories that mislead client and clinician.

# CHAPTER 4

# Accuracy and Confidence

*It isn't so astonishing, the number of things that I can remember, as the number of things I can remember that aren't so.*

—Mark Twain

Although Mnemosyne's capacity for error is well known, it is often under-estimated. Popular assumptions about mnemonic accuracy float with the tides of cultural metaphor, from Aristotle's wax tablet through Augustine's caverns to Atkinson's information processing computer. The computer metaphor's favor among memory researchers has waned since the 1970s, but it is still alive and well elsewhere. For example, one-third of the credentialled psychotherapists who responded to Michael Yapko's 1992 survey agreed with the statement that "the mind is like a computer, accurately recording events as they actually occurred."[1] A more common analogy among the lay public is the video camera, a false resemblance that is reinforced around the clock through the national American pastime: television. A growing number of prime-time television shows rely on scenes in which main characters recall the past in perfect living technicolor that preserves every detailed nuance of the original event. These scenes artificially eliminate the blurred focus, empty gaps, incompatible fragments, chaotic chronology, and false features that a more realistic portrait of remembrance would include.

Were we to ask people whether they trust the televised representation of memory that I have described, most of them would probably say no. And it is true that in rational moments of careful thought, we recognize that normal memories are blurred, fragmented, and chaotic. But amid the pressures of everyday living, our actions and assumptions refute that rational understanding. We say we know that memory is fuzzy, yet we unconsciously expect others to describe past events infallibly; we even accuse them of lying if they do not. We say we know that memories are fragmented, yet in courtrooms, clinics, and counseling sessions we unconsciously anticipate detailed histories without gaps or fragmentation. We say we know that the precise sequence of events during a particular episode may be remembered chaotically or not at all, yet we unconsciously assume that anyone of standard IQ who experienced an episode should be able to recount it with chronological veracity. We accept the imperfection of memory at an empirical level but not at a phenomenological one, perhaps because our own recollections emerge from the neural mist with an iron-clad feeling of certainty. In everyday living, I, too, succumb to the temptation of blind faith in my recollections despite years of concentrated study corroborating the errors of reminiscence.

In fact, memory is not at all like a computer or a video camera, nor is it objective or infallible. We accept these metaphors not for their propriety but because in a society that is increasingly monitored by technology, we want our machines to mirror our lives. The comfort of such beliefs is exceeded only by their danger. A better metaphor for memory is as a theater of the past, "a dynamic medium of experience imbued with drama and feeling, and invigorated by the inherently human capacity for narrative creation."[2] Although the gist of most episodic and autobiographical recollections is correct, smaller details—sometimes very important ones—are often wrong even when we feel confident about them. Decades of cognitive research have demonstrated repeatedly the errors of memory that occur despite strong confidence in their historical accuracy.


## FLASHBULB MEMORIES

Ulric Neisser, the cognitive revolutionary whom you met in chapter 2, recently conducted a study that is particularly convincing in its demonstration of mnemonic fallibility outside of the scientific laboratory.[3] He and a colleague, Nicole Harsch, asked college freshmen to write down their memories of the *Challenger* explosion on the morning after it occurred. As part of a brief classroom exercise, the students wrote a narrative description of their experiences, then answered specific questions about the circumstances under which they learned of the explosion: where they were, what they were doing, who informed them of the disaster, what time of day it was, and who else was present. This kind of vivid emotional event often produces what cognitive psychologists call a flashbulb memory  in which the very moment and detailed context of discovering a catastrophe are seared into the mind like a hot branding iron pressed against cool flesh. Cultural disasters often form the basis for flashbulb memories; varying generations of Americans, for example, are likely to have flashbulb memories of the attack on Pearl Harbor, the first landing on the moon, President Kennedy's assassination, President Nixon's resignation, or Princess Diana's tragic death in a high-speed car crash. That the students participating in Neisser and Harsch's study perceived the *Challenger* explosion as a highly emotional event is verified by their own reports of feeling "shocked," "stunned," "sickened," and "horrified" upon hearing that the space shuttle carrying seven people had burst into flame.[4]

Nearly three years later, forty-four of the college students were asked once again to write a description of the episode and to answer the same questions specifying the context in which they first heard the news. Responses were compared to the previous records, based on the reasonable assumption that the original descriptions—recorded in writing less than one day after the event—were accurate. The comparison showed that *not one* of the subjects' memories was entirely correct. One-quarter of the subjects answered all five of the context questions incorrectly, and an additional half of the subjects answered most of the questions incorrectly. When the data were analyzed—not by individual subject but by individual question—42 percent of the students' memories were completely wrong, and an additional 27 percent were partly wrong. Only 30 percent of the answers to specific questions concerning the students' memories of this vivid event were accurate.

Faced with such unexpected inaccuracy, the researchers decided to contact the subjects a third time for an interview that would investigate the depth of their memory loss. During each personal interview, researchers provided retrieval cues and exercises designed to help the former students recall their original experiences. Specialized techniques produced no improvement whatsoever, nor did the use of salient cues based on the researchers' knowledge of each subject's original response (for example, "Is it possible that you already knew about the explosion before seeing it on TV?"). The most drastic attempt to prompt recall transpired when the researchers gave subjects their original three-year-old questionnaires, expecting that when the students read their own responses, some glimmer of accurate memory would emerge. Instead, almost all the subjects expressed great surprise on seeing three-year-old documents filled out in their own handwriting that contained descriptions conflicting so strongly with their own recollections. Not only had their original memories of the explosion disappeared, but three-quarters of the students didn't even remember completing a questionnaire regarding the *Challenger* explosion.

Despite the inaccuracy of the subjects' flashbulb memories of the *Challenger* explosion, their confidence in those memories was high. Ninety-one percent of the subjects reported a greater than neutral level of confidence in their recollections. Twenty-five percent of them said they were "absolutely certain" of their memories. These elevated degrees of confidence may be partly mediated by the strong ratings of visual vividness that most subjects reported. In other words, the highly vivid nature of these incorrect memories—like a flash photograph of an imaginary belief—may have fooled subjects into believing they were true. Another possibility is that mislocations in time or place may account for such undue confidence. In mislocations, a remembered event really did happen but at a different time or in a different place than we believe. Neisser's analysis of John Dean's Watergate testimony provides many examples of mislocations, which are thought to be common mistakes in normal autobiographical memory.[5]

Flashbulb memories, then, which cognitive psychologists once believed were more accurate than standard memories, are just as likely to be incorrect regardless of their vivid, detailed nature. In the study of *Challenger* memories, this inaccuracy persevered despite the increased encoding strength that was caused by writing down the original experience. Furthermore, as demonstrated in that study and others, inaccuracy remains regardless of the rememberer's strong confidence that the memory is correct. In fact, we now suspect that the primary difference between flashbulb memories and standard recollections is not found in accuracy, degree of vividness, level of detail, or amount of emotion, but merely in the degree of confidence with which they are held.[6]

When we inspect more mundane memories, accuracy fares no better. After researchers were given permission to check official transcripts for verification, a group of college freshmen were asked to recall their high-school grades. Overall, subjects recalled only 71 percent of their own grades correctly. When senior-level grades that students had earned in the previous one or two semesters were analyzed separately, the accuracy rate remained at 73 percent. In addition, the subjects produced a recall curve that declined consistently as the grades decreased, so that grades of A were recalled correctly 89 percent of the time, but grades of D yielded only 29 percent accuracy. (No sense dwelling on the negative, as my D students sometimes say, but of course it is also true that students with poor memory for examined content are likely to exhibit poor memory for other information as well.) In keeping with the fact that human memory usually operates to enhance rather than impede self-image, 80 percent of the errors in recall served to inflate the actual grade. Grades of A produced a significant correlation of medium size between the subjects' accuracy in recall and their confidence in knowing the grade. However, the confidence levels that subjects reported for their memories of B, C, and D grades were completely uncorrelated with accuracy.[7]

## EYEWITNESS TESTIMONY

Accuracy of normal recall has been scrutinized with the greatest zeal in explorations of eyewitness testimony. This area provides especially fertile ground for such investigation because of its long history in experimental psychology, its reliance on methodologies that are less artificial than much of what has defined other types of memory research, and its practical importance in the real world of courtroom law. Eyewitness memory research dates back to 1900 when Alfred Binet—better known for his development of the Stanford-Binet IQ test—examined the effects of misleading questions on children's memories.[8] By 1908 enough research had been conducted to warrant Hugo Münsterberg's monograph on the fallibility of eyewitness memory.[9] Following the behaviorist hiatus, eyewitness research blossomed again during the 1970s and remains a vigorous area of cognitive psychology today.

Although it has been fruitful, memory methodology since Ebbinghaus has tread primarily in the dreary tradition of the artificial laboratory. Proceeding beyond that apex of ecological invalidity, the nonsense syllable, experimental psychologists eventually selected words as the most favored stimuli to be remembered in standard memory experiments. Faces, voices, names, facts, and spatial locations were used only as unpreferred substitutes, and memories for events, emotions, and autobiographical episodes were almost entirely ignored until Neisser insisted that we pay attention to the facets of memory that actually matter in everyday living. Decades of research in which hordes of subjects were made to recall long boring lists of unrelated words—an act we never carry out in real life—are partly responsible for the scorn and disregard that our scientific contributions to society's understanding of memory have received from professional psychologists and members of the general public. The obsession with isolated words as stimuli is likely to teach us more about the psychology of faux language processing than about memory itself.[10] Yet, even that idea is often ridiculed despite preliminary studies of early amnesia that suggest strong dissociations between episodic memory and lexical knowledge, including vocabulary, pronunciation, spelling, and the appropriate use of words.[11]

I do not mean to imply that science must always be conducted in realistic natural settings to be useful or important, nor do I intend to suggest that every laboratory experiment is unrealistic. Some of my own research, in fact, falls directly within the mainstream of tightly controlled laboratory science conducted under artificial circumstances. However, I do believe that a more ecologically valid program of inquiry would have attracted the kind of public attention that a basic understanding of human memory requires. From the start, eyewitness testimony research held firmly to the need for ecological validity, producing methodologies that were based on well-simulated versions of reality even though ethical considerations prevented the staging of real crimes. Analyzing people's recollections of an event—even a staged event—is a much more realistic study of human memory than is dissecting a subject's ability to recite a list of unconnected words.

The study of eyewitness testimony also benefits from its practical importance. During the 1960s, prior to the topic's resurgence, the rate of false convictions in the United States was estimated at 5 percent, a rate that would send tens of thousands of innocent citizens to prison each year.[12] Eyewitness testimony was, and still is, the most important evidence that jurors consider in determining guilt. In fact, one British survey yielded a 73 percent conviction rate in trials for which there was no evidence against a defendant except one eyewitness's identification.[13] Applications of eyewitness testimony research have trickled into American courts of law during the past twenty years in the form of judges' instructions to jurors, revised interrogation and identification techniques, and expert testimony regarding the fallibility of memory. Such instruction is intended to reduce the likelihood that innocent citizens will be jailed on the basis of one bystander's fuzzy and fragmented recollection.

For all three of these reasons—its history, its realism, and its practical significance—the cognitive study of eyewitness memory provides information that can be used in determining the accuracy of autobiographical and episodic recall in everyday life. A general review of the literature by psychologist Alan Fruzzetti and his associates supplies solid information based on experimental findings that have been replicated in many studies over many years. With respect to the witness, we know that the most accurate observers tend to be young or middle-aged adults since correctness and completeness decline among children and the elderly. Children are also more suggestible than adults, although subsequent chapters will show that we adults are much more suggestible than we care to admit. The common presumption that police are highly trained in eyewitness identification and face recognition, which encourages jurors to place extraordinary confidence in police testimony, is trampled by empirical studies demonstrating that eyewitness memory performance among police officers is no more accurate than within the general population. Eyewitnesses are more likely to identify accurately a perpetrator of their own race than one of a different race. In addition, the practice of viewing books containing photographs of known criminals impairs accurate identification of the observed perpetrator. Seeing hundreds of faces merely interferes with the memory of a perpetrator's face.[14]

With respect to the event, it's hardly surprising that longer exposure to a criminal's face enhances later recognition accuracy. Less obvious, however, is the fact that people tend to grossly overestimate exposure duration. This means that a witness may easily and unintentionally sway a jury by vowing that she observed a criminal for two and a half minutes when she actually saw him for only thirty seconds. This is exactly the extent of overestimation that one group of psychologists obtained among subjects who watched a simulated bank robbery on videotape.[15] The type of face makes a difference, too. Typically, unattractive people or those with distinctive facial features are easiest to identify accurately. The existence of a weapon in an event draws attention away from the person holding the weapon, hindering the accuracy of later identification. Excessive violence, whether including a weapon or not, is also known to impair the accuracy and the detail of a memory.[16]

In these kinds of studies, exactly how inaccurate are people when asked to identify the perpetrators of simulated crimes or to answer factual questions about videotaped events? In general, although they differ as a function of subjects and situations, inaccuracy rates tend to hover between 25 percent and 30 percent; that is, slightly more than one-quarter of the information people remember under such circumstances is typically wrong. For example, 29 percent of all subjects who were asked to identify the person who stole money from a wallet in a three-minute videotape chose the wrong individual.[17] The same inaccuracy rate appeared earlier in this chapter when college freshmen were asked to recall their high-school grades.

A different group of researchers asked two thousand museum visitors from all walks of life, aged five to seventy-five, to answer factual questions about the events in a film clip showing a man walking through a threatening mob, being nearly run down by a car, then collapsing after being struck with a club. Twenty-six percent of their answers were wrong even though an informational sign near the exhibit encouraged viewers to try to remember the events while watching the film.[18] Because most eyewitness memory researchers limit their subjects to college students, the museum study is especially valuable in verifying that similar degrees of inaccuracy emerge when the range of subjects is broadened to include more of the general population. In fact, after isolating the data produced by museum visitors who happened to be college students, these researchers discovered that the college students were significantly more accurate than all other groups, with a 21 percent rate of inaccuracy. This finding suggests that eyewitness memory research, which is monopolized by the college student subject, underestimates the degree of inaccuracy that the rest of us produce when recalling a previous event.

## THE MISINFORMATION EFFECT

Standard inaccuracy rates increase dramatically when experimenters introduce subtle manipulations such as those used during police interrogation and courtroom cross-examination. When misleading information, often in the muted form of a single incorrect word, is presented to subjects after they have observed an event, a robust "misinformation effect" typically increases subjects' standard inaccuracy by 20 to 30 percent.[19] This effect occurs in both children and adults, and is no less apparent among college students than the general population despite the students' lower base rate of inaccuracy.[20] All of us, it seems, are inclined to alter our memories in accordance with misleading information.

To gain a better idea of how the misinformation effect works, let's walk through one of the first studies to produce it. In 1974, cognitive psychologists Elizabeth Loftus and John Palmer wanted to determine whether a subtle word change in post-event questioning might alter eyewitness reports. They designed an experiment in which one hundred subjects watched the same short film of a traffic accident, then answered a series of questions about what they had seen. One of the questions provided the primary experimental manipulation: Half of the subjects were asked, "How fast were the cars going when they hit each other?" The other half were asked, "How fast were the cars going when they smashed into each other?" After seeing the film and answering the questions, subjects were thanked for their participation and told that the experiment was over.[21]

Loftus and Palmer reasoned that the manipulation in the wording of that one question might cause subjects' memories of the event to change. They predicted that subjects who believed the cars had merely "hit" each other would recall the accident as a minor one in which both vehicles were traveling at low speeds. However, subjects who believed the cars had "smashed into" each other would probably recall a more severe accident at higher speed. Sure enough, subjects who were asked how fast the cars were traveling when they "smashed into" each other reported a significantly faster speed than those who were asked how fast the cars were traveling when they "hit" each other. The manipulation of only one word during questioning had altered subjects' estimates of traveling speed even though every subject had seen the same cars traveling at the same rate.

A further test of the predictions came one week later when the subjects were asked unexpectedly to return for the second part of the experiment. This time subjects were asked a few more questions about the accident, including "Did you see any broken glass?" In fact, no broken glass was present at the filmed scene of the accident. However, more than twice as many subjects who believed that the cars had "smashed into" each other reported broken glass than did subjects who believed that the cars had "hit." Results showed a statistically significant misinformation effect caused by changing only one word during the kind of questioning that often takes place after a real car accident or crime has happened.

Over the years, in hundreds of misinformation studies conducted all over the world, experimenters have found it quite simple to add completely nonexistent properties—from shards of broken glass to an entire barn—to subjects' memories merely by altering one or two words in a question. Loftus herself, the leading psychologist in the field of eyewitness memory for over twenty years, supplies a sample of errors culled from the scientific literature, each consistent enough to produce a statistically significant impairment: "Stop signs are recalled as yield signs, hammers are recalled as screwdrivers, traffic signs are recalled as stop signs, Coke cans are recalled as cans of Planter's peanuts, *Vogue* magazine is remembered as *Mademoiselle*, green plastic pictures are remembered as yellow, breakfast cereal is remembered as eggs, a clean-shaven man is recalled as having a mustache, the word *Yukon* on a T-shirt is remembered as *Nixon*, and a man named Dr. Henderson is remembered as being named Dr. Davidson."[22]

In keeping with scientific understanding of human memory, people are confident in their misinformed recollections, insisting that the broken glass, yield signs, eggs, and mustaches really were there.[23] Moreover, they are often able to describe such items in great detail, explaining how much nonexistent glass was scattered over the road, how the invisible eggs were cooked, and what type of vaporized mustache was seen.[24] The presumption that detailed memories are more likely to be accurate is simply not borne out by empirical research; on the contrary, the literature demonstrates unequivocally that detail is as likely to be present in a true memory as in a false one. Furthermore, misinformed memories issue with the same speed as genuine memories do, so hesitation or verbal faltering provides no indication of a recollection's veracity. Misleading information is also more likely to be accepted by subjects when it is presented by someone they perceive as knowledgeable, a fact that psychotherapists should take to heart when working with their clients.[25]

The precise mental processes that cause the misinformation effect to occur have received extensive investigation. Is an original memory obliterated by misinformation, blended into it, or never stored in the first place? Do subjects forget the source of misinformation, incorrectly recalling that it was provided during the event rather than during the post-event questioning? These and other questions form the crux of a debate over the misinformation effect, which I consider in chapter 5.[26] But the fact that the misinformation effect is genuine, and not merely an experimental artifact, has been verified repeatedly.[27] We may not know what causes it, but everyone agrees that it exists.


## CONFIDENCE IN REMEMBERING

Attempts to uncover a solid relationship between confidence and accuracy have also been a prominent part of eyewitness memory research. Here, practical significance is paramount: In the United States since 1972, the degree of confidence that a legal witness exudes during testimony is considered one of only five criteria for determining whether she has identified the correct perpetrator or not. Presumed levels of confidence, then, play directly into the determination of whether a defendant is found guilty, despite the fact that "confidence" is displayed by a wide variety of inadvertent means. For example, a witness's clothing, manner of speech, degree of eye contact, and posture may suggest a degree of confidence to jurors that even the witness does not feel. Worse yet, legal reliance on confidence defies several decades of empirical research showing that accuracy and confidence are usually not correlated to any statistically significant degree.

Specifically, correlation coefficients for the relationship between confidence and accuracy in eyewitness memory range from .08 (virtually nonexistent) to .42 (moderate), according to a meta-analysis of thirty-five studies.[28] The higher coefficients are obtained only when witnesses experience optimal viewing conditions for a long period of time, so that the perpetrator can be observed clearly and at length. In real-life situations, however, eyewitnesses seldom enjoy such prime circumstances. Independent authors of multiple literature reviews, each combining results from a large number of relevant studies, all agree that confidence is not related to accuracy in any meaningful degree. In general, confidence actually accounts for less than 10 percent of the variance in an eyewitness's accuracy, but jurors trust it to such a degree that their assumption of an eyewitness's confidence accounts for 50 percent of the variance in their beliefs concerning that eyewitness's accuracy.[29] The fact of the matter is that a highly confident witness is about as likely to be wrong about a memory as to be right.

Overconfidence is common to several areas of cognitive performance. Studies of metamemory (knowledge about one's own memory performance) show that students, for example, tend to be more confident in their ability to answer test questions than their performance warrants. Illusions of knowing are consistent across academic domains; they appear in mathematical reasoning, verbal comprehension, reading inference, vocabulary, and spatial analysis, to name only a few. As annoying as such overconfidence may be to those who need to determine personal or legal truths, it undoubtedly serves the valuable purpose of boosting self-esteem. In addition, approaching a task with confidence, even when that confidence is unfounded, usually helps us to perform better than we otherwise would.

The overconfidence effect has not been studied in depth across more practical domains of everyday, nonacademic experience. A few research reports provide interesting preliminary information, however. One pair of psychologists obtained a surprisingly strong correlation ($r$ =.75) between subjects' confidence and the accuracy of their memories for information heard on the news, although the strength of the relationship declined rapidly as questions became more difficult.[30] Several interpretations of this result are possible. Perhaps we have more practice at gleaning information from the news than we do at taking mathematical examinations, for instance, and are therefore better able to assess our knowledge. The researchers also admit that none of their test questions was particularly difficult, so that confidence and accuracy may have been related only by virtue of task simplicity. It is also likely, however, that a methodological change in this study is responsible for the strong correlation: These subjects did not select confidence ratings until after they had seen and answered each question. The process of assessing each question and thinking through their answers may well have tweaked original confidence levels.

The disparity between confidence and accuracy also emerges in studies of everyday autobiographical memory. An investigation of people's ability to remember the daily events of their own lives, as recorded in personal diaries, furnishes some illumination. Every evening for four months, subjects wrote about three events that had happened to them on that day. Each event was described in detail, including the physical environment in which it transpired and the subject's personal reaction to it. When the four-month recording period ended, experimenters used the diaries to create recognition tests containing forty-five statements of events that had occurred in a particular subject's life, mixed with events that had not occurred. Recognition tests of this sort were administered to every subject individually, at intervals ranging from one to twelve months after the original episode took place.[31]

Across the entire twelve-month period, subjects' ability to correctly recognize events that had occurred in their lives remained around 90 percent—quite high compared to the standard accuracy rates of 70 percent for secondhand observations of simulated crimes. Of course, the act of choosing three events per day and writing detailed accounts of them would boost memory in itself. Subjects' corresponding ability to correctly reject events that had not occurred in their lives was quite low, however, as evidenced by false alarm rates that climbed steadily from about 35 percent to 50 percent as the months went by. In other words, nearly half of the time they said that an event really had transpired in their lives when in fact it had not. Like Mark Twain, these subjects were fairly accurate in recognizing autobiographical events that had occurred, but quite poor at recognizing as false events that had not occurred.

When the participants in this study took the recognition tests, they rated the confidence of their responses to each stated event or non-event. The confidence ratings proved to be no different for correct responses than they were for incorrect responses, and they did not change over time even though accuracy continued to decrease as the retention intervals became longer. These results for daily autobiographical events, then, demonstrate the same relationship between confidence and accuracy that we have seen in studies of eyewitness testimony and flashbulb memory: People think they know exactly what happened in the past, but in reality they often do not.


## EVENT DATING

Some experimental psychologists have also investigated the ability to recall the time at which an event occurred. We use time as a cue for memory frequently, not only in courtrooms and clinics but also in daily conversations with friends, asking when a particular event occurred as a way of jogging one's memory for the event itself. But once again common practice does not match empirical knowledge: Time is well known among memory researchers as one of the worst cues for recollection despite the likelihood that temporal organization of autobiographical events probably abets a sense of personal history.[32]

Memory for when an event occurred is reliable only when reconstructed from external aspects of the recollection. Therefore, rather than acting as a cue for recollection, datings are constructed by prior knowledge of the event. No evidence exists as yet, despite some searching, that memories are tagged for time when they are encoded in the brain. Furthermore, errors in dating increase by a constant proportion to the amount of time that has passed so that dates are off by about one day for each week that has elapsed since the to-be-remembered event occurred.[33] Such errors follow systematic biases of several types: First, we tend to "telescope," so that events from long ago seem more recent; hence the common experience of being surprised that it has really been twelve years, not eight or nine, since we saw Aunt Sally or five years, not three, since a close friend got married. Second, highly memorable events seem more recent. Was it really two years ago that my father had his motorcycle accident? Seems like last month. Third, memory for absolute dates—the accident happened on July 11, or was it the

21st?—tends to be very poor, whereas memory for the day of the week is better, and memory for the time of day that an event occurred is usually best. Finally, repeated episodes of a similar nature—"repisodes," to use Neisser's terminology—are especially prone to errors of dating because they seem to blend together into a general schema.

Certain cues do help people locate a date more accurately, although, as I mentioned with respect to early childhood memories, pinpointing the exact date is usually impossible after months or years have gone by. Any kind of natural boundary provides a beneficial cue, such as the beginning or end of an academic semester or the physical context of a specific season that involves certain temperatures, clothing, activities, and landscapes. Important events—holidays, weddings, funerals, moving to a new neighborhood, starting a new job—also act as mental landmarks for dating a memory. Routine behavior that occurs regularly on certain days of the week or times of the day may aid event dating. Because the sequence of a series of events is usually preserved, date retrieval may also be cued by encouraging the rememberer to think through related events in chronological order.

## NORMAL INACCURACY

All in all, inaccuracy is a normal and natural part of human memory. Some of the mental functions that lead to it, such as forgetting and interference, are valuable processes that help us lead intelligent adaptive lives. I have emphasized memory's fallibility here because too often we imagine that recollection is—or should be—absolute, perfect, a direct analog to the computer or video camera. This attitude causes significant problems in many settings of psychotherapy. Mental health practitioners must be aware, I believe, that even the most confident client's recollections are mental constructions that contain errors, that all memory is "an intricate stew of truths and mirages."[34] This feature makes the therapist's job more important and more challenging; the therapist must responsibly interpret the underlying meanings and prospective actions that the simmering mixture of individual truths and personal mirages dictates, a task far more difficult than it would be if clients' autobiographical narratives could be accepted at face value. As time elapses between an original event and its recollection, these constructions and reconstructions layer upon themselves, producing an ever greater likelihood of inaccuracy and distortion. The inaccuracies we have explored in this chapter are based on several months or, at most, two or three years of retention; recounting events that occurred twenty or thirty years ago is an extremely rickety process that is rife with error.

I am not suggesting that it is the clinician's job to determine a client's absolute truth. In most cases, such determination would be impossible, and even if it weren't, the knowledge would seldom serve the therapeutic purpose anyway. It is crucial, however, not to misuse a client's recollections as if they were the absolute truth. If the ultimate purpose of therapy is to help people understand and accept themselves so that they can learn to take appropriate actions and create coherent belief systems, then mirages of a life are at least as important as the truths, perhaps more so. In addition, clients should never be encouraged to believe that their memories are perfectly accurate. This caveat, in turn, need not suggest in any way that the client is lying; if only a smattering of solid empirical knowledge about memory is imparted to clients in the therapeutic setting, they will appreciate the distinction between natural inaccuracy and intentional falsehood as well as we do.

A point that is often overlooked in clinical discussions of memory fallibility is that it is not only the client whose memory is fallible. No normally functioning individual is exempt from errors of memory. Therapists themselves are equally prone to mistakes in their own recollections, including their recollections of the clinical sessions in which clients provide the information that creates a platform for further treatment. Common aids, such as written notes or tape recordings, may be very useful in avoiding the natural biases of memory, but even they do not eliminate the problem.

Having established that memory is often wrong, allow me now to back down ever so slightly in admitting that the primary features of many of our recollections remain intact. If you recall going for coffee with a friend last week, chances are excellent that you really did even though you may be wrong about which day of the week you met, the particular shirt he was wearing, or whether he was carrying a folder of papers. After all, even the standard inaccuracy rate of 30 percent for unmolested eyewitness memory means that a full 70 percent of what we remember is correct. In accepting empirical facts showing that secondary, but sometimes critical, aspects of memory can be inaccurate, we need not rush to the other extreme in suspecting that everything we remember is wrong. Harvard University's Daniel Schacter, a cognitive scientist who explores the mental and physical underpinnings of remembrance, refers to this paradox as the "fragile power" of memory, in which its limitations do not reduce its influence. As Schacter says, "Even though memory can be highly elusive in some situations and dead wrong in others, it still forms the foundation for our most strongly held beliefs about ourselves."[35]

# CHAPTER 5

# Construction and Distortion

*Memory is like a frustrated painter, never fully satisfied with his work, always adding*
*or deleting detail, images, impressions, light and shadow, thought, ideas, whatever will*
*make the remembered moment unique, make it telling, give it substance, whether real*
*or imagined.*

—Harry Middleton

Maybe it was Wilder Penfield's research that clinched the twentieth-century presumption of an infallible memory. Penfield is the Canadian neurosurgeon who elicited vivid reenactments of the past among patients whose brains he stimulated by electrode while removing regions that were damaged by epilepsy. Because the brain itself contains no pain receptors, such procedures are sometimes done without general anesthesia so that the patient can guide the surgeon's knife cognitively by carrying out simple mental tasks. As Penfield stimulated specific locations inside their brains, his patients reported a myriad of experiences: hearing voices at a carnival, seeing faces from the neighborhood, feeling the sensations of familiarity, listening to music.[1]

Scientific reports like these led many psychologists of the time, both practitioners and researchers, to suspect that all previous experiences are stored permanently in the labyrinth of the human brain, ready to be extracted in gluttonous detail as soon as the right cue comes along. Penfield's findings were pumped into general media circulation, then reiterated in psychological textbooks for nearly twenty years before a serious critical evaluation of his work was published. The evaluation pointed out that 92 percent of Penfield's attempts to evoke memories by brain stimulation failed completely. The remaining 8 percent of cases, on which the entire idea of permanent memory hinged, usually produced perceptions that were nonspecific, and none of them were corroborated as memories of real events.[2] As usual, Penfield's study was welcomed with a flurry of sensationalism that far exceeded the public attention given to the later critique, so that even today the collective memory of a permanent store lives on long after the flawed research has died.

The belief that remembering is a process of certainty, akin to plucking an old photo from the attic chest, is reflected in our language: People frequently "recall," "retrieve," "recollect," and "recount" events from memory; but in common parlance and even in psychological argot, we seldom "construct," "compose," and "create" the past. Most of the lay public also seems to assume that accuracy is highly desirable in memory, that it holds many benefits but no sacrifices. "If only I had a better memory . . ." is a concept on which many a wealthy self-help author has capitalized. But is accuracy really so golden?

I think not. It is surely annoying to forget a name, but if we forgot nothing, our minds would drown in the memories of exactly which space our automobiles had occupied each time we parked or precisely what time every day's appointments had occurred. Even a few months' worth of such accuracy would become inanely cumbersome. If our memories were not subject to interference, we might conquer Macintosh Microsoft Word and PC Word-Perfect simultaneously, but important new knowledge would be jettisoned in favor of preserving old information. Without the cognitive capacity for categorization, our lives would be spent in the mental abyss of instances and anecdotes. Even the simplest features of language acquisition could not proceed properly if "cat" referred to only one particular feline animal. The loss of ability to infer would leave us skipping doltishly across the surface of our books, art, and music with no depth of meaning, so that perusing an Impressionist masterpiece would be equivalent to glancing at a whitewashed fence. Even distortion has a purpose: to create a meaning that lends personal substance to a moment and molds it into the framework of self, just as the frustrated painter adds a dab of color here and there.

All of these processes—forgetting, interference, categorization, inference, and distortion, as well as construction, interpretation, and assumption—are desirable functions that help us live intelligently. Without them we would be more accurate but much less adaptive. These normal processes of memory can occur at any stage, from the original perception of an event through encoding, consolidation, and storage, and eventually to reconstruction. Each stage is susceptible to the unconscious biases of personal experience, existing knowledge, mental attention, cultural expectation, and self-enhancement. Those who righteously intone their immunity to such biases are merely fooling themselves; illusions are part of everyday life, whether past, present, or future.

## CONSTRUCTIVE PERCEPTION

At its most basic level, what we remember depends directly on what we perceive. Psychological perception is based on physical sensation, of course—on the chemical and electrical processes that occur in the eye, ear, nose, mouth, and on the skin, and in their corresponding areas of cortex. The eye points toward a particular scene, picks up the play of light and dark, transduces it into a pattern of electrical stimulation, and transmits that stimulation through the brain until it arrives at the visual cortex in the back of the head. All along the way, however, the mind runs rampant with unconscious hypotheses as to what the scene might be. These hypotheses are created from our memories of past experiences, existing knowledge, expectations, and needs. Because memories are idiosyncratic, each of us perceives the same event in a different way, a difference that ranges from minuscule to monumental. The conscious perception of a scene, then, comprises an intertwined combination of external reality and internal expectation.

Examples of visual and auditory illusions are so plentiful as to have become the cornerstone of many a standard undergraduate course in human perception. One of my favorites is the young woman/old woman illusion, dubbed the "wife/mother-in-law" in less politically correct times. Most young people who look at the drawing (Figure 5.1) see the young woman first. Only with conscious effort can they construct a view of the old woman in their minds. However, most elderly observers of the drawing see the old woman first and, similarly, must use conscious effort to see the youthful beauty. Furthermore, regardless of age, people who have first been exposed to drawings of other young women are more likely to see a young woman in the ambiguous figure, but the opposite is true for those who have first been exposed to drawings of old women.[3] Who we are and what we have done determines what we see—even when we are all viewing one drawing

Figure 5.1

that produces only one set of physical sensations. The power of internal ex-pectation is so compelling that many observers of this illusion have trouble seeing anything other than what they first believed the drawing portrayed. Readers who experience the same difficulty may be able to alter their per-ceptions by noting that the young woman's chin, necklace, and ear are the old woman's nose, mouth, and eye, respectively. In addition, the young woman is looking away from us, exposing the back side of her jaw, whereas the old woman is looking more directly to the left.

Auditory perception also depends on who we are and what we know. Trained musicians, for example, tend to hear music analytically, while un-trained listeners hear it holistically. In other words, a musician's knowledge and training causes her to perceive the multiple overtones in a musical note that untrained listeners do not hear. One musical note causes one physical sensation, but the conscious perception of that note differs from person to person. In accord with this perceptual difference, the right hemisphere—

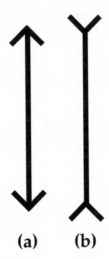

**(a)    (b)**

Figure 5.2

long noted in the popular press as specialized for music—is in fact not primarily responsible for the trained listener's musical perception. Instead, the left hemisphere, which tends to govern the more analytical functions of the brain, is used extensively when musicians listen to music. The right hemisphere, with its preference for more holistic functions, dominates musical perception only in untrained listeners.[4]

Differing perceptions of the same physical stimuli appear across people of divergent cultures as well, although the effect usually depends less on purely cultural features than on properties of the physical environment. Cross-cultural studies of human perception date back to 1901, when common European illusions were presented to members of non-European cultures. In the Müller-Lyer illusion, a frequently cited example, most North Americans see a line bounded by standard arrows (Figure 5.2a) as significantly shorter than a line bounded by inverted arrows (Figure 5.2b) even though a ruler will verify that both lines are actually the same length. This common illusion is seen quite differently by people whose habitat contains dense vegetation and few carpentered corners. Such environments reduce human experience with right angles and limit long views of linear perspective. In fact, the earliest cross-cultural investigation demonstrated that people from the tropical Murray Islands are significantly less prone to the Müller-Lyer illusion than are European subjects. Other studies followed, verifying the difference and extending the research to show that the percentage of perceived discrepancy in length between the two lines reaches 19 percent for industrialized Western subjects, while the comparable figure for African Bushmen is no greater than 1 percent, a whopping difference by psychological standards. Western adults are also less susceptible to the Müller-Lyer illusion than children, perhaps because analytical skills that are acquired in late childhood and adolescence reduce visual inference.[5]

To separate the effects of habitat from ethnicity, a more recent investigation measured the degree to which the Müller-Lyer illusion was seen among two groups of Navajo people living on the largest reservation in the United States: those who had lived primarily in round hogans, and those who had lived primarily in rectangular houses. As expected from previous research, many more Navajos who lived in angular homes reported seeing the illusory difference in line length to a significantly greater extent than did Navajos who lived in round hogans.[6] Physical environment, and not ethnicity, thus appears to impel the illusory phenomenon.

If two individuals can look at a stimulus as simple as two identical lines and judge them to differ by only 1 percent versus by as much as 19 percent, it should come as no surprise that the complex events of everyday life can create vast perceptual disparities across various people. That we have differing memories of the same event is to be expected. In fact, we should be puzzled not at the degree of difference between two people's memories of the same episode but at the remarkable degree of similarity, given the invisible machinations of human perception.

## THE ENCODING PROCESS

Once perceived, an experience is held momentarily in short-term memory and may then be encoded into long-term memory. The perennial assumption that all experiences are stored cannot be corroborated within the limits of science: An episode or fact that cannot be recalled might never have been encoded, or it might have been forgotten. Separating the two interpretations has proved impossible. Given present knowledge about the effects of attention, mental set, context, and personal significance on memory, my opinion, which is shared by numerous cognitive scientists, is that many—indeed, most—daily experiences are never stored. Such slavish devotion to encoding would certainly not be economical in an adaptive brain, and, let's face it, most of our minute-by-minute experiences fall into the category of useless trivia that, if memorized, would provide little advantage over the long term. Mental capacity is better spent on those aspects of our lives that are worth remembering.

Encoding is most likely to occur for events or facts that fit the organizational framework of one's existing knowledge and self-image. In psychotherapy, this compatibility can be a boon or a curse: Clients who have a strong self-image will accumulate memories of positive experiences that help them maintain their confidence, while the greater majority of people seeking psychological help—those with poor self-image—will store episodes that bolster their negative beliefs. Fortunately, individuals with low self-esteem can be taught to remember positive experiences.[7]

Information that is processed in depth is much more likely to be encoded than is information processed at shallow levels, so mental activities of deep elaboration and active application are effective methods of encoding new material.[8] The American educational system would be vastly improved if more teachers mined the brain's penchant for deep processing. Active learning exercises help students tremendously in consolidating memories for the long term, and they can be every bit as effective for clients whose psychotherapy attempts to alter personal self-image. A very short list of such exercises would include creating examples, talking or writing about a to-be-remembered topic, debating its pros and cons, transforming information into a wide variety of different media, involving people actively in events that convey specific knowledge, and putting new memories to use in multiple applications.

Rote repetition, as well as the mere intent to remember, are nearly useless in moving information from working memory into long-term stores. Likewise, attempts to encode and store material that is not personally important to the individual usually fail. For more than fifteen years I have had to look up the number of neurons estimated to reside in the human brain every time someone asks. The request usually comes from people whose areas of expertise lie outside cognitive science and who therefore assume that the number of neurons in an average brain is a significant fact that any good cognitive scientist should know. But actually, such information is trivia to the discipline; it is the organization and physiology of connections between neurons that teach us how the brain works, not the sheer number of 100 billion cells or 60 trillion synapses.[9]

Although many theorists have attempted to explain long-term encoding over the past century, the most current spate of explanations relies on the premise of neural activation patterns. According to these theories, the memory of one simple experience is not represented by one neuron. Instead, bits and pieces of the experience are scattered across a wide swath of the posterior brain lobes through a network of distant but connected neurons, so that the memory of one simple experience requires a large number of individual neurons to be activated simultaneously. Because the synaptic connections in the network are more important than the neurons themselves, we sometimes say that the memory trace is represented in the emptiness of multiple synaptic gaps rather than in the solidity of the cell bodies that comprise brain tissue. Furthermore, the new unions that are formed to represent an experience are strongly influenced by the strengths and weaknesses of existing connections that represent past events and declarative knowledge. Portions of these existing connections are linked to the newly formed conjunctions, a merger that can either enhance or distort memory. Both new connections and old increase their strength with use, so that frequent activation of a particular neural pattern allows the memory it embodies to be retrieved more easily.[10]

Support for this generalized class of activation theory is ample, thanks to recent advances in neuroscience. Animal studies demonstrate that new synapses are created by novel events, both in youth and adulthood. When the new synapse is formed, an electrochemical process known as long-term potentiation causes the freshly joined neurons to enjoy a boost in excitatory potential for several days, allowing a temporary period during which the new memory can be activated with ease.[11] More dramatic structural changes continue to occur throughout life in brain regions that are especially plastic, like the hippocampus, and they persist across a wide range of species who are exposed to similar learning conditions. In response to a particular experience, new synapses form within minutes, and dendrite growth is measurable within only a few days. Furthermore, neuroscientists have shown that these changes are caused by learning and are not merely a by-product of physical activity or mental exercise.[12]

Explorations of memory's physiological underpinnings exploded with new information during the 1990s, helping to explain the electrical and chemical bases of remembering in neurons. However, little is known about other brain processes that may be equally important. Vascular development in response to a novel experience, leading to an increase in blood vessels surrounding certain brain regions, has not yet received the attention it deserves. Likewise, scientific suggestions that gonadal hormones, such as estrogen, progesterone, and testosterone, may influence human memory and cognition have been largely ignored. Furthermore, neuroscientists are just beginning to delve into behaviorally driven molecular changes at the level of gene expression.

Even experiences of great personal significance that are selected for encoding in a neural network can become distorted far beyond the level of error already admitted by perceptual bias. First, not all of the bits and pieces of a perceived experience are represented by neural synapses. Some are lost entirely, leaving holes in the network's representation of the memory. These holes are often filled unconsciously with information based on inference or generalization, much like the blind spot of the human eye is overcome by the brain's ability to patch the visual gap with educated guessing. In both cases, we remain unaware that a hole existed or that it was filled. Second, a competing neural connection that happens to be linked to the network of a given memory may have the strength to override synapses that have become weakened with disuse. When this happens, a piece of erroneous information is injected into the memory, without conscious awareness that it is wrong. Again, the processes of inference and generalization operate to keep us unaware of the error.

Empirical studies of inference show that it operates during the perceptual, encoding, storage, and retrieval stages of remembering. One team of investigators presented statements that are common in commercial advertising, then asked subjects to judge the truth of related inferences that were presented immediately or some time later. One sample stimulus began by querying subjects: "Tossing and turning again? Having trouble getting to sleep? Get a good night's sleep and feel refreshed in the morning. Buy Dreamon sleeping pills, the ones in the purple package." Subjects later judged the truth of a related test statement: "Dreamon sleeping pills will make you get a good night's sleep and feel refreshed in the morning." The results indicated that 50 percent of these inferred claims were judged immediately as true, a larger percentage than most people would expect. When a retention interval was inserted prior to the true/false judgments, the percentage of inferred claims that were accepted as true shot up to 75 percent.[13] I find it rather frightening that people base half to three-quarters of their memories on questionable inferences even when listening to advertisements that ought to increase their skepticism.

Aside from competing neural connections and representative holes in the network, an even more powerful source of distortion at the stage of encoding is located in themes of self. British psychologist Martin Conway has suggested that an individual's plans and goals, along with discrepancies between his present self and a possible self that is either desired or feared, combine to form motivating themes.[14] These themes, whether conscious or unconscious, help determine which autobiographical experiences and declarative facts, and which parts of a given experience or fact, will be encoded for the long term. Suppose, for instance, that a sixteen-year-old boy hopes—perhaps unconsciously—to demonstrate his adult manliness by driving a fast sports car with great skill. Attainment of the goal, signified by a successful high-speed adventure, is likely to be encoded firmly as a piece of autobiographical information that helps him build the desired self-image. If, on the other hand, the high-speed drive resulted in stripped gears and scraped fenders, the teenager's brain would be less likely to encode those parts of the experience that cast a shadow over his desired concept of himself as a skilled adult male. Alternatively, his brain could solve the problem by failing to encode the notion that high-speed driving is related to manliness and by prioritizing the concept that manliness is better measured in other ways.

Research has borne out Conway's theory by demonstrating that experiences of thematically compatible goal attainment are indeed remembered with vivid detail. Memory cues based on discrepancies between actual and ideal selves are also more likely to elicit recollections than are cues that are related to the event but not to the self-discrepancy. Autobiographical memory searches based on the chronological organization of past experiences are effective for only the first year or two of storage, whereas searches based on personal themes of self lead to successful retrieval of older experiences. Furthermore, most people recall the scenes of even their recent memories not in chronological order but in clusters surrounding the most distinctive detail. Often, that detail focuses on an issue of personal self-creation.[15] All in all, the evidence stacks up in favor of the notion that themes of self are very powerful memory aids and should therefore be applied frequently in both clinic and curriculum.

## DISTORTION DURING STORAGE

After an experience has been firmly encoded in a distributed pattern of neural activation, it is still not immune to distortion. An engram, or pattern of neural connections that represents a past experience, weakens naturally over time, especially if it is not activated regularly. During long-term storage, the twin processes of forgetting and interference operate on a daily basis to loosen the mind's grip on particular pieces of information. As you know, Ebbinghaus was the first to study forgetting scientifically. The results of his studies have been replicated hundreds of times since he memorized nonsense syllables, and they have been extended to paint a picture of forgetting that travels far beyond the ecologically invalid stimuli that he favored. Ebbinghaus's forgetting curve showed that 50 percent of the new nonsense syllables that he intentionally memorized were forgotten within one hour. Within nine hours, 60 percent of them were gone, but the rate of forgetting slowed radically as the hours and days progressed so that after a month had passed, only about 70 percent of the material had been forgotten, leaving 30 percent in long-term memory.[16]

Later experimenters have obtained the same pattern of forgetting, whereby rapid loss of new information within the first few hours levels off over a matter of days and weeks. However, different types of stimuli cause a less dramatic amount of forgetting: Rhymed poetry, for example, is forgotten much less quickly than nonsense syllables are, and about 70 percent of one's memory for personal events tends to be retained for as long as six months.[17] Nevertheless, the shape of the forgetting curve persists even with these more memorable stimuli. Forgetting is an important adaptive process that operates in every normal brain.

Interference also affected Ebbinghaus's results. During one year of data collection, he memorized over twelve hundred lists of stimuli, with thirteen nonsense syllables in each list, and he worked through the set of twelve hundred lists 163 times![18] It should not be startling that the stored trace of a syllable like "zud" might interfere with the creation of a new memory for the syllable "zuf." Extant knowledge often interferes with our ability to learn something new; hence the common finding that the most memorable information will be compatible with past experience, current organizational framework, cultural assumptions, and present self-concept.

The same sort of interference influences previously stored autobiographical memories. Retention of personal events is created through three types of knowledge. The first type, event-specific knowledge, is comprised of details pertinent to one episode, such as the details of your conversation last month with a particular physician. Roughly speaking, it is the same as an episodic memory. The second type is general-event knowledge, defined as schematic understanding; it might be represented as typical conversations with typical physicians. The third type of knowledge contributing to the storage of auto-biographical memories is lifetime-period knowledge. This is a category of abstraction that characterizes a time in one's life, like a year of visiting different physicians in an effort to assign medical diagnosis. As might be expected, interference is most disruptive to autobiographical memories stored at the event-specific level. Its effect is milder on the superordinate categories of general-event and lifetime-period knowledge.[19]

After initial encoding is complete, new engrams whose neural connections have been activated only once or twice go through a process of consolidation. Complete consolidation, which allows the engram to be retrieved reliably in the future, takes months or years of interleaved learning in which the memory is activated at increasing intervals and in different physical or conceptual contexts. The medial temporal lobe aids consolidation by coordinating the simultaneous activation of multiple neurons scattered across numerous physical locations in the brain. Although a full physiological explanation remains elusive, we do know that sleep enhances consolidation and that the REM state of dream sleep may be predominantly effective. Such results are corroborated by inveterate knowledge in cognitive psychology that greater recall is displayed when learning is immediately followed by periods of sleep. In addition to its neurological effect on memory consolidation, sleep also strengthens a new memory by reducing interference from other activities. Even a brief nap can help.[20]

## DISTORTION UPON RETRIEVAL

More is known about memory construction and distortion during the retrieval stage than during the preceding stages of perception, encoding, consolidation, and storage. The cues used to elicit recollection, along with the internal and external context during retrieval, help to determine exactly what will be recalled. As Schacter says, "The 'memory' in a neural network model is not simply an activated engram. . . . It is a unique pattern that emerges from the pooled contributions of the cue and the engram."[21] Because the retrieval cue alters the engram, each successive recollection of a particular memory changes the trace that is stored. In other words, we literally cannot retrieve the same memory twice because it is dynamic rather than static. Repeated retrieval prevents forgetting but increases the amount of unconscious alteration that occurs. Contrary to popular assumption, recalling an experience again and again does not solidify it into an immutable rock of knowledge.

Physiologically, the brain carries out episodic retrieval with the help of many cortical regions. As I have previously said, the neural connections that represent stored information are distributed throughout the brain in various, mostly posterior locations. To assemble and activate a given neural network, the medial temporal lobe, including the hippocampus, acts as a pointer that indexes various distributed locations. PET studies show that the right prefrontal lobe is especially active during episodic retrieval, while its counterpart on the left lights up during episodic encoding.[22] Theories based on neuroscientific findings suggest that the prefrontal cortex may also play a primary role in evaluating the information that is activated; that is, in determining whether a given piece of information adequately serves the purpose for which it is being retrieved. The thalamus, buried within the central portion of the brain, serves as a connecting station that links the evaluative work of the frontal lobes with the distributed network of posterior storage. Therefore, associative retrieval that occurs automatically (*kitchen-chair-table*) seems to require the use of medial temporal lobe and hippocampus, but strategic retrieval that requires effort (imagining the kitchen chairs in your childhood home) relies more on the prefrontal cortex. If this sounds complex, just wait until we know more about how the sophisticated ingredients of neurotransmitters, glial development, blood vessels, sex hormones, and molecular gene expression fold into the memory recipe.

Scientific investigations proliferate with respect to the ways in which retrieval can alter an existing memory. To provide only a few examples, one pair of British psychologists found that the same memory, recalled multiple times, resulted in different and sometimes conflicting details each time, even when the same retrieval cues were used.[23] Another team of investigators altered subjects' memories of voice tone by manipulating retrieval cues of facial expression. All subjects heard and encoded the same neural voice in an initial stage of the experiment. Later, subjects who saw a smiling face as a retrieval cue recalled the corresponding voice as pleasant; those who saw a scowling face recalled the corresponding voice as irritating. In fact, there was no relationship whatsoever between facial expression and tone of voice in the experimental stimuli.[24] The form of a question alters retrieval as well. Multiple-choice questions are more likely to elicit errors in recollection than are open-ended questions answered with a continuous narrative.[25]

Another study demonstrating retrieval alteration was based on the Freudian distinction between field memories and observer memories. In a field memory, your participation in a scene is represented from the personal viewpoint that precludes seeing yourself, so that you are remembering the event from the same position in which you experienced it. Observer memories have been altered to create an external viewpoint that allows you to see yourself in the remembered scene, as if you were both a participant and a bystander. In the experiment on retrieval alteration, subjects were asked to remember personal life events in which they had played significant participatory roles. Recent memories were more likely to fall into the field memory category, while older memories tended to be remembered from the observer point of view. When the researchers manipulated retrieval cues, subjects who were told to focus on their emotions recalled more field memories, whereas those who were told to concentrate on the objective facts of an event recalled more observer memories.[26] Later researchers demonstrated the releasing of emotion from certain memories by asking subjects to purposefully change a field memory into an observer memory. Subjects reported that the original memory seemed less emotional when they imagined seeing themselves in it from the vantage point of an objective onlooker. The memory itself and its attendant emotions were altered by a simple change in the method of retrieval.[27]

Different cues lead to divergent memories partly because a network of neurons can be entered from any one of its thousands of connections. Some portions of each connected network will be stronger than others by virtue of more frequent activation. For example, your memory of the most recent wedding you attended is captured in a large number of synaptic gaps. Some portions of the network represent your knowledge of the bride; others represent your knowledge of the groom; still others signify the type of cake that was served at the wedding reception; and so on for each encoded feature of the entire event. If the bride happens to be your coworker, the portion of your wedding memory that contains information about her might be activated and altered every day as the two of you work together. Conversely, if you do not know the groom well, information about him is probably limited to the circumstances of the wedding and will tend to remain relatively static and frequently inactivated. Over a period of months, the bride portion of your wedding memory gains strength, while the groom portion becomes weaker. Ensuing retrieval cues, about either the bride or the groom, may cause different portions of the entire wedding memory to be activated. Only the stronger features are likely to enter consciousness. In all likelihood, then, you will probably recall more about what your coworker, the bride, did at her wedding than you will recall about the activities of her new husband during the ceremony.

When the weaker nodes of a network are not activated during retrieval, unconscious construction fills the holes with acceptable knowledge. Such knowledge is plausible within the framework of the overall memory, but it is often inaccurate. Holes are patched with inference or generalization, or by a related node that is not actually part of the original memory but works effectively as a decent substitute. In this manner, activated memories usually feel complete when they become conscious; the brain works hard to prevent our realization that a hole ever existed. And once a hole is filled, it becomes part of the original memory that will be re-encoded and stored again.

As is true for encoding, the activation of a memory during retrieval depends not only on its frequency of usage but also on its compatibility with self-concept. Knowledge that fits with our personal understanding of ourselves, that does not create a discrepancy between the current self and ideal self, will be more easily recalled. Furthermore, because the self is every bit as dynamic as the memories that create it, the portions of an experience that can be recalled today may be very different from the portions of the same experience that can be recalled next year. In other words, what is uppermost in one's quest for the ideal self will change at various times so that present desires determine what will and will not be remembered. Of course, the process of composing a memory according to internal goals is usually entirely unconscious.

When we provide ourselves with retrieval cues, we are likely to choose the ones that match an encoding fairly well. If the cake at that wedding, for instance, was terribly important to you—maybe because you own a wedding cake business or must select the cake for a relative's upcoming ceremony—you will be likely to cue your own memory of it appropriately. In real life, however, someone other than the rememberer usually selects the retrieval cue. One person's question or cue seldom matches another person's encoded response. If you encoded the taste of the cake, the unique method by which it was decorated, and a likely list of its ingredients, but then you were asked whether its decorations matched the color of the bridesmaids' dresses, you might be unable to respond on the basis of your memory. The memory then appears weak when in fact it is merely being called upon via the wrong cue.

Wedding cakes aside, the process by which retrieval is cued becomes crucial in psychotherapeutic settings. The troubled psychological client often suits the description, to a disconcerting degree, of the individual who is most prone to memory distortion. Such an individual is highly suggestible, capable of developing quick rapport with a sympathetic listener, liable to accept authority without question, and unable to concentrate on a specific issue for more than a few moments. His unconscious inclination toward excessive memory distortion is exacerbated by the very existence of a therapist in the recall environment—regardless of the therapist's skill or the client's honesty. Any cues that the therapist provides to elicit the client's memories will change those memories to some degree. And all of these factors, including the altering effect of a clinician's cues, are even more potent when the engram is impoverished to begin with, such as when it is very old or very hazy. Memories that have not been activated for many years, and are cued in a clinical setting by even the most highly trained therapist, are likely to be profoundly distorted.

## SOURCE AMNESIA

Errors attributed to source memory are among the most frequent roots of distortion. Here, the memory of an event or fact is retained, but information as to its source is muddled. For instance, you may recall learning something about a phenomenon dubbed the reminiscence bump, and you may remember enough about it to describe the effect accurately. However, source memory may prevent you from recalling exactly where you acquired the information: Was it in this book or another? Was it in chapter 2 of this book or chapter 4? Was it something you read or something you heard from a colleague? Anyone who has become frustrated with the need to document sources in written manuscripts can sympathize with the feeling of source amnesia. Already a major factor in memory distortion, it can only increase in today's hyper-connected technological world.

An excellent example of distortion caused by source amnesia is found in recent research concerning the misinformation effect, in which eyewitnesses who are provided circuitously with misleading information later recall the incorrect assertion as being true. Thus, an eyewitness who is asked how fast a car was traveling when it passed the yield sign will likely recall a yield sign later, when in fact what she saw was a stop sign. The cause of the error seems to be source memory: Eyewitnesses encode the yield sign but do not recall whether the source of that sign was their original perception of the event or the questioning provided a few minutes later by experimenters or police interrogators. Returning to the neural network momentarily, the missing source information is filled in with whatever data is represented by the strongest synaptic connection, whether it is correct or not. And the strongest connection is often the most recent one, hence the bias toward misinformation. Source amnesia is so complete in these cases that people usually experience little consternation, advancing their incorrect answer with confidence because it fits the rest of the memory network so well.[28]

If distortion is a common feature of normal human memory, and if remembering is more accurately characterized as constructing knowledge than retrieving it, why do we feel so confident that our memories are veridical representations of reality? While this question still receives less inspection than it warrants, a few facts have emerged. Frequent rehearsal, such as that which occurs prior to courtroom testimony, adds to one's sense of false confidence, as does familiarity with the cues and contexts surrounding a retrieval attempt. Reinforcement from authority figures, such as attorneys, judges, police officers, educators, and mental health professionals, can also increase confidence levels without concomitant increases in veracity. In addition, the retrieval of event-specific knowledge, rather than lifetime-period or general-event knowledge, may bolster confidence because of the vibrance and specificity that are typically included in such autobiographical memories. Our societal acceptance of the assumption that vivid detail signifies accurate recollection is also to blame; this falsehood is routinely reinforced in newspaper, magazine, television, and cinematic descriptions of memory as well as in the American legal system and many of our most prominent clinical settings, both medical and psychological.

Theories of constructive memory are not new. In fact, the German biologist Richard Semon, who coined the term "engram," presented a highly constructive view of remembering, including an explanation of memory distortion, in 1904.[29] Freud offered a different but equally constructivist theory in his essay on screen memories dated 1899.[30] Frederick Bartlett's research, conducted during the 1920s and 1930s, provided empirical support for the active construction of memories caused by an interaction between the to-be-remembered material and the rememberer's prior knowledge and cultural expectations. In 1932, he published a monograph detailing such evidence, including the famous "War of the Ghosts" experiment in which British subjects were asked to recall a brief story of Pacific Northwest Indian lore that they had heard earlier. Bartlett found that the subjects frequently omitted details that were not consistent with their British backgrounds, added nonexistent details that were consistent, and created nonexistent rationalizations for those parts of the story that seemed confusing.[31]

At a more general level, interdisciplinary scholarship concerning memory construction and distortion has grown rapidly in the past few years and is likely to continue in the future. Philosophers have offered a deeper understanding of the potential for creation that is inherent in memory as well as an intriguing journey into the notion of memory as truth. Marcel Proust, Vladimir Nabokov, and James Joyce form only a tiny subset of novelists who place memory distortion squarely in the center of literature, reminding us along the way that, for all its flaws, memory is one of the most enriching and universal aspects of human life. Recent trends in literary analysis combine the linen of traditional literature with the silk of postmodern philosophy, weaving a field in which the construction and creation of memories become primary concerns. Historians wrestle with the veracity of a growing revisionism, and political scientists grapple with the effects of collective memory on nationalism. Everywhere we look, it seems, there are good reasons to believe that memory is constructed and distorted on a regular basis, with unconscious neurological intent, and in purely natural ways. Why we have persisted in assuming that memory is like a video camera, in the face of such historical background and compelling evidence to the contrary is a perplexing cultural question.

# CHAPTER 6

# Memory and Mood

*Still the last, sad memory hovers round and sometimes drifts across like floating mist, cutting off sunshine, and chilling the remembrance of happier times.*

—Edward Whymper

To what extent in everyday life are our memories affected by our emotions or moods?[1] One well-known psychologist reports that when embarking on the study of mood-dependent memory during the 1970s, he was teased by academic friends for "even bothering to demonstrate such an 'obvious' triviality."[2] A decade later, mood and memory research had become a jumbled icefall of intricate contradictions that spurned even the most dedicated scientists. Today, we are finally making sense of the field's complexities through a combination of methodologies. As is so often the case, what appeared to be transparent was actually opaque.

The relationship between cognition and emotion is especially important when applying the results of psychological science to the riddles of clinical psychotherapy. It is also an interconnection about which experimental psychologists have been frequently misunderstood. Critics argue that academic psychology has ignored emotion entirely on the reductionistic assumption that all mental phenomena can be reduced to cognitive processes or brain physiology. But in fact the study of emotion has not been ignored during much of psychology's history. Witness the 1890 James-Lange theory of emotion that remains in contention today, the classical conditioning studies of the 1920s that exploited the link between emotion and cognition in developing methods of eliminating fear, the investigations of weapon focus in eye-witness memory that were conducted during the 1960s and 1970s, or the recent explorations of emotional effects on learning since cognitivism ousted behaviorism forty years ago. Nor does the greater scientific attention devoted to cognition necessarily imply a reductionistic mind-set. Many psychologists who specialize their research by creating a temporary separation between cognition and emotion would never argue that emotion is an object unworthy of psychological science. On the contrary, most cognitive scientists agree that the relationship between cognition and emotion is of primary concern and that we now know enough about isolated cognitive and emotive processes to fruitfully study their interaction in tandem. No complicated discipline can begin by investigating everything simultaneously.

That greater curiosity is now paid to the link between emotion and cognition is undeniable. The journal entitled *Cognition and Emotion*, established in 1987 and devoted entirely to this link, receives over 120 manuscripts each year, and several recent books promote "a genuine interweaving" of cognitive and emotional processes at the neurological level.[3] Antonio Damasio, for example, believes that cognition and emotion are intimately intertwined in the realms of logical reasoning, planning, problem solving, and rationality. He goes so far as to say that irrational emotions and feelings are required for rational thought, and backs his assertion with results gleaned from his experience as both neurologist and experimental psychologist.[4] We now know that some of the same brain structures mediate both emotional and cognitive functions.[5] If you want to achieve the most rational thought processes, keeping a cool head may be detrimental.

Specific investigations of emotional effects on memory have been undertaken since at least the 1950s, with philosophical exploration of the topic significantly predating that. It is a basic fact—"obvious," some might say, before they delve into the field—that emotions, moods, physical environments, and bodily states do alter human memory. If the memory of an event is constructed and stored while you are angry, for example, you will be more likely to recall the event later if you are again in an angry mood. Bodily states, such as intoxication, and physical environment have similar consequences. Anyone who has walked through the corridors and classrooms of his elementary school twenty years after leaving it will have experienced context-dependent memory, usually resulting in a flood of recollections that seemed nonexistent prior to the visit. The relationships of mood and state to human memory are likely to be crucial to therapists when applied both as a technique for enhancing clients' recall and as a basis for interpreting their voiced reminiscences. Not a few observers have pointed out as well that the clinician's own memories of a client's situation and treatment are swayed by mood.

## VIVIDNESS, CONSISTENCY, AND ACCURACY

We might enter the literature on mood and memory by asking whether emotional memories differ from unemotional ones.[6] Ample evidence exists to support the fact that events suffused with emotion are remembered more vividly and more consistently over time than are unemotional events, although the conditions under which these outcomes occur tend to be complex. Regardless of the emotion under study (anger, fear, delight, disgust) or the stimuli used in scientific tests (words, events, daily activities), a strong positive correlation persists between the emotionality of an experience and the vividness of its recollection.[7] Research in this area is dispersed over a variety of laboratory and naturalistic settings, normal and abnormal subjects, natural and induced moods, and positive and negative events, yet it remains consistent with respect to vividness. Even highly traumatic events are most likely to be remembered brilliantly.

Why emotional events are recalled with such long-lasting vibrancy remains an open question, however. In both naturalistic and laboratory settings, inquiries into emotional memory are restricted by the number of potential factors confounding the results. For example, emotional events may induce intense memories because they tend to be personally significant, because they receive a great deal of attention, or because they are accompanied by physiological arousal. Important events tend also to be rehearsed frequently—either silently as we ruminate on them, or aloud as we talk about them—and they may be rehearsed differently as well. One pair of psychologists have proposed that "one not only thinks more about emotional events than neutral events; one also thinks about them in a different way, in more personal, more psychological terms, and less in schematic or abstract ways."[8] Any event having the same personal importance, whether emotional or not, might produce equally sharp clarity over time.

The fact that emotional events are recalled vividly and consistently does not mean that they are recalled accurately. As we have seen, even the most vivid memories—like those of the *Challenger* explosion—can be inaccurate, and vivid inaccuracies can be maintained consistently for entire lifetimes.

Memory is actually less accurate for the details of emotional materials than for the details of nonemotional materials. The irony of such permanently vivid inaccuracy is not lost on researchers in the field: "It is our most detailed, seemingly most complete, memories that are the memories most likely to contain fallacies. . . . Many psychologists would endorse this striking claim and, more specifically, the claim that emotionality does indeed undermine memory accuracy."[9] However, those same researchers go on to say that we can trust most of our emotional memories to be accurate. If it sounds as though I'm saying that emotional memories are both accurate and inaccurate, you're right. Welcome to the icefall.

Making sense of such confusing contradictions is possible, though it requires a willingness to bypass easy answers and look deeply into the literature. The Easterbrook hypothesis, named after the psychologist who proposed it in 1959, provides a plausible, if partial, explanation.[10] Easterbrook argued that the physiological arousal experienced during emotional events causes mental attention to narrow into a heightened focus. This, in turn, creates a memory that is vivid and accurate for the central gist of the event but incorrect and cloudy for peripheral details. When pressed to recall peripheral details that were never encoded, we unintentionally reconstruct, creating a coherent story that smoothes out the unconscious holes in our recollections. This effect has been demonstrated repeatedly in research studies since 1959.[11] Its best-known example may be weapon focus, in which eyewitnesses to a crime cannot identify the perpetrator holding a weapon but are very good at recalling information about the weapon itself.[12] Several studies have even shown that people remember emotional scenes as being more spatially compact than they really were, whereas they remember neutral scenes as more broadly inclusive, as if an internal photographer were switching between a telephoto and a panoramic lens.[13]

The Easterbrook effect means that we can trust only the focal gist of a retrieved emotional event and not the details. Detailed vividness, of either the center or periphery, should not fool us into accepting the reminiscence as necessarily accurate. In practice, however, we commonly use peripheral details to verify that memories are true. After all, it is not the gist but the details that convince juries during courtroom hearings, physicians during medical diagnosis, police officers during interrogation, and sometimes mental health professionals during clinical sessions. Our dependence on peripheral detail is misplaced, fashioning a false sense of confidence in both parties to the memory. Furthermore, what qualifies as "focal" or "peripheral" is subject to a great deal of argument, depending on who is being asked. For instance, the innocent victim whose eyes are riveted to the wrong end of a gun is likely to consider that weapon—and the finger on its trigger—to be "focal," while the face behind the gun and attached to the trigger finger is considered "peripheral." Local detectives, investigating the crime later, would probably hold the opposing view.

Source amnesia may also play a role in the inaccuracy of memory for the details of an emotional event. Indeed, when subjects recall emotional stories they have read, they make fewer errors in describing plot than control subjects do, but more errors about the main character's motives or reactions.[14] Interestingly, these errors in motive are mediated by the subjects' emotions at the time they read the story, recalling their own emotionally based motives as part of the narrative even when such motives would directly contradict the story itself. Thus, a subject who feels frightened upon reading of a surgeon's decision to slice an artery is likely to report later that the confident surgeon herself was frightened, although that was not at all true. By confusing the source of the emotion, we tend to produce inaccurate memories that can lead to a false understanding of the original event.

What about consistency? The lasting nature of emotional memories is caused by a delay in normal forgetting rather than an unusually strong encoding of the original event. In other words, compared to neutral events, emotional events produce poor levels of recall immediately after they occur but they are forgotten more slowly, leading to an apparent enhancement of memory over time.[15] The slowed process of forgetting explains another of the many contradictions in this area of study: When asked to recall an emotional event that occurred only a short time ago, memory is impaired relative to baseline; when asked to recall an emotional event that occurred long ago, memory is enhanced. This outcome may be partly explained by the fact that strong emotions do not subside immediately, so that the rememberer may still be upset when asked to recount the event soon after it occurred. There is more to it than that, however. Perhaps there is something about emotion—maybe physiological arousal—that ultimately alters the process of consolidation. This suggestion is borne out by recent neurological data that is considered more thoroughly in the chapter on memory for trauma.

To summarize thus far, memory for emotional events is characterized by graphic but unreliable detail, consistency over time, accuracy for the central gist, corresponding inaccuracy for peripheral features that may nonetheless be extremely important, delayed forgetting, and an unconscious tendency to fill gaps with plausible—but often false—explanations. In addition, like all memories, those that capture emotional events are subject to unconscious cognitive biases that work to alter self-image and maintain comfortable trends in thinking. These trends and biases may be positive or negative, depending on the emotion and on the remembering individual. Because they can be changed with strategy and practice, they also provide beneficial applications to the clinical setting.

## MOOD DISORDERS AND MEMORY

A standard finding within the area of cognitive biases is that normal people in everday life find pleasant events most memorable, while depressed individuals retrieve a panoply of unpleasant reminiscences. This effect remains robust regardless of the number of negative events that an individual has actually experienced. It also appears within the same individual at different times. In one study, patients whose depression varied cyclically were asked to retrieve personal memories related to neutral word cues. As expected, patients who were depressed at the time retrieved far more negative memories than positive ones. The outcome was reversed during nondepressed times of the cycle, so that the same patients then retrieved more positive than negative memories.[16] The effect stands even when differences in emotionality ratings are controlled, demonstrating that people are not merely rating particular memories as more negative because of their depression. A meta-analysis of numerous studies in this area indicates that depressed people recall 10 percent more negative than positive memories, while nondepressed individuals recall 8 percent more positive than negative memories, for a sizable (18-point) total difference.[17] This sort of emotional priming generalizes across naturally depressed patients and normal subjects in whom sadness is temporarily induced, as well as across a variety of cueing methods and different types of tasks.

In addition to retrieving fewer positive remembrances, people who are clinically depressed also retrieve less specific memories. Mark Williams, a British psychologist who studies the connection between memory bias and emotional disorders, has determined in a number of well-controlled studies that overgenerality is a hallmark of reminiscence in depressed individuals.[18] Although positive memories are most susceptible, overgenerality is also seen in negative memories held by depressives. In one of Williams's investigations, subjects were asked to retrieve specific personal memories. Control subjects who were given the cue word "angry" recounted specific situations, such as "with my supervisor on Monday." Suicidal patients who received the same cue word supplied overly general circularities, such as "when I've had a row."[19] Making the cue words more specific did not help the suicidal patients to generate precise memories. Williams went to some trouble to rule out alternative explanations for these results, confirming that overgenerality was not a side effect of the drugs taken by suicidal patients nor was it limited to memories of older events whose specific details would naturally have been lost over time.

The size of the overgenerality bias is impressive. One study showed that depressed individuals' memories were specific only 40 percent of the time, while control subjects' memories were specific 70 percent of the time.[20] Thirty percentage points is a huge disparity by the standards of psychological research, especially when the researchers' success in matching the two groups for age, education, and semantic performance is taken into account. Failure to provide specific memories is a common characteristic of clients with depression and posttraumatic stress disorder, but not among those with anxiety disorders, and it is also seen frequently in frontal amnesics, people with right-hemisphere damage, and normal young children.[21] Equally intriguing, overgenerality lingers even after emotionally disordered patients have recovered to the point of experiencing very little mood disturbance. Usually, individuals who offer overgeneral memories remain unaware of their behavior and therefore fail to comprehend requests for greater specificity. To them, vague abstractions seem like perfectly normal memories.

Overgenerality is currently viewed as a function of "mnemonic interlock," in which retrieval efforts occur continually at shallow levels but go no deeper; therefore, rumination of the same general idea ("I'm bad, I'm bad") repeats itself.[22] Unfortunately, this description begs the more important question: Why does overgenerality—or mnemonic interlock, if we must—occur so rampantly in the depressed population? A good dose of speculation has been administered to this query, with some alternative explanations appearing more likely than others, but no solid answers are available yet. Overgenerality in recollection might be a cognitive style developed long before the onset of depression, and if so, it might even contribute to the evolution of the disorder. This possibility is partially supported by the finding that overgenerality among both normal and disturbed individuals is more likely to occur during times of unusual stress. But it is also possible that depressed patients use overgenerality as a protective strategy to prevent rumination of negative details, a strategy that then erodes their memories of positive details as well. Continued insistence on vague abstractions creates perceptual habits in which specific features of an experience are literally not perceived or encoded, exacerbating the memory's weakness. Overgeneral memories may also be easier to provide than specific memories if the patient's primary objective is to please therapists and experimenters into going away. Depressed individuals might also wish to avoid sharing personal details with others; on this matter, however, Williams points out that "patients show similar recall failures during therapy sessions after a great deal of trust has been established and many painful areas already discussed."[23]

Whatever the reason, we do know that the patients who provide the most overgeneral memories are least likely to recover from their depression. On the other hand, those who recall specific events in detail—especially positive events—are most likely to resume normal lives.[24] Detailed examples of behavior, held in memory, can be crucial for solving problems effectively; without them, a client's database of information is completely impoverished, and he will be unable to proffer the level of detail needed to think of potential solutions that might work in specific settings. Overgeneral memories also inhibit effective psychotherapy: The client who says, "I'm always bad at everything," but cannot offer precise situations is unlikely to improve her emotional intelligence. As an example, disturbed mothers who immediately classified their children's misbehavior as "bad" without encoding specific memories of it were unable to get along with their offspring. Equally disturbed mothers who learned to encode and retrieve the details of individual events significantly improved their relationships with their children.[25]

Fortunately, memory biases of overgenerality can be altered. Williams recommends the judicious use of anamnesis, a therapeutic strategy in which clients are asked to deliberately recall recent autobiographical events while the therapist provides memory instruction.[26] Because many people assume it is best not to remember difficult situations, the therapist can begin to help simply by explaining why detailed memory is important for both negative and positive events. Clients are more likely to embrace such precision once they are aware that it will improve problem solving by generating potential solutions. As their recollections proceed, patients can be praised for detailed reminiscences, encouraged to identify memories that lack detail, taught to generate specific cues that will improve the search for specific memories, reminded to think about details while perceiving new events, and asked to record the details of daily events in diaries. These strategies are then practiced frequently both in the clinical setting and in everyday circumstances until clients are able to encode and retrieve precise details of their autobiographical memories with little effort.

## MOOD CONGRUENCE AND DEPENDENCE

Congruence between mood and memory, in which bad moods lead to bad memories and vice versa, is not limited to people who experience mental disorders. All of us are vulnerable to the phenomenon. In fact, most of the research on mood congruence has been conducted using normal subjects. Under everyday circumstances, mood mediates memory in a manner that preserves positive self-image, categorizes knowledge, and deepens both cognitive and emotional understanding. It may also operate as a regulatory force, balancing negative moods with positive information and countering positive feelings with negative knowledge.

Mood congruence refers to the normal tendency to remember the words, faces, activities, and events that most closely match our moods of the moment, just as depressed individuals tend to remember depressing events. For all of us, sad stimuli are more memorable when we feel sad, and happy stimuli are more memorable when we feel happy. The effect is larger and more consistent for positive moods than for negative moods when moods are artificially induced, but this difference disappears with autobiographical memories encoded under natural conditions.[27] In everyday life, then, positive events are likely to lodge in our minds when they occurred during pleasurable times, but negative events will be especially hard to forget when they occur during difficult times. Just as the thought of pregnancy causes many women to notice every mother with a young baby, positive attitudes can increase positive memories that will, in turn, boost the positive attitude. This spiral is beneficial in creating a positive self-image, but obviously it can be very harmful when turned to negative use. In general, the mood congruence effect is well known, remaining robust for both experimental recall of word stimuli and natural recollection of autobiographical event memories.

But nothing about the human psyche is simple. The reverse phenomenon of mood incongruence has also been demonstrated, although less frequently. One research team discovered to their surprise that people who did well on an exam or were questioned on a sunny day were more likely than control subjects to produce sad memories.[28] Since that first discovery of mood in-congruence in 1990, the effect has been replicated several times. Researchers speculate that a balancing strategy is in use, allowing good news to be inter-spersed with bad as a form of mood regulation. Potential motives for the de-sire to dampen a good mood have been supplied by one of the original investigators. Specifically, people might inhibit good moods "to promote re-alistic thinking, to avoid distraction . . . , to motivate oneself to work hard, [or] to protect oneself against future disappointment."[29] Social motives would include the desire "to behave appropriately . . . , to be considerate . . . of others, to conceal one's mood from others, [or] to influence other people's moods."[30] It appears, then, that there are many reasons for reducing the hap-piness of a good mood.

Mood-dependent memory is also a feature of normal reminiscence. The resemblance between the terms "mood dependence" and "mood congru-ence" often leads to confusion, but there are important distinctions between the two concepts. Specifically, mood congruence refers to an effect of the stimulus itself: A sad event is more memorable when we feel sad. Mood de-pendence is not caused by the stimulus: Any event is easier to recall when our mood at the time of encoding is similar to our mood at the time of re-trieval. Although mood congruence is a stronger and more reliable phenom-enon, mood dependence is also quite forceful under the right circumstances, generating roughly 90 percent recall improvement among depressives and 50 percent among normal college students.[31] To add to the confusion in ter-minology, its effects also meld with those of mood congruence. That is, mood dependence is most likely to occur when the material to be remem-bered actually creates the mood that is later recaptured during retrieval, as is often the case in autobiographical situations.

Since the mid-1970s, hundreds of studies have been published demon-strating mood dependence. In one of the earliest investigations, moods were induced hypnotically in normal college students, who then learned four lists of neutral words, one each when they were feeling either happy, sad, afraid, or angry. Recall was most accurate in all four moods when subjects at-tempted to retrieve the words under the same mood they had experienced while learning the words. For example, a given individual was better able to recall neutral information while in a fearful mood if she had also learned it while in that same mood. Subsequent research replicated, generalized, and extended this basic finding, establishing its existence in semantic, episodic, and autobiographical memories.[32]

One prominent theory of mood dependence—the "emotion network model"—suggests that each different emotion (such as happy, sad, disgusted) is represented in the mind by an organizing feature that pulls related information together into an individual category. When that organizing feature is activated for any purpose, neural activation automatically spreads to the related bundle of information so that we are more likely to become aware of that information and less likely to become aware of information clustered under other emotional organizing features.[33] Whether each organizing feature represents emotions along a unidimensional or a multidimensional valence is still under careful consideration. Unidimensional representation would imply that each emotion can be represented along one continuum, stretching from very happy to very unhappy, for example. Multidimensional representation argues that each emotion is represented by two to eight different valence dimensions, creating concurrent vectors that form a rich collage of the information bundled within any one emotional organizing feature.

Although the studies of mood dependence during the 1970s and early 1980s demonstrated consistent effects, later investigations fell under the penumbra of spotty replication and discrepant results. From the mid-1980s to the early 1990s it seemed that the more we learned about mood-dependent memory, the less we knew. Eric Eich, a cognitive psychologist at the University of British Columbia who leads the research on mood and remembrance, imposed some order on the recalcitrant results by identifying four features of mood dependence that are critical in producing the effect. First, mood dependence is strongest for information that is generated internally rather than externally. Thinking about a situation, or even imagining it, increases the boost that mood provides to later recall. Second, highly specific cues tend to impair mood-dependent memory. Therefore, it is best to encourage people to recall an event by inducing a mood similar to that felt during the experience of the event, then allowing the individual to recall freely without questions or comments from the listener. In this way the rememberer is generating for herself not only the recalled material but also the cues to its retrieval. Third, a sturdy and stable mood must be experienced, both at the time information is encoded and at the time it is retrieved. Although natural moods are best, induced moods can be effective. Finally, the fourth of Eich's recommendations for consistent mood dependence in memory is to consider level of arousal in addition to the usual dimensions of emotional valence. Increased arousal usually heightens the mood dependence effect.[34]

Mood induction has been criticized on several occasions as an artificial technique that is unlikely to fool people into experiencing certain feelings. Subjects themselves, however, argue that induced moods are actually quite realistic, especially those that are created with Eich's continuous music technique.[35] Some research has even been conducted to establish the validity of this technique in producing specific moods. Chapter 11, which is devoted entirely to methods of enhancing retrieval, contains a full description of the procedure.

Eich's identification of the four features that provide an organizational framework for mood-dependent memory has been very helpful in moving the research forward. But what does it mean for the psychological practitioner? To contemplate these features in a more practical light, mood-dependent memory is especially likely to occur with internal processing of remembered events, free recall of the ensuing memories, implicit aspects of the event as key points, potent feelings of affect, and heightened arousal—all central or potential traits of the therapeutic context. That clinicians may apply the research on mood-dependent memory to their clients' benefit is clear, although greater investigation into the potential pitfalls of such techniques is needed.

## STATE AND CONTEXT DEPENDENCE

Mood may also be at the root of other memory dependencies that have proved themselves perverse. Like the early research on mood-dependent memory, initial investigations into state and context dependence seemed transparent. In one of the best-known studies, a group of underwater divers was asked to memorize words in one of two physical environments—either while sitting by the side of a Scottish lake or while hovering under water near the bottom of that lake. As you might expect, recall was better—46 percent better, in fact—when the learning and retrieval conditions matched. Divers who learned the words at the bottom of the lake were much better able to recall them when placed again in the same physical context. Likewise, divers who learned the words while sitting lakeside experienced significant improvements in memory when sitting lakeside during retrieval.[36] Soon thereafter the same effect was obtained using an assortment of physical environments and bodily states, including alcohol intoxication, amphetamine use, and barbiturate consumption. Although I would never suggest that retrieval be enhanced by getting drunk or diving to the bottom of a local pond, it is true that context is a potent mnemonic cue. That is why victims and eyewitnesses often experience a surge of recollections upon returning to the scene of a crime.

But later studies of state and context dependence elicited puzzling results. Situations in which we were certain to obtain significant differences between match and mismatch conditions did not pan out, while those that held no promise whatsoever engendered positive outcomes. Although investigations of state and context dependence are still marked by confusion, Eich argues that mood may be at the center of the mystery. Perhaps an individual's internal context when in a particular environment or situation is more important to memory than is his external location in the physical realm. Eich points out that this would explain the fickle nature of results on classroom testing. Classrooms can be matched or mismatched at learning and retrieval with little effect because the act of taking a difficult test creates internal feelings that are about the same in any classroom. Similarly, state-dependent memory based ostensibly on the use of drugs such as amphetamines and barbiturates may in reality be a mere by-product of the mood changes induced by the drugs.[37]

Although bodily state and physical environment do indeed have the potential to alter human memory, Proust's assumption that taste and scent elicit reminiscence may not be entirely redeemed. Memory's dependence on aroma is still elusive despite decades of cognitive research and known neurological connections between the olfactory nerve, which is responsible for our sense of smell, and the hippocampus. Although it seems likely that the flavor and aroma of the madeleine would have helped Proust's teatime memory to come wafting back in that famous passage from *Remembrance of Things Past*, replicable empirical demonstrations of the phenomenon are lacking. My office mate in graduate school spent months studying the relationship between memory and aroma, storing his experimental materials—papers that reeked of cinnamon, apple, and cherry scents—in the office where he and I frequently studied. Alas, the scents had no effect on his many subjects and served only to make me hungry. Cognitive scientists do not fully grasp the connection between remembrance and aroma just yet.[38]

Mood congruence and mood dependence are better understood at this time than are state dependence and context dependence. There is no doubt that emotions and moods stimulate memory. But is it also possible that emotions and moods cause us to perceive events differently even before they are remembered? One series of studies suggests that the answer is yes.[39] When feeling happy, for instance, we are more likely to pay attention to happy events, quicker to perceive happy words, and better able to discriminate happy faces. The same perceptual congruence occurs with other emotions as well. Emotional influences on perception are seen in everyday life, with researchers in the field noting that "we see people with whom we are in love as more attractive than people whom we hate, . . . the same dark alley looks more ominous when we are afraid than when we are not, and . . . foods that are usually appealing look unappetizing when we feel disgust."[40]

## MEMORY FOR EMOTION AND PAIN

Although emotional feelings usually aid memory, most people are poor at remembering the emotions themselves. This inability may be more directly related to language than to memory, given the weakness of words in expressing the infinite nuances of a complicated emotion. However, some research suggests that language may not be the only factor. For example, although the shadings of both pleasant and unpleasant emotions are difficult to describe linguistically, people consistently have more trouble recalling the intensity of negative emotions than positive emotions. Interestingly, when pressed to guess at the intensity of a previously felt negative emotion, most people overestimate.[41]

Mental health professionals who rely on popular diagnostic tests that require clients to answer questions about their past emotions, such as the Minnesota Multiphasic Personality Inventory (MMPI) or the California Psychological Inventory (CPI), might be startled to learn that no published studies demonstrate accurate recall of emotion, either in emotional intensity or emotional frequency. Nevertheless, comprised largely of statements that require memory for personal emotions, the MMPI remains the most widely used psychological test in North America. In addition, it is applied in more than fifty countries around the world and has been translated into more than 115 foreign languages. Upwards of twelve thousand technical articles and books have been published on its use.[42] In stark contrast to the MMPI's popularity, a thorough search of the psychological literature prior to 1997 uncovered no evidence whatsoever that people—normal or disturbed—are able to remember their emotional pasts with anything resembling the kind of accuracy that such diagnostic tests entail. Some psychologists might argue that the initial development of personality inventories by comparison between normal and disordered populations alleviates this problem. However, the use of such tests has widened in scope to such a degree in recent years as to render this argument meaningless for the majority of people to whom the tests are administered.

In addition, the most widely used diagnostic manual in the world for various types of mental disorders, the *Diagnostic and Statistical Manual* (presently DSM-IV), encourages clinicians to base their diagnoses of affective disorders largely on a patient's memory for emotions. Questions like "How often do you feel depressed?" and "How long does the feeling last?" are quite difficult to answer with accuracy given the weakness of normal memory for emotions.

Although studies of memory for physical pain are very rare, a few do exist.[43] With the help of his colleagues, Eric Eich has established the occurrence of pain congruence in memory, demonstrating that people's current level of pain alters their memories of chronic pain experienced in the past. More specifically, when their level of current pain was low, subjects reported that the discomfort they felt one week earlier was less excruciating than they had said it was at the time.[44] Another study showed that current menstrual pain hindered normal women's ability to retrieve pleasant autobiographical memories to a statistically significant degree. Furthermore, the same pain significantly increased access to unpleasant autobiographical recollections, but only when the subjects were simultaneously experiencing a negative mood. (Almost all of them were—as anyone who has lived in pain would expect.)[45] Thus, at the very time positive attitude may be most important in relieving physical pain, our memories seem to operate against us. As if to verify that supposition, chronic pain is strongly correlated with clinical depression.[46]

Memory for physical pain is as critical to medical diagnosis as memory for emotion is to psychological diagnosis. The next time you visit a physician, think about how much of the experience is based on your assumed ability to recall and compare differing degrees of physical pain or psychological discomfort under a variety of past circumstances. Everything we know about human memory points to the opportunity for grievous error in such diagnostic recollection. Yet, despite their radical influence in physical and mental diagnosis, the topics of memory for pain and emotion have been sadly neglected in empirical research. Such neglect represents, in my opinion, an irresponsibility among experimental psychologists and cognitive scientists that the disciplines of psychology and psychiatry should never have allowed. Traditional Western medicine—long the bastion of empirical science—has condoned the same level of ignorance. We spend millions of dollars investigating every hair on a diseased earthworm, but we take our assumptions of accurate memory for granted.

Just as medical, psychiatric, and psychological diagnoses are made every day on the basis of patients' faulty memories for physical pain or emotion, the physicians and psychotherapists making those decisions are subject to identical vulnerabilities—being human, after all. In fact, one investigator surveyed sixteen psychologists and found that none of them could remember their own initial plans for the clinical treatment of twenty of their patients. They even expressed surprise when shown written copies of their initial plans, which were one year old at the time the research study was conducted.[47]

Looking at the study of mood and memory from a broader perspective, one caveat comes to mind. The notion that "emotional memories" may be stored and retrieved differently from "nonemotional memories" might convey the implication that some memories have no emotion attached to them whatsoever. On the contrary, I would argue strongly that memory is seldom emotion-free or moodless. It is the type and degree of emotions or moods, and the manners in which they change—cyclically, whimsically, or causally—whose effects are being investigated most productively. Although the vagaries of language sometimes encourage us to speak of "nonemotional" memories, no one is really suggesting that any memory can be devoid of feeling.

Given that caveat, a quarter-century of research has established that emotions and moods do indeed affect our memories for all kinds of events, knowledge, and information. To say that we don't know much about the relationship between memory and mood, and that we therefore have little knowledge to apply to practical settings, is little more than a display of personal ignorance. Mood causes all of us to perceive and remember events differently from the way we normally do, and it can be a boon to recall in certain situations, just as the reenactment of a physical context or bodily state inspires memories to come rushing back. Furthermore, positive mood is as effective in favoring pleasant recollections as negative mood is dangerous in perpetuating nettlesome remembrances. Therapeutic strategies based on such research findings can help troubled individuals use their memories to create healthy attitudes.

Emotions make our recollections more vivid and more consistent, but they cannot overcome Mnemosyne's occasional pockmarks of inaccuracy. In this respect, the peripheral details of an event suffused with emotion are likely to be remembered less accurately than are those from an event that was relatively bland. Focal aspects of the more emotional situation are remembered well, however, a finding that has been obtained in hundreds of empirical studies and should therefore lay to rest the assumption that emotional memories are frequently lost.

# CHAPTER 7

# Memories for Trauma

*Remembering seemed unwise. They never knew where or why she crouched, or whose was the underwater face she needed like that. Where the memory of the smile under her chin might have been and was not, a latch latched and lichen attached its apple-green bloom to the metal.*

—**Toni Morrison**

No other topic within the field of human memory today is as controversial or consequential as the study of memories for trauma. Authors pale at the thought of grappling with its scientific ambiguities, political pitfalls, and choleric debates. Some succumb to the temptation to change its conflicting shades of gray into black-and-white answers that are clear-cut but misleading. Potential readers, by contrast, may be eager to turn first to this chapter when perusing the book, as if it can act as a representative test whose outcome determines whether the entire volume is worthy of their time. What most therapists need are solid conclusions leading to meaningful treatments for real human beings in deep despair; what most of the research offers are questions, uncertainties, and conflicting results.

Although a few conclusions are now available from the scientific literature on traumatic memory, I do not pretend to supply easy answers in this chapter. Instead, I ask readers to join me in exploring the questions, traveling the twists and turns of a highway that surely goes somewhere but still seeks its final destination. As a point of departure that models the topic as a whole, we begin with a contradiction.

In 1989, the American Psychological Association's flagship journal presented the results of a survey of sixty-three individuals who were considered experts in eyewitness testimony. Almost all of them had Ph.D.s in psychology; three-quarters had authored at least one article concerning eyewitness testimony, with a mean of six relevant publications each; and roughly half had testified in court as expert witnesses in that field. The authors of the survey presented a series of statements to these experts, asking them to rate their level of agreement with each assertion on the basis of their familiarity with relevant evidence. Two of the statements are especially pertinent to our inquiry: First, 79 percent of the psychologists agreed that the evidence was favorable, generally reliable, or very reliable for the claim that "very high levels of stress impair the accuracy of eyewitness testimony." Second, 51 percent agreed that the evidence was favorable, generally reliable, or very reliable for the statement that "eyewitnesses have more difficulty remembering violent than nonviolent events."[1]

Yet if we compare those results with published assertions from some of our most respected neuroscientists, psychologists, cognitive scientists, and psychiatrists, a different view emerges. Prominent neuroscientist James McGaugh writes, "The evidence . . . leaves little doubt that events that are characterized as arousing, emotionally exciting, or stressful are generally well remembered."[2] Psychologist Sven Christianson, whose research has focused on the effects of stress on eyewitness memory for over fifteen years, argues that "the results from . . . studies of real-life events suggest that highly emotional or traumatic events are very well retained over time."[3] Cognitive scientists Katharine Shobe and John Kihlstrom report that "the preponderance of laboratory evidence indicates that memory is more likely to be enhanced than impaired by high levels of emotion and stress, so that memories for trauma are distinctive, long-lasting, and easily retrieved."[4] And psychiatrist Lenore Terr, a clinical practitioner with extensive experience in treating traumatized clients, says, "I found that every one of the [twenty-six] kidnapped children retained detailed, precise memories of what had happened, even in the later study. . . . The Chowchilla memories stood out in sharp light, as if the whole scene had been lit with a magnesium lamp. Nobody repressed. And nobody forgot."[5] On the one hand, then, we have sixty-three experts in eyewitness testimony who largely agree that trauma impairs memory, while on the other hand we have the very top researchers from relevant areas of expertise arguing that trauma improves memory. What gives?

## METHODOLOGICAL CHALLENGES

To address that question responsibly, a side trip is in order through the ethical and methodological mine fields of traumatic memory research. Simply put, the topic is very difficult to study. The American Psychological Association's guidelines for ethics, along with our own personal principles, preclude the development of laboratory studies that induce trauma. In other words, we cannot put a loaded gun to a subject's head, then ask what he remembers about the event later. We can, of course, create experimental conditions that provoke mild stress, but such laboratory experiments are rightfully criticized for their fictional nature. Less artificial studies involve interviewing people who have endured truly traumatic experiences that occurred naturally, providing the requisite degree of reality but opening the door to a host of confounding variables that muddy the results. For example, in real situations, researchers have no control over an individual's physical distance from the event, level of emotional stress, degree of physiological arousal, vantage point, ability to perceive an event unfolding very rapidly in darkness, extent of physical injury, or motivations to cooperate with police or psychologists. Validation is also problematic—outside of the laboratory, how can we be certain that what a witness or victim remembers is an accurate representation of what actually happened? Although it is important to use a wide variety of methods, both laboratory and lifelike, none of them is trouble-free.

These methodological problems lead to a situation in which consumers of the research must accept responsibility for evaluating it with a critical eye. Many of the studies done on memory for trauma are flawed in some way, often by lack of control or lack of realism. Sometimes this cannot be helped; researchers do the best they can to conduct a preliminary inquiry, knowing that their designs are not perfect. On other occasions, the design could be improved but is not, perhaps because of ignorance or haste. Either way, swallowing the results of flawed studies without chewing over their methods first is quite dangerous, especially if those results are to be applied directly to traumatized clients. Even highly educated practitioners who are not well versed in the details of research methodology are likely to accept flawed studies as good evidence. It's an easy error to make. And those with less training avoid the original studies entirely, leaning instead on information from pseudo-authorities who have plenty of slick conclusions but no background in memory research.

To the widespread existence of flawed methodology in this area, we must add conceptual confusion. Some researchers in the field consider the normal death of elderly parents a "traumatic" event; others reserve the term for the axe murders of one's own preschool children. There are no clear boundaries in the literature between "stressful" events and "traumatic" or "emotional" events, nor are there criteria for deciding why one person's " difficult experience" is another's "severe trauma." "Arousal" is also confusing even though it has been earmarked as a key feature of the inquiry: Are we talking about autonomic arousal, cortical arousal, or excited behavioral response? Arousal of the reticular activating system or arousal of the hypothalamic/limbic system? Is trauma chronic or acute? Is all stress negative? And are we investigating the typical creation of traumatic memories, or are we more interested in understanding rare instances of dissociative amnesia? None of these issues has been resolved adequately despite their implicit appropriation as cornerstones of the quest.

Here is a topic, then, that is riddled with methodological challenges and conceptual confusions but is critically important to thousands of professionals who must find a way right now to help their tormented clients. But to get the most accurate snapshot of the problem, we must stir in the explosive powder of popular controversy, fueled by rampant media sensationalism. Under these conditions, the best of scientists are misquoted and misunderstood, the worst are welcomed as instant experts, responsible psychologists on all sides are run through the wringer of righteous indignation at their dearth of knowledge, and—worst of all—the truly desperate are left stranded in the spotlights without receiving any real help. Even within the quiet cloisters of science, popular impetus has an effect: We race toward quick solutions, we present too many preliminary explorations as if they are replicated fact, we spend little time explaining our work, and we publish flawed research that would normally rot in a file cabinet. It's no wonder that the area is difficult to comprehend.

## DOES TRAUMA IMPAIR MEMORY?

Many people assume that the contradiction among experts as to whether trauma impairs or improves memory is irresolvable. But it is not. Resolution is indeed challenging, but with careful analysis of all the underlying factors, we can reach some important conclusions. First, we must look more closely at evidence for the idea that trauma impairs memory. Two significant clues

to the puzzle are the fact that most of this evidence predates studies showing that trauma improves memory and that most of it is derived from laboratory studies instead of naturalistic observations.

Some of the earliest and most frequently cited investigations demonstrating memory impairment under stress were conducted by showing films to
subjects participating in traditional experiments. In many cases, all subjects
saw the same film, with the exception of a brief section that was violent in
one condition but nonviolent in another. In one of these classic experiments,
for example, a two-minute video showing a simulated bank robbery contained either a fifteen-second clip of a boy being shot in the face or a fifteen-
second clip of the manager calming employees after the robbery had
occurred. When asked later to provide the number on the boy's football jersey, which had been visible for two seconds in both versions of the film, only
4 percent of the subjects in the violent condition were able to do so. By comparison, 28 percent of the subjects in the nonviolent condition identified the
number correctly, suggesting that violence does impair memory.[6] Similar experiments done around the same time, during the late 1970s and early 1980s,
produced analogous deficits in recall among subjects who had seen violent
versions of a film. These deficits occurred for actions carried out by characters in the scene and for physical descriptions of the characters. Another
well-known study demonstrated that both recall and recognition were less
accurate for written descriptions shown with mutilated faces than they were
for the same written descriptions shown with normal faces. In each case, the
violence of the stimuli seemed to hinder subjects' abilities to remember what
they had seen.[7]

Evidence of traumatic impairment from these laboratory simulations was
bolstered by clinical reports of memory disturbances including psychogenic
amnesia, dissociative identity disorder, and fugue. All of these disorders are
known to result from severe psychological trauma that, for a variety of reasons, an individual is unable to handle in a normal manner. Without doubt,
they are compelling examples of radical memory loss following trauma and
have been appropriately cited as evidence for impairment by trauma. In
psychogenic amnesia, the occurrence of a traumatic event shuts down autobiographical aspects of memory, leading to total but temporary loss of personal information. Episodic memory of the event itself is also lost, but both
types of memory are usually regained soon after the traumatic experience is
over. For example, incidents of rape that initially cause psychogenic amne-

sia—a consequence that is extremely rare, by the way—are almost always recalled a few hours later in disturbing detail.[8]

Amnesia for episodic and autobiographical information following a traumatic event is seldom psychogenic, however. Much more often, physical injury incurred during the event is responsible for the subsequent memory loss. This is especially true for closed head injuries, which can be difficult to identify, allowing for the potential, but incorrect, conclusion that the amnesia is psychogenic rather than organic. A widely known example of post-traumatic amnesia from organic causes is the case of Trevor Rees-Jones, the bodyguard who barely survived the high-speed car wreck that killed Princess Diana in 1997. He experienced severe head injuries, was administered massive amounts of anesthesia during hospitalization, and sustained a total loss of consciousness for many days. Despite these problems, police and paparazzi alike expected Rees-Jones to explain precisely upon his recovery the events that led to the crash, as if such extensive physical damage could not possibly have jostled the internal video camera that human memory is incorrectly assumed to be. Of course, upon resuming consciousness, Rees-Jones was unable to remember any portion of the crash or the events leading to it. Seven months later, he recalled little more than "flashes of a female voice."[9]

Distinguishing between psychogenic and organic amnesia is seldom that easy. To return to the example of the rape victim, we often have no knowledge of the likelihood or extent of possible injury to the brain. We rely instead on symptoms of the amnesia itself. Organic amnesia following physical trauma is usually generalized to several memory systems, including episodic, semantic, and, to a slightly lesser extent, autobiographical. Recovery from organic amnesia is often gradual, with older memories returning first, although in a spotty and haphazard manner. By contrast, psychogenic amnesia is frequently limited to autobiographical recollection and very specific episodes, such as the traumatic event itself. Recovery of all memories typically occurs all at once, only a few hours after the amnesia began.[10] There are exceptions, of course: The categorical separation of physical and psychological is often difficult to reconcile with the more realistic human combination of the two.

Psychogenic fugue occurs when an individual flees her life and assumes an entirely different identity, often replete with a new name, home, family, and friends. The flight is preceded by extreme stress that cannot be handled normally, either because the stressful events themselves are too difficult or because the person experiencing them does not know how to cope. Loss of memory for the individual's original identity and all its trappings can continue for many years. When memory does return, it often comes back fairly quickly and thoroughly, but memory for the identity assumed during the fugue is then usually lost. In other words, activating one set of autobiographical memories seems to inhibit the other set. A related disturbance occurs in dissociative identity disorder (DID) which, as most readers of this book are likely to know, results in the same sort of memory compartmentalization from one identity to another. The upshot of such severe dissociation is that one individual may be psychologically divided into several selves, each of whom holds memories separate from the others.

Although these dissociative disorders are prime examples of extreme memory malfunction caused by trauma, whether they should be treated as evidence for typical forms of traumatic memory impairment is another matter. Despite their frequent mention on  television talk shows and appearance in soap operas, novels, movies, documentaries, and newspaper and magazine stories, the mental disorders of psychogenic amnesia, fugue, and DID are very rare. Fugue, for example, occurs at a national prevalence rate of only .2 percent,[11] while DID has increased substantially in recent years, to 1 percent.[12] Should the study of memories for trauma be focused on a few rare individuals, or should it be trained on the vast majority of everyday folks who occasionally experience trauma and have trouble dealing with it? My opinion is the latter. The greater the number of people to benefit from memory scholarship, the better.

## DOES TRAUMA IMPROVE MEMORY?

The impairment side of the story, then, rests primarily on laboratory simulations done prior to the mid-1980s and on rare cases of psychological disorders that cause extreme deficits. Given this evidence, why do most 1990s experts argue that psychological trauma improves memory? The evidence for their belief comes mainly from studies of real-world violence, which show that most people who have experienced severe trauma remember it all too well. Indeed, many of them cannot forget the episode despite their forceful efforts. Added to such naturalistic evidence is a sprinkling of recent laboratory explorations as well as clinical experience with posttraumatic stress disorder (PTSD).

From the clinical front, evidence of memory loss in dissociative disorders is offset by evidence of recollective brawn in PTSD, a psychological disturbance marked by the total inability to forget traumatic memories that are so vivid they seem alive. The most trustworthy estimates of the lifetime prevalence of PTSD fall within 1 percent to 3 percent of the general American population.[13] The likelihood of experiencing PTSD increases with the number of repeated exposures to trauma. Contrary to everything we know about ordinary forgetting, the frequency and strength of these traumatic recollections increase over time. But in keeping with neurobiological evidence of a chemical connection between arousal and memory, PTSD patients exhibit higher levels of sympathetic nervous system functioning than do healthy subjects or patients with other anxiety disorders. Such excessive arousal occurs both while PTSD patients are reexperiencing traumatic memories and while they are resting under normal conditions. Traumatic memories in PTSD usually occur in all-or-none fashion; that is, they seem to emerge into conscious awareness whole or not at all. Furthermore, the focus on old memories can cause new events to be suppressed.[14] Observations of brain waves show that PTSD sufferers have significantly higher neural thresholds for experiences of new events than do healthy subjects. A higher threshold would make new experiences less salient, as if the brain sells itself into reexperiencing the past at the cost of living the present.[15]

The vigor and permanence of PTSD memories is mirrored among normal subjects who experienced trauma long ago. In addition, they display strong accuracy, something that is difficult to verify among PTSD sufferers. In one study, seventy-eight victims of the Nazi holocaust were questioned forty years later about their memories of specific concentration camps. These survivors had written reports of the camps at the time they were liberated, allowing the accuracy of their later remembrances to be verified by comparison with the earlier reports. Almost every one of the seventy-eight subjects in this naturalistic study recalled personal experiences as well as general camp conditions with great accuracy and impressive detail.[16]

Another real-life investigation involved interviewing thirteen witnesses to a murder, four to five months after it had occurred. Accuracy was verified by comparing the witnesses' memories with police reports taken a day or two after the murder. By these standards, recall was very accurate, yielding almost no deficit when compared to the earlier reports. Moreover, those witnesses who reported feeling the greatest degrees of arousal at the time of the murder produced the highest accuracy at the time of recall many months later. Their mean rate of correct recall was 88 percent, quite impressive compared to the typical laboratory study of memory for nontraumatic materials.[17]

Lenore Terr's naturalistic study of twenty-six children in Chowchilla, California, who were abducted on their school bus and buried alive for twenty-seven hours, also shows that trauma leads to excellent memory in great detail. Every one of her subjects fits this description. When interviewed just after the abduction ended, the twenty-six reports displayed remarkable consistency, [18]and when tested four to five years after the kidnapping took place, the children's reports matched the results of the earlier interview.[19] Terr, puzzled by the indication that some individuals do not remember traumatic events while others do, later theorized that different types of trauma have varying effects on memory. Specifically, she proposed that Type I trauma, characterized as a single unusual event, improves memory, while Type II trauma, characterized as a number of repeated events over time, impairs memory by virtue of psychological strategies designed to avoid pain.[20]

Unfortunately, there are some problems with the theory. First, we have already seen that with increased repetition of traumatic events the heightened recollections of PTSD are more likely to occur, not less. Second, Terr presented only one study to verify her suppositions, and so far, few other researchers have joined the probe. Third, that one study contains several flaws that undoubtedly contaminated its results: confounding variations in subject age, intimate knowledge of certain individuals through extensive psychotherapy, and the lack of a control group for comparison. Fourth, naturalistic studies that have filled these potholes have yielded results showing significantly stronger memory for all traumatic episodes, as opposed to neutral events, regardless of the amount of repetition. And fifth, repeated memories of any similar episodes are commonly blurry because of interference among the various events. This repisodic memory is a standard feature of ordinary forgetting that could explain the posited weakening of remembrance following repetition of any event, not just a traumatic one.[21] Further research and replication by independent laboratories may eventually prove Terr correct, but for now the evidence simply does not support her theory.

In addition to evidence of its accuracy and detail, other naturalistic studies sustain the view of traumatic memory as strong and confidently held. Studies of people's personal memories show that more intensely emotional recollections receive higher confidence ratings than do less emotional reminiscences.[22] Suggestibility is reduced as well, so that memories of stressful situations are less easily disrupted by the misinformation effect that alters standard eyewitness memories.[23] In addition, intense memories are more easily retrieved, whether they are positive or negative in valence.[24] And like the remarkable finding among PTSD patients whose traumatic recollections become stronger over time, studies in which normal individuals keep diaries of episodic events demonstrate that upsetting episodes stimulate memories that violate everything Ebbinghaus knew about forgetting.[25]

We need not rely exclusively on real-life studies for evidence that traumatic memories tend to be accurate. In one experimental investigation of nearly four hundred college students, 26 percent of the subjects who observed a neutral event depicted in photographic slides recalled the color of a woman's clothing correctly when tested later. But subjects who observed a matching emotional event—the same woman lying injured—were much more accurate: 70 percent of them recalled the color correctly. That's a large difference.[26]

To return to our original query—whether trauma impairs or improves remembrance—it should be obvious by now that a very real difference exists in the literature. Some studies, particularly laboratory simulations conducted prior to the mid-1980s, demonstrate that memory is hindered by traumatic events. Others, including most of the naturalistic real-life studies and many of the experimental investigations in the 1990s, show that memory is enhanced by psychological trauma. Clinical corroboration falls equally on both sides of the fence: Although rare disorders like fugue and psychogenic amnesia are defined by striking recollective deficits, the more common ailment of PTSD demonstrates remarkably vigorous memories that defy the laws of normal forgetting.

Such contradictions are perfectly normal in science. Preliminary explorations serve to make us aware not of the conclusions but of the many conundrums that are inherent in a topic. The topic of traumatic memory is no exception, but its disparities have received more attention because of publicity that rendered preliminary investigations into what appeared to be a solid body of replicated knowledge. Most media blitzes don't distinguish between a rough sketch and the finished portrait. Like Steven Spielberg, they create something even when it isn't there.

## RESOLVING THE CONTRADICTION

In seeking a reconciliation among contradictory results, cognitive scientists have uncovered a number of previously uncontrolled factors that we now know are critical in comprehending how the mixture of trauma, stress, and arousal impacts human memory. Specifically, traumatic memory is (1) better for central detail than for peripheral detail, (2) better among victims than among bystanders, (3) better when tested after a delay than when tested shortly after the trauma, (4) better when tested for recognition than recall, and (5) better when the items to be remembered are part of the trauma itself. Early studies that did not take these factors into account often produced misleading results. For instance, the first entry on the list goes back to the Easterbrook hypothesis discussed in chapter 5. As is true for emotional memories, we now know that central details are remembered more accurately from traumatic events than neutral events, while peripheral details are remembered more accurately from neutral events than traumatic ones. Research designed prior to this discovery often employed memory tests that inadvertently asked subjects for peripheral details, thereby producing results suggesting that memory for trauma was worse than memory for neutral events. Had those tests included questions about central details, the opposite result would have been exposed.

The classic experiment that I described earlier as evidence of memory impairment, in which subjects saw a simulated bank robbery on film, provides a more concrete example of the problem. Subjects in the neutral condition saw a young boy playing in the parking lot as the robbers ran away. Those in the violent condition saw that boy being shot in the face. The boy was visible for the same brief amount of time in both conditions. To test subjects' memories, the critical question requested all of them to supply the number on the football jersey that the boy was wearing. Given our understanding of the Easterbrook effect, it is no wonder that this question—referring to a completely peripheral detail—produced evidence of impaired memory for the film.[27] Most of us who were faced with such a grisly scene in real life would attend to more important central details—the murderer's clothing and physical features, the weapon used to shoot the boy, the boy's injuries, the rush to secure medical help. Who cares about the number on the back of the poor kid's shirt?

Recent laboratory simulations that take such methodological issues into account corroborate the Easterbrook claim with respect to traumatic memories. One study in which subjects observed a series of slide photographs presented a mother and son on a walk. In the violent condition, the boy was hit by a car; in the neutral condition, he walked past that car. As expected, questions concerning central details of the scene were answered more accurately by subjects in the violent condition. However, when peripheral questions were asked, no significant difference materialized between the two groups of subjects.[28] Although we may be tempted to criticize the earlier study of the simulated bank robbery as hopelessly flawed, we must remember that it (and others like it) served the important scientific purpose of generating a perplexity that was resolved by later inquiry. Because of such studies, we now know more about how traumatic memories actually work.

Naturalistic research also verifies the fact that traumatic memory is better for central detail than for peripheral detail. Interviewing a pool of witnesses who had seen twenty-two real robberies demonstrated that central details were quite memorable in their minds even though contextual information was not.[29] Likewise, when four hundred randomly selected people were asked to recall their most traumatic memory, a statistically significant correlation appeared between the amount of emotion reported and the number of central details recalled.[30] In general, there is now a great deal of research, from the laboratory and the real world, corroborating the fact that central details are more memorable than peripheral ones in our recollections of traumatic events.

Other factors have also helped us understand why so much of the early laboratory research indicated that trauma leads to memory impairment. Whether we place subjects in the simulated position of victims or bystanders is important enough to alter results. Recent studies are quite convincing in their display of more accurate memories among the victims of a trauma than among the bystanders as long as physical injuries do not preclude recollection.[31] The time of testing—soon after the trauma or following some delay—also makes a difference that early researchers were not aware of. Consolidation processes in the brain seem to occupy the memory trace so that it cannot be retrieved reliably just after a traumatic event has occurred.[32] Nor would we expect a victimized individual, one who is frightened, confused, and maybe hurt, to overcome his immediate state of shock quickly enough to provide a coherent report of what happened. I am reminded of Margaret Atwood's statement: "When you are in the middle of [living] a story it isn't a story at all, but only a confusion; a dark roaring, a blindness, a wreckage of shattered glass and splintered wood; like a house in a whirlwind, or else a boat crushed by the icebergs or swept over the rapids, and all aboard powerless to stop it. It's only afterwards that it becomes anything like a story at all. When you are telling it, to yourself or to someone else."[33]

Because they can provide the same kind of context that aids mood-dependent and state-dependent remembrance, cued tests of memory often enhance traumatic memory retrieval. Recognition tests, in which a remem-berer is given correct information along with incorrect distractors and asked to discern between them, usually lead to increased accuracy rates in laboratory simulations. Recall tests yield lower accuracy because they do not provide cues to either the original memory or its context.[34]

Finally, the ways in which to-be-remembered information is related to the trauma are very important. As Christianson has pointed out, "The issue of interest is what an eyewitness remembers about a traumatic event, not what the witness is able to retrieve from memory in the midst of the traumatic experience."[35] Several early studies of traumatic memory focused on the latter; more recent research looks carefully at the former. Thus, information that is directly associated with the stressful emotions of trauma is more likely to be recalled or recognized than information that was presented contiguously but bears no causal relationship to an individual's feelings of extreme distress.

At this time, cognitive and behavioral evidence from both laboratory and natural settings leans toward the same conclusion: Trauma enhances the strength, vividness, permanence, and accuracy of normal memory. That this conclusion is not necessarily true for every traumatic situation experienced by every human being need not sway us from its power. Every rule has exceptions, but we still need to know the rule. Many potential reasons exist for the enhancement of memory under traumatic conditions. Christianson argues that boosts in early perceptual processing, such as attention, focusing, and motivation, allow a traumatic event to be perceived especially clearly. Improved perception is then followed by unusually potent conceptual processing in which the event is mentally rehearsed in an elaborative way many times over.[36] Such rehearsal is especially likely to occur naturally for stressful events that are tainted with strong emotional meaning. Both repetition and elaborative rehearsal are standard aids in memory improvement, regardless of whether the information to be remembered is traumatic or bland.

## IS TRAUMATIC MEMORY ORDINARY?

Is it fair to apply our extensive knowledge of ordinary memory to the way people's minds work when faced with a devastating catastrophe? This question rests at the heart of science and scholarship on traumatic recollection.

Some authors have implied that a separate and qualitatively different memory system retains and retrieves knowledge of traumatic events. Therefore, they imply, there is little need for practitioners who specialize in treating trauma victims to learn the principles of ordinary memory. As you might expect, I heartily reject this implication on the basis that all memory is an inherent part of psychological self that cannot be ignored in any therapeutic situation, whether the client has been traumatized or not. Stepping beyond that point, however, whether traumatic recollection really is subserved by an autonomous brain system is an empirical question that remains open. Some highly respected scholars have argued that it is, including those who participated in a recent Human Capital Initiative Committee funded jointly by the National Science Foundation and the American Psychological Society. These researchers point out that traumatic memory is unusually accurate and that it is subserved by a brain structure known as the amygdala that seems to have little effect on unemotional remembrance.[37]

Opponents argue that the evidence for such beliefs is insufficient. Mnemosyne's accuracy in recounting disaster can be explained equally well, they contend, by thinking of traumatic memory as differing merely in degree, not kind, from ordinary episodic or autobiographical memory. Furthermore, although the amygdala is critical in creating emotional recollections, it does not necessarily follow that other neural structures involved in semantic, episodic, procedural, or autobiographical memory do not also subserve traumatic remembrance. Perhaps we simply have not yet uncovered all the functions mediated by such structures. In addition, neurobiological evidence of the chemical mechanisms by which all types of memory may be strengthened or weakened lends support to the notion that traumatic memory is just a heightened kind of recollection based on general principles that are already known.[38] For these reasons, a majority of cognitive scientists believe that we should continue to gather meaningful data before postulating the existence of yet another separate memory system.[39]

Either possibility may be borne out in the future. However, memory experts do agree that certain popular characterizations of the potential difference between traumatic and ordinary recollection are wrong. Specifically, we can easily refute the notion that traumatic memory differs—according to one writer—by virtue of being somatosensory, implicit, iconic, difficult to recall, confused, unconscious and involuntary, rigid, solitary, often forgotten, nonverbal, state-dependent, and evoked by cues.[40] First, copious corroboration in the form of hundreds of laboratory and naturalistic studies, as well as clinical cases, exists to prove that most traumatic memories are in fact easier to recall, less confused, and less frequently forgotten than their ordinary counterparts. Second, typical remembrances are frequently implicit, iconic, rigid, solitary, nonverbal, state-dependent, and evoked by cues. Therefore, if a qualitative difference exists between brain systems for typical memories and traumatic ones, it must be based on some subset of features other than these. In addition, any special system for traumatic memory would have to include mechanisms that lead not to impaired memory for trauma but to improved recollections of traumatic events.

## THE NEUROLOGICAL BASIS OF TRAUMATIC MEMORY

Although there is much more to learn, huge strides have been taken since the late 1980s in understanding the neurological underpinnings of emotional and traumatic memory. The amygdala has been established as the primary neurological structure for expressing and learning fear, and it is now thought to be critical in the formation of traumatic memories.[41] Damage to the amygdala in humans impairs the normal expression of emotion, leading to flat affect across a variety of typically stimulating situations.[42] Because fear and anxiety are primary issues in clinical settings, research into the functioning of the amygdala should be as relevant to professional psychotherapists as it is to cognitive scientists and neurobiologists. If a special system exists for traumatic memories, it undoubtedly includes the amygdala.

Furthermore, recent investigations have led to the intriguing suggestion that two anatomical systems, not one, may subserve traumatic recollection. I emphasize that the findings leading to these suggestions have not yet been replicated or interpreted to the degree of depth that we would prefer, so I offer them only as speculation at this time. Joseph LeDoux, professor of neural science and psychology, proposes that two separate pathways in the brain can lead to the creation of emotional memories. One travels through the thalamus, which mediates sensory information, on to the hippocampus, and then into the amygdala. This pathway is marked by rapid transmission of electrical impulses, allowing for raw information to be carried quickly to the amygdala. The other pathway also goes through the thalamus, but from there it goes to the higher level sensory cortex and then into the amygdala, bypassing the hippocampus entirely. This route allows raw information to be interpreted along with its surrounding context before arriving at the amygdala, and it therefore proceeds slowly.[43]

Abundant clinical and neurological evidence shows that the hippocampus is critical for the development of declarative memory. After all, as discussed in chapter 3, when H. M.'s hippocampus was removed, he was rendered immediately bereft of all ability to form new declarative memories. The fact that one of the emotional memory systems bypasses the hippocampus could therefore be considered a substantive—albeit speculative—clue to the possible existence of a neuroanatomical specialty for emotional or traumatic remembrance. We must keep in mind, however, that both emotional memory pathways operate simultaneously in normal adults. The hippocampus is therefore hard at work during the creation of both emotional and declarative memories even if it is not always necessary for emotional memory.

The tempting corollary of this speculation—that babies store emotional memories by virtue of one pathway before the other is fully developed—is highly unlikely. Although the hippocampus is not mature enough to sustain memory in infancy, it is equally true that the higher order sensory cortex used by the secondary pathway is puerile as well. And whether the existence of two neural pathways to emotional memory will ever explain the discord between facts and feelings in the retelling of traumatic events remains to be seen.

The chemical effects of acute stress are also critical to an understanding of memory for trauma. Corticosterone, vasopressin, and epinephrine are stress hormones produced naturally by the human body as part of the sympathetic nervous system's "fight-or-flight" response. These hormones increase memory retention when they are naturally secreted or externally administered immediately after new information is presented. This salutary effect occurs regardless of whether the information to be remembered is declarative, episodic, autobiographical, emotional, or nonemotional.[44]

Artificial administration of stress hormones is sometimes carried out in the experimental laboratory to investigate the chemical mediation of memory under controlled conditions. From these investigations we have learned that the time of administration and the dosage amount are both important factors. If the hormone is injected during information presentation or more than one hour afterward, it has no effect on memory, suggesting that hormonal regulation is particularly pertinent to the processes of consolidation.[45] Furthermore, if the dosage is too low, no effect is seen; if it is too high, memory is impaired rather than enhanced.[46]

A more concrete explanation of how stress hormones such as epinephrine work on the amygdala to create traumatic memories might be helpful.

Briefly, acute stress resulting from some event causes the body to secrete increased epinephrine. This jolt of epinephrine, in turn, boosts the amount of glucose in the blood. Glucose is the brain's primary source of fuel, so it travels to the brain and causes the amygdala to form an especially distinct memory of whatever was happening. Neither the epinephrine nor the glucose operates by directing the amygdala as to which event should be remembered. That determination is strictly chronological—whatever was happening just prior to the sudden infusion of extra glucose will enjoy a sturdy grip on memory. Furthermore, electrical stimulation of the amygdala immediately after an event enhances memory in much the same way, probably because electrical stimulation causes epinephrine to be released. The combined action of epinephrine and glucose that I have described works to enhance all kinds of memory, not just emotional or traumatic memories.[47] I take the liberty of applying their action primarily to traumatic memory because a traumatic event is most likely to elicit a sudden increase in epinephrine under natural conditions.

With additional research and full replication, these findings may help us explain the discrepancy between enhanced memory for most traumatic events and impaired memory in rare cases. Perhaps moderately traumatic events are customarily accompanied by a moderate rise in stress hormones, causing memory enhancement, while severely traumatic events cause extreme secretion of the same stress hormones, leading to memory impairment. Along the same lines, different neurotransmitter systems are known to operate in different ways. Some natural chemicals, such as acetylcholine and glutamate, tend to improve memory formation; others, including endorphins and GABA, impair it.[48]

Studies of classical fear conditioning, in which a frightening stimulus causes a learned fear response to develop, indicate that hormonal oversecretion is not always required for memory enhancement. These fear responses include the passenger's rapid inhalation of air when a driver unexpectedly brakes a car, or the pounding heartbeat we feel after stepping near a rattlesnake. They occur very rapidly. It takes only five milliseconds (five one-thousandths of one second) for neural impulses to travel from the amygdala to the startle pathway, much less time than would be necessary for hormonal release and uptake. Despite hormonal inactivity, classic fear responses are often learned after only one negative experience, and they are very difficult to extinguish over time.[49] With many counter-experiences, individuals can learn to control a fear response, but it is never erased.

The operation of chemical systems on memory structures in the brain is vastly more complex than my description implies. The neurobiological literature leaves no doubt that multiple brain structures as well as multiple hormonal and neurotransmitter systems work in parallel fashion to form memories, traumatic and otherwise. Furthermore, different chemistries interact in complicated ways, each altering the normal function of many others. Imagine a cascade of constantly changing chemicals, both bodily hormones and neural transmitters, each helping us to remember or forget one tiny piece of an event. Add to that the many different structures in the brain that help us form and retrieve memories: the hippocampus, amygdala, prefrontal cortex, sensory cortex, associative cortex, cerebellum, and basal ganglia, for a start. All of these regions interact in their own sophisticated ways, some being more receptive to certain chemicals than others. Because chemicals injected into local brain sites cause specific memory tasks to be enhanced or impaired, while systemic injections operate similarly across a number of tasks, some neuroscientists suspect that the structural system plays a more important role in enhancing and impairing specific memories than does the chemical system. If so, all memories would be formed by the complex action of hormones and neurotransmitters, but memories with differing content would be determined by the ways in which these chemical systems operate at different locations in the brain. Time—and a great deal more investigation—will tell.[50]

Despite the fact that our knowledge is not complete, current research in cognitive science offers important information on the creation, consolidation, storage, and retrieval of traumatic memories. I have tried to present a smattering of that information here, selecting preponderant evidence that is widely accepted within the discipline and pointing out a few speculations that are intriguing but not yet trustworthy. The topic of traumatic memory carries tremendous importance not only to individuals but also to our society as a whole. It therefore deserves careful analysis steeped in equal amounts of intelligence and compassion. Critical evaluation of the research—whether clinical, cognitive, or neurobiological—should be welcomed by all psychological professionals.

The last chapter of this book discusses in detail my concern that the clinical and experimental sides of psychology will never bridge the chasm they have created between each other. If that concern is borne out, I have little doubt that our understanding of traumatic memory will remain dangling in the maw of a vengeful debate that serves no one. But if we form sound research teams that include clinical practitioners and experimental scientists, working together from preliminary design through conclusive interpretation to therapeutic application, we may develop a deep understanding of traumatic memory, helping our discipline and our public at the same time. There may be no other area in all of psychology that cries out more plaintively for true interdisciplinary collaboration between clinical and experimental specialists.

# CHAPTER 8

# Implicit Recollection

*One is no more than a visitor in the mansion of memory, and most of the rooms one does not enter.*

—Esther Salaman

I often have trouble consciously recalling a close friend's telephone number despite my ability to dial it without looking in a directory. Some might say that my fingers know the number even though my mind does not. We have all probably experienced the same phenomenon—if not with telephone numbers, then perhaps with the entry code to a photocopy machine or the identification number for an automated bank account. When we use the numbers without thinking, they are correct; when we try to think of the numbers without using them, they are wrong.

So emerges the distinction between implicit and explicit memory, a disparity that is with us during every moment of our lives but was ignored for nearly a century of scientific scholarship on human memory. Many terms have been used to characterize the distinction. In addition to explicit and implicit memory, we have terms like declarative and nondeclarative, direct and indirect, knowing and remembering, or memory with awareness and memory without awareness. With advances from psycholinguistic inquiries on word retrieval and neuropsychological investigations of clinical amnesia, the entire subfield of implicit memory research erupted during the mid–1980s and has enjoyed growing attention ever since. Because it is so indirect and unconscious, implicit memory is a slippery concept to define. The ability to perform such motor skills and procedures as typing and riding a bicycle is implicit, but so are certain cognitive skills, such as completing word fragments and answering test questions correctly with no conscious awareness of how we know the answers. By contrast, explicit memory includes conscious awareness of the material that has been recalled, usually with a fair idea of how that knowledge was gained.

## HISTORICAL BACKGROUND OF IMPLICIT MEMORY RESEARCH

Daniel Schacter, the contemporary expert on memory who was mentioned in previous chapters, sees René Descartes as the first prominent thinker in a historical span of two millennia to have mentioned implicit memory. Intriguingly, he did so in the context of childhood trauma, conjecturing that frightful events may affect one's brain throughout life although no conscious memory of the experience remains. After Descartes' brief comment in 1649, Gottfried Leibniz wrote on the topic at greater length in 1704. One hundred years later, according to Schacter, a French philosopher known as Maine de Biran published what appears to have been the first extensive discussion of implicit memory. By 1870, as psychology's official founding approached, the physiologist Ewald Hering argued that implicit memory deserved considerable attention, pressing as far as to chastise other researchers for their shackled explorations. Hering's admonitions apparently had some effect because soon thereafter the study of human memory was basking in the scholarly sunshine of the 1880s, the decade that presaged memory's renaissance a century later.[1]

During the 1880s, implicit memory was investigated in the context of such psychic phenomena as automatic writing and neurological amnesias in which procedural abilities were preserved. As a corollary to his studies of explicit memory using nonsense syllables, Hermann Ebbinghaus described what he saw as a large category of implicit remembering and even went as far as to develop a scientific method of measuring it. His savings method involved waiting until all explicit memory of a list of nonsense syllables had disappeared, then measuring the time to relearn the same list. Because some implicit memory of the syllables remained without his awareness, less time was needed to relearn a list than to learn it in the first place, and the resulting difference was calculated as a savings score. Experimental psychology continued to dip a wary toe into implicit memory with the work of Edward L. Thorndike, O. Poetzl, Clark Hull, and William McDougall, who coined the terms implicit and explicit memory in 1924. But immersion was still half a century away.

Meanwhile, in the neurologists' quarter of the 1880s, Freud and Janet played a significant role as well, developing their theories of psychopathology on the basis of implicit memories. Freud believed that childhood traumas—or, in a later version of his theory, traumatic fantasies during childhood—were kept from awareness by an involuntary process of repression, effectively preventing the traumatic memory from emerging into consciousness.[2] These repressed memories, however, could still exert a powerful pull on behavior. Implicit memory is not the same as repressed memory, but this early psychiatric work is compatible with the notion that memories in general are not always open to conscious recollection.

Once the heyday of the 1880s had passed, almost all the research done on human memory concentrated on explicit recollection. Several plausible excuses merge to explain this tunnel vision. First, psychology was founded in an era during which science in any form was exalted. Because explicit memory was much easier to study using scientific methods, it tended to receive the most attention. Second, the stultifying effect of American behaviorism dictated that unobservable phenomena were not worth investigating, a pronouncement that certainly ruled out the study of implicit memory. Any psychologist who wanted a job in the United States from 1920 until about 1960 would have had to blind himself to the truly intriguing empirical questions of human behavior, like the Lady of Shalott turning away from her mirror. Even the relief of cognitive psychology in 1960, with its freedom to look inside the black box and its emphasis on unconscious mental processes, failed to revive interest in implicit memory. To this day most dictionary definitions of "memory" assume conscious recollection.[3]

## IMPLICIT RECOLLECTION AMONG AMNESICS

Today, the study of implicit memory represents an interdisciplinary amalgam of psycholinguistics, neuroscience, and experimental psychology, proceeding in the best of cognitive science tradition. Through this work we have demonstrated the existence of implicit recollection across a plethora of tasks, both in real life and in the scientific laboratory. Several of the tasks have been carried out in different modalities, showing that implicit memory occurs within visual, auditory, and tactile modes of sensation.[4] Within normal subject populations, implicit memory is seen across a wide range of ages, from before eight to after eighty. Tests of brain-damaged populations demonstrate the same kinds of implicit abilities, despite variations among many different cognitive deficits and neurological loci of lesions. The early glimmers of gold seen in amnesics' surprising abilities to remember implicitly, along with normal priming phenomena in lexical access studies, have panned out to create a new field of investigation that holds tremendous promise for neurological advances as well as real-world applications to education, development, social determinations, cognitive abilities, and psychotherapeutic settings.

One of the best-known stories of implicit memory in amnesics comes from Edouard Claparède, whose 1911 anecdote is still passed along to most undergraduates taking their first college course in human memory. Claparède is the infamous psychologist who hid a pin in his palm before shaking hands with an amnesic woman. Later, the pin-pricked amnesic, having no explicit memory of meeting Claparède before, refused to shake hands with him. Because she remained willing to shake hands with others, Claparède concluded that the amnesic patient held an implicit memory of being pricked with the pin.[5]

Contemporary amnesics display implicit memory as well. One of the earliest discoveries surrounding H. M.'s profound memory loss was that, despite constantly forgetting where he was and who he was with, H. M. was able to do pursuit rotor and mirror tracing skills. Both of these motor tasks were used in experimental testing during the 1950s and 1960s. They require the ability to copy by hand a random pattern of lines, while those lines are being generated by a machine. Most normal subjects find the tasks awkward on the first or second attempt, but with practice they are able to acquire some skill. By virtue of his nonexistent memory, one would expect H. M. to trace poorly each time he was asked to try, as if each session were the first. Instead, H. M. displayed nearly normal ability to learn the pursuit rotor and mirror tracing skills. This was quite a surprise to his psychologists. After all, this man could not store even the briefest or simplest explicit memory and was unable to recall his own age, his father's death, or any person he met.[6]

Further research on other amnesics showed that they, too, were able to learn new motor skills. In addition, many of them could learn the cognitive skills needed to complete the Tower of Hanoi puzzle, another experimental task requiring practice in moving blocks from one peg to another in a particular order. Most amnesics perform well on the Gollin figure test, a series of picture fragments that allow a simple object to be identified. Cognitive mapping is also possible—for instance, H.M. knows where the bathroom is and how to get there when he visits the laboratory at which he is occasionally given neurological tests. If you ask him to recall the room's location explicitly, he cannot do so. But if he wanders down the hallway, he can find the bathroom without error on his own.

Bolstered by these early observations, psychologists began to systematically test the procedural skills that amnesics had learned prior to their brain injuries. Frequently practiced sports routines, for example, were often preserved, so that the amnesic who used to ski probably still could but would have to be reintroduced to skiing partners at the bottom of the run. Procedural preservation is not limited to amnesics; it also occurs in people who experience alcohol-induced blackouts, drug-related amnesias, psychogenic amnesias like fugue, and dissociative identity disorder. In his review of the implicit memory literature, Schacter points out that amnesics who cannot remember a thing explicitly are nonetheless able to "learn fictitious information about people, . . . produce bits and pieces of recently presented stories, . . . learn to program a microcomputer, . . . acquire preferences for previously exposed melodies, . . . and spot a hidden figure more quickly after a single exposure to it."[7] At the same time, they do not remember ever hearing the fictitious information, learning of the people, hearing the stories, sitting down at the computer, listening to the songs, or seeing the hidden figures. Neurologist Oliver Sacks' books contain similar case studies.[8] The explicit memories are gone, but the implicit knowledge remains.

## IMPLICIT MEMORY AMONG NORMAL INDIVIDUALS

While neurologists and psychiatrists were discovering the unseen abilities that their amnesic patients possessed, experimental psychologists and psycholinguists were exploring the mechanisms used to access one's vocabulary, or lexicon, at a rate speedy enough to accommodate the remarkable human capacity for language comprehension and production. Careful speech production proceeds at a rate of about two words per second, with much faster dialogue occurring among people who know each other well. Average reading speed is about four words per second, and it can be increased with practice.[9] Even at these impressive rates, we frequently speak, listen, or read for hours without pause, seldom becoming tired. The study of lexical access inspects certain facets of this everyday ability that most people gloss over. In what way, and by what means, are words organized and stored in the mind? How do we unconsciously access or retrieve precisely the word we need exactly when we need it? And given the vast number of syntactically connected words that we use in a typical day, compared to the tiny number of daily errors we make in retrieving the right word, why is lexical access so impervious to error? When errors do occur, what neurological or cognitive events cause them?

The research conducted to answer these questions often involves presenting college students with hundreds, sometimes thousands, of words upon which some boring task must be performed. In one of my own psycholinguistic studies done years ago, which thankfully remains unpublished, each of nearly five hundred subjects stared at a computer screen and named isolated words aloud for over an hour while I cranked out statistical analyses in an effort to support a complicated pet theory about primed associations among words stored in the mental lexicon. Priming studies are the kind of laboratory research at which psychological practitioners sometimes scoff; it is tedious, abstract, difficult to understand—and its results often seem meaningless. Even I eventually abandoned that particular study for its ephemeral artificiality.

But ostensibly meaningless research sometimes packs a surprise. To general amazement, priming studies went on to become the cornerstone of experimental investigation in implicit memory. In one standard paradigm, subjects study a long list of words, then take either an explicit or an implicit memory test. Explicit tests usually involve recall, in which subjects write down or say aloud the words they remember from the list, or recognition, in which subjects review a list of words and choose only those they remember studying. These explicit measures of memory have been used since Ebbinghaus's time. Implicit tests take a variety of forms but most commonly include perceptual identification, word fragment or stem completion, homophone spelling, or lexical decision.

In the perceptual identification test, subjects are presented with an extremely brief view of a word—usually about 30 milliseconds (three one-hundredths of a second). Such brief presentation leaves one with the feeling that nothing has been seen except a brief flash of dim light, so subjects are encouraged to merely guess at what the stimulus might have been. The results of implicit memory experiments show convincingly that their guesses are often correct when the word was primed by its appearance on the original study list. Word completion tests require subjects to fill in the blanks, so that after studying a word like "dimple," they are asked to guess the puzzle "d _ _ p _ e." Their performance is compared to guesses on similar puzzles for control words that were never studied. Stem completion is similar; people receive test stimuli like "con___." If the word "concept" was on the original study list, subjects usually supply it, as opposed to equally plausible words like "connote," "confluence," or "consensus." Homophone spelling simply involves writing down homophones ("pare") as an experimenter says them aloud. Implicit memory is displayed when the spelling ("pare" or "pear" or "pair") duplicates the word originally studied. And lexical decision, a time-honored task of traditional psycholinguistic experimentation, requires subjects to determine very rapidly whether a string of letters forms a known word or not ("barker" or "bekran"). Response times are faster for words that were primed than for words that were not.[10]

Scores of studies have now been completed in which amnesic individuals were given a list of words to study, then asked to complete explicit and implicit tests of this sort. Because most profound amnesics have no memory of ever seeing the list of words by the time they finish studying it, their performance on explicit tests of recall or recognition is miserable. Usually they are unable to remember even a single simple word from the list. However, all of the implicit tests I've described yield memory performance among amnesics that is no different from the performance of control subjects with perfectly normal memories. In other words, the same amnesic who can't remember seeing the original list of words nevertheless identifies those words in very brief perceptual presentation, completes fragments of those words correctly, spells homophones in accordance with the original forgotten list, and makes lexical decisions significantly faster to words on the list than to matching control words that were never seen. Such results have been obtained with individuals who have suffered a broad assortment of brain injuries or diseases leading to their amnesia.[11]

Instructions to amnesic subjects can alter this pattern of results. Specifically, if after studying a list of words, amnesics are encouraged to use that knowledge on an upcoming implicit test, results suffer. But if they are encouraged to merely guess, as in playing a word game or solving a puzzle, their implicit memory produces normal results. Many of us have probably experienced this phenomenon at some time in our lives. Actors learning their lines, equestrians performing in the show ring, and professors teaching class often remark that their performance remains strong only for as long as they trust it. When doubt creeps in, conscious awareness begins to take over, and performance deteriorates.

Studies of normal subjects produce similar levels of implicit priming, although of course they also display decent performance on explicit memory tests. Here, however, we must be careful to rule out the possibility that subjects are applying their explicit knowledge to an implicit test. For example, a non-amnesic subject faced with a word completion test might pretend to guess at the words when in fact she remembers them from the original study list. Several pieces of evidence suggest that such strategies are not used. First, when debriefed after the experiment has ended, subjects say they did not strategize in any way. Second, they are often as surprised as the experimenter to learn that their performance on "guessing games" was so good. Third, results compatible with implicit memory persist even when the opportunity to strategize is strictly controlled in laboratory experiments. Fourth, and most persuasive of all, implicit and explicit memory tests produce statistically independent results within the same subjects for the same materials. In other words, whether a given subject explicitly recalls or recognizes a given stimulus is completely independent of whether that person implicitly knows the same stimulus, and vice versa. Such stochastic independence stands as compelling proof that implicit memory is not merely a methodological artifact.[12]

## DIFFERENCES BETWEEN IMPLICIT
## AND EXPLICIT OPERATIONS

That strong powers of implicit memory are observed in both normal and amnesic populations is critical. It shows that implicit memory is not simply an add-on substitute for the "real" memory that amnesics don't have, and it suggests a neurological process that is diffuse enough to avoid obliteration when brain disease and injury strike. Generalizing the results across two disparate populations also aids in the development of new methods of inquiry, advances in measurement and testing that may prove useful in many arenas. Our nascent ability to measure indirect knowledge in normal populations has already allowed us to explore the differences and similarities between implicit and explicit memory systems. What we find is surprising.

We know that explicit memory is aided by deep, elaborate forms of processing such as visual imagery, semantic conceptualization, and intricate application. We know that explicit memory is seldom affected by the sensory modality through which information comes; whether visual, auditory, or tactile, knowledge is easily translated into a generic trace that can be accessed through different modes without altering content or meaning. We are aware that explicit recognition decays rapidly over time when tested in certain ways but seems to persist when tested by other means. Interference hinders explicit recall and recognition, pictures produce explicit memory that is superior to words, and conscious reflection usually helps to recreate direct memories. Explicit performance is best when stimuli are generated by subjects, or at least determined from context, rather than presented in isolation. We know also that alcohol hampers explicit memory. These are facts of memory, the foundation on which generations of undergraduate psychology majors have built their knowledge.

Imagine, then, how startling it was to confront a way of knowing—implicit priming, to be specific—that contradicted each of these known facts. Contrary to our understanding of explicit memory, implicit priming is not aided by deep or elaborate processing. It is strictly bound by modality, so much so that the drawing of a common object does not reliably prime the name of that same object. It decays rapidly on exactly those forms of measurement that preserve explicit knowledge, but it perseveres with measurements that produce rapid loss of explicit memory. Interference has little effect on implicit priming, words produce superior performance to pictures, and conscious reflection is the kiss of death. Isolated stimuli are best at priming themselves; self-generated stimuli are worst. And alcohol's detrimental effects on explicit recollection disappear when implicit knowledge is tested. Although similar dissociations are found within the field of explicit memory itself, it is these differences, and the possible reasons for them, that have captured the attention of so many cognitive scientists. Priming is perverse.[13]

## THEORIES OF IMPLICIT REMEMBRANCE

Prominent theories of implicit memory fall into two categories: neurological and cognitive. Schacter believes that implicit memory is subserved by a special neurological system that is separate from those that Tulving has proposed for semantic and episodic types of recollection. Evidence favoring this theory stems mostly from the research on amnesic patients. Somehow, the argument goes, implicit memories are sustained despite the destruction of the limbic system and diencephalon, brain structures that are known to play a significant role in creating explicit memories. One way of explaining this conundrum is to hypothesize that those structures are used strictly for explicit reminiscence, while others as yet unidentified are employed only for implicit knowledge.[14]

We might well wonder, though, why it is necessary to postulate a new neurological system for implicit memory when each part of it has already received a full accounting. Tulving's original set of memory systems includes semantic, episodic, and procedural memories. The procedural system is widely thought to include knowledge of skills and habits as well as some forms of conditioning. Most memory scholars see priming as falling within the procedural system.[15] Indeed, Schacter himself presents priming as "a form of memory that is little affected by semantic or conceptual factors."[16] Why, then, do we need yet another brain system for a type of memory that includes skills, habits, conditioning, and priming?[17]

Schacter's response to this question points us back to dissociations in neurological deficit. Although amnesics' implicit memory is most often displayed on tests of familiar vocabulary or procedural skills, it is true that they can also use recently acquired words and new facts on implicit tests without awareness that they have obtained this knowledge.[18] Furthermore, amnesia that occurs for different reasons can create different types of deficits. For example, patients with Alzheimer's disease display poorer priming than other amnesics do, perhaps because their damage extends into areas of association cortex. Their ability to learn new motor skills is preserved, however. On the other hand, patients with Huntington's disease, whose basal ganglia are damaged, show normal priming ability but little capacity for motor skill learning. Considering both of these populations simultaneously, one form of implicit memory (priming) appears to require intact association cortex, while another form of implicit memory (motor skills) needs fully functioning basal ganglia. On the basis of such evidence, Schacter argues that the catch-all category of "procedural memory" is unable to explain such dissociations.[19]

But if we were to postulate a separate brain system to account for every dissociation known to exist in the memory literature, just how many independent systems would we be talking about? This is part of the argument against neurological systems theory that is presented by Henry Roediger, an experimental psychologist at Rice University whose extensive research in the area of implicit memory has made him a leader in the field. The human mind is complex enough that literally thousands of dissociations exist between apparently different types of memory and, more critically for the present debate, within them. When a significant foundation of neurological and cognitive evidence amasses to require the postulation of yet another new brain system, that is the direction theory must take. After all, the ultimate purpose of a psychological theory is to provide a real accounting of how the mind actually works. It may indeed work by the autonomous but interactive functioning of thousands of neurological modules, but Roediger insists that we have little reason to believe that just yet.

Roediger proposes instead that implicit memories are processed in cognitive ways that differ from those used to retain and retrieve explicit memories. It is these differences in cognitive processing, and not the brain structures underlying the process, that cause dissociations to occur in tests of implicit and explicit memories. Unfortunately, just as Schacter cannot specify which brain structures might comprise a neurological implicit memory system, neither can Roediger identify which processes would embody the cognitive implicit memory system. He suggests that the modality-specific and presemantic nature of priming makes it an ideal candidate for what cognitive psychologists have long referred to as bottom-up processing. This means that direct information from the stimulus itself is given priority, with little aid from conceptual knowledge. Roediger proposes that explicit recall and recognition occur with greater unconscious attention given to background experience and context than to the stimulus itself. This form of processing is known as top-down.[20]

Roediger's proposal has its weaknesses. Much of what is known about explicit and implicit memory does not fall within the simplistic categories of top-down and bottom-up processing. That is, many aspects of explicit remembering are not top-down, just as a growing amount of implicit knowledge fails to fit the confines of bottom-up processing. Furthermore, differences in processing, while capable of sweeping cognitive effects in normal individuals, do not account for much of the research showing implicit memory among amnesic populations. We simply do not know at this time which theory is correct. Both are plausible, both are supported by some evidence in their favor, and both are refuted by other evidence implying they are wrong. What often happens in such cases is that both theories are found to operate simultaneously at different levels, just as competing theories of color vision were eventually resolved. This outcome is especially likely when cognitive and neurological mechanisms are being proposed since both operate simultaneously at all levels of psychological functioning.

The possibility of a separate neurological system for implicit memories may tempt some people to connect the implicit/explicit distinction with the traumatic/ordinary distinction that was considered in chapter 7. Although such a dualistic mapping is convenient, it is highly likely to be incorrect. As we have seen, most traumatic memories are disturbingly explicit, and many ordinary memories are completely implicit. In addition, autobiographical and episodic memories are usually so rich that any given instance cannot be cubbyholed into only one classification. The memory traces that represent one episode are likely to contain pieces of implicit knowledge and pieces of explicit knowledge, as well as a mixture of semantic, episodic, and procedural chunks, some retained and some constructed. Away from the theoretical armchair, it is almost impossible to classify any one memory as entirely implicit, purely semantic, or completely veridical.

## "BODY MEMORIES"

Psychotherapists who are familiar with the increasingly popular notion of body memories might point to them as an example of an implicit memory that is related to trauma. This idea is worth discussing at some length if only for the influence it exerts on the current pop psychology scene. The original metaphor is that the body "remembers" what the mind forgets. Certainly it is true that mind and body work together in integrated fashion, that the knowledge underlying many physical and mental skills is unconscious, that physical relaxation of the body can improve mental affect and function, and that frequently practiced body movements—whether practiced for athletic or psychological reasons—become automatic over time. There is no doubt that the brain sometimes directs the body to react in particular ways that may be related to forgotten experiences. In addition, we know that somatization disorder is a very real affliction in which psychological conflict is manifested by physical symptoms in the human body. I am not aware of a single cognitive scientist or experimental psychologist who actively resists these facts. However, to accept the metaphor of body memory literally is an entirely different matter.

A disturbing number of popular authors today argue that the muscles, tendons, joints, and organs of the human body are literally capable of remembering information, especially traumatic information. To those who question this startling assertion, as I once did, I offer quotes so that such writers can speak for themselves:

"The body stores and re-enacts traumatic memories." (Whitfield, 1995, p. 243)
"Trauma is stored in somatic memory." (van der Kolk, 1994, p. 253)

"Our physical bodies always remember sexual abuse." (Fredrickson, 1992, p. 93)
"A person may have forgotten a traumatic experience, but their [sic] body somehow remembers it." (Whitfield, 1995, p. 245)
"[We] map out very clearly the psychological content of different muscles and link them to the time of their first activation." (Marcher, as quoted by Bernhardt, 1992, p. 290)

Not one of these quotes is taken out of context, nor is there any suggestion in the original documents that they were written tongue-in-cheek, figuratively, or metaphorically. Furthermore, in writings on body memory, the word "body" does not include the human brain. To explain how the alleged process works and how therapists can make use of it, we are told:

"Body memories [are] unconnected to the present or the self and undiminished by the passage of time. . . . [They] are primary, prior to any narrative, and they may well surpass the victim's narrative ability because they pass beyond his knowledge . . . [They] are intrusive and incomprehensible . . . They obey none of the standard rules of discourse." (Culbertson, 1995, p. 178)
"The body stores memory as energy. . . . Whenever a part of your body is touched that was hurt, the stored or blocked energy can be accessed." (Fredrickson, 1992, p. 146)
"[Body memories are] clues as to what's happened to you if you are lacking specific memories of your abuse." (Black, 1997, online)
"As certain places on the body are touched or certain movements are made, memories of abuse may surface." (Fredrickson, 1992, p. 98)
"Therapists who have assisted trauma survivors in their long-term recovery have observed traumatic memories manifesting themselves in the body in numerous ways." (Whitfield, 1995, p. 244)
"The details themselves, all I knew at first, are my most basic and concrete sorts of memories, which were clearly in my body." (Culbertson, 1995, p. 187)

No evidence—clinical, experimental, or anecdotal—is provided to support these statements. Occasionally, a footnote is supplied, but a quick dash to the library verifies that while the source may nod blithely to the general topic, it provides no evidence establishing the existence of body memory. A few authors attempt to contradict the antiscience rhetoric so typical of body memory discussions, apparently hoping to persuade readers by virtue of scientific authority. For example, Whitfield writes, "Scientists are intensively studying the body's role in memory. They no longer believe that the brain is the only repository for feelings and memory."[21] This statement piqued my curiosity. I asked four research assistants to conduct a thorough literature search on body memory using the most widely known psychological, psychiatric, and biomedical computer databases in existence. From these searches emerged a grand total of four scientific articles on body memories, all speculative and none particularly "intensive." Of course, this does not include reports on bodily complaints that accompany disorders like PTSD, somatization, and conversion because there is no reason to believe that these experiences are instances of body memory. The fact that troubled individuals occasionally experience physical pain that can be alleviated by massage and/or psychotherapy does not mean that muscles have memories.

The idea of body memories grew out of long-established knowledge concerning psychosomatic illness. Freud and Janet believed that dissociated memories could cause physical aches and pains as well as the better known conversion symptoms that seemed neurological and led to a diagnosis of hysteria. Both world wars provided clinical evidence of combat amnesia that is accompanied by psychosomatic symptoms. Under conditions of war, however, some of those cases may have been caused by undiagnosed physical illness or injury suffered during the combat experience. Victims of the 1991 Gulf War, whose leaders denied repeatedly that chemical warfare had been used before finally admitting that it had, will attest to the humiliating falsehood of being told for several years that a serious physical illness is all in one's head. Concentration camp survivors also report psychosomatic complaints, although their symptoms, too, might have as strong a basis in physical torture and malnutrition as in psychological terrorism.[22]

Much of the bodywork therapy employed today comes from the theories of Wilhelm Reich, one of Freud's disgruntled students who broke away from the master to develop his own brand of psychotherapy in which both body and mind were treated simultaneously to cure neurosis. Reich believed that psychological stress was held in the body by muscular tension that creates "armor." This tension weakens specific physical areas that subsequently become prone to disease. Such tension usually begins in childhood, before we are old enough to know how to cope with psychological pain. For example, a child fighting back tears might tense the muscles near her eyes, throat, chest, diaphragm, and abdomen, leading eventually to physical problems in these locations. Reich developed techniques of physical massage, body movement, and breathing instruction to ease the tension, thereby eliminating the armor in both body and mind while freeing energy.[23] Contemporary offshoots of Reichian therapy include Energy Stream, Core Energetics, Bioenergetics, and Pathwork. Although they are occasionally cited by authors of works on body memory who are starving for a footnote, none of these schools of thought have taken the unwarranted leap of insisting that memories are literally held in the body.[24] Even Reich, whose career ended in the disgrace of American imprisonment for fraud, did not imply that the muscular tension of armor was a body memory; instead, he argued merely that psychological feelings would surface as physical tension was released. The ensuing loss of psychological inhibition might then lead to the brain's release of a memory into conscious awareness.

Danish body psychotherapist Lisbeth Marcher reaches substantially farther toward the literal notion of body memory in her development of Bodydynamics therapy. Bodydynamics involves "testing the psychological content of each muscle independently of others" and inferring how that content can be applied to a client's psychomotor development during infancy to understand his "present life, character structure, and . . . life history."[25] One of the examples she uses to describe her theory of body psychotherapy is that of a client whose psychological desire to push others away is manifested in tight triceps muscles. Once this "diagnosis" has been established, Marcher activates the triceps by touching or moving them, while simultaneously working through the psychological distancing issues in talk therapy.

Although body psychotherapy is by no means limited to clients with somatization or conversion disorders, it is these ailments that are often connected with the notion of body memory. Such disorders have a very long history (conversion dates to 1900 B.C.),[26] though the terminology for each of them has varied dramatically over the centuries. According to DSM-IV, these disorders are much more common in women than men. The most frequent physical complaints expressed by somatizers are nausea, abdominal bloating, vomiting, diarrhea, and food intolerance. More generally, gastrointestinal or gynecological disturbances are often suspected, both linked to abdominal pain. The DSM-IV diagnostic criteria for somatization disorder include "a history of many physical complaints beginning before age 30 years, . . . four pain symptoms, . . . two gastrointestinal symptoms, . . . one sexual symptom, . . . and one pseudoneurological symptom, . . . [none] fully explained by a known general medical condition, . . . [and] not intentionally produced or feigned."[27]

Most notably, this list of diagnostic criteria does not require that the patient exhibit any symptoms of amnesia or other memory deficit.[28] In addition, one study showed that more than three-quarters of posttraumatic stress disorder patients complain of somatic symptoms, yet in none of them is there any indication of amnesia, repression, or even successful suppression of traumatic memories.[29] On the contrary, these patients' somatic complaints are accompanied by remarkably indelible memories of traumatic events. Comparable prevalence rates and somatization data are not available for populations in which extreme personal trauma has not occurred. It is quite possible, therefore, that similar numbers of undiagnosed physical complaints are experienced by individuals whose bodies have no trauma to remember.

And what of the DSM-IV criterion concerning medical diagnosis? It means that the very existence of somatization disorder, along with the notion that past history of trauma is held implicitly in body memories, is based on the medical establishment's inability to diagnose every human ailment approaching a laboratory. This is absurd. Many medical diseases are notoriously challenging to identify, with hundreds of thousands of patients traveling from one specialist's office to the next without success. In fact, the American Medical Society noted sheepishly in a 1997 study that close to half of American adults report that they, their relatives, or their friends have been misdiagnosed by medical doctors in the past.[30] Conversion disorder provides more of the same evidence: One-quarter of male and one-third of female conversion disorder patients are later found to be suffering from a medically known neurological illness that was simply not diagnosed. Comorbidity is very high as well, with conversion symptoms being extensive in patients who also suffer from head injuries, multiple sclerosis, central nervous system tumors, brain seizures, antisocial personality disorder, depression, anxiety disorders, and/or alcoholism.[31] No wonder they complain of physical ailments. Likewise, anorexics and bulimics are said to experience body memories when complaining of somatization symptoms that include nausea, vomiting, stomach cramps, diarrhea, and abdominal pain.[32] Why should we believe that such symptoms, so clearly related to the poor nutritional habits of serious eating disorders, are evidence of memories held in the body and not the brain?

The very real existence of mental disorders that are defined or accompanied by psychosomatic complaints does not require or even suggest the concomitant existence of body memories. Rather, those disorders—and the innocent victims who suffer them—are demeaned by such a ludicrous explanation. Muscles, tendons, joints, and organs are not capable of creating a memory trace, storing it over time, or allowing access to it for later retrieval. Neurons do that. We've been snookered by a metaphor gone terribly awry. Ra of Thebes was the first to state, in 3000 B.C., that the heart—not the brain or the muscles—is the primary site of mental processing, and this false belief endured in ancient Hebrew, Hindu, Chinese, and Greek cultures. Even Aristotle, so accurate in many of his speculations about human memory, perpetuated the error. But we now know that memories are formed, retained, and retrieved in the human brain and that muscular reactions are also governed by the human brain. Sports commentator Scott Hamilton's insistence that a figure skater with the flu has nothing left to rely on but "muscle memory" is easily dismissed. She still has a brain, Scott.[33]

Body memories are not good examples of implicit knowledge, but the skills, procedures, habits, routines, and other abilities that we use every day are. Our brains are full of remembered knowledge that seeps out in indirect ways, helping us through our lives without expecting credit in return. The field of implicit memory may have been slow to conceive, but now, fully born, it holds the promise of a childhood and adolescence that portend well for the future. Applications are likely to be extensive: from the formation of social impressions to our attributions of people's actions and beliefs; from a deeper understanding of affective knowledge such as moods and fears to diagnosis and treatment of psychopathology; from preschool to postdoctorate education in formal settings; and from youth to old age in memory maturation.[34] The lamp of implicit memory will illuminate all of these facets of human life.

# CHAPTER 9

# Hemispheric Differences in Memory

*The man bent over his guitar,*
*A shearsman of sorts. The day was green.*
*They said, "You have a blue guitar,*
*You do not play things as they are."*
*The man replied, "Things as they are*
*Are changed upon a blue guitar . . . "*

—**Wallace Stevens**

Ever since Roger Sperry's work hit newspapers in the 1970s, distinct functions of left and right cerebral hemispheres have captured public imagination with the force of a medieval clock. Stories of split brains catapulted into virtually every American magazine during the 1980s, stories that usually mingled a few facts with a glut of fallacy. By the end of that decade, few citizens of the United States had not heard that language and logic cleave to the left, music and art to the right. That this belief was so oversimplified as to be largely irrelevant to our understanding of normal mental functions carried little consequence in the melee. To this day, journalists announce the existence of two brains in every head—a "left brain" and a "right brain"—paying little attention to the rapid transfer and mutual integration of information that occurs relentlessly between hemispheres. Scholars of lateralized

135

function contend that "few areas of scientific inquiry have generated so much interest from so diverse an audience."[1]

The discovery of differences in hemispheric functioning[2] is often credited to Paul Broca who, in 1864, averred that damage to the left side of the brain was linked to language disturbance, or aphasia. In fact, however, some twenty-eight years earlier at a French medical society meeting, Marc Dax had presented over forty cases of aphasia in which the left hemisphere was damaged. On the basis of this evidence, he insisted that speech was governed by the left hemisphere, but his proclamation was ignored. Dax's presentation remained forgotten until his son published it three decades later in an unsuccessful effort to prove that Broca had appropriated the elder Dax's ideas. Broca soon became the lightning rod for an academic quarrel over the existence and purpose of hemispheric differences, a controversy still vigorous today.[3]

A contemporary of Broca's, Hughlings Jackson, published a lengthy treatise on cerebral laterality in 1874, adding to the squabble his supposition that the left hemisphere was dominant in most normal brains. Even the celebrated Pavlov undertook some of his investigations with the intent of studying functions governed by independent hemispheres.[4] But it wasn't until Roger Sperry's work with split-brain patients that the necessary research methods and surgical techniques were honed sharply enough to provide reliable evidence that the left and right hemispheres operated in different ways. Throughout the 1970s, Sperry and his colleagues at Caltech in Pasadena, California, tested patients whose severe epilepsy had been curbed by commisurotomy—the surgical separation of the left and right hemispheres by severing a band of connecting fibers called the corpus callosum.[5] In 1974, cognitive neuropsychologist Dahlia Zaidel collaborated with Sperry to produce the first study of memory in split-brain patients, opening a new path of research which Zaidel has since followed.[6] Soon Sperry's lab had verified the clinical propositions that speech and most aspects of verbal memory were governed by the left hemisphere, while many features of visual memory were subserved by the right hemisphere.[7] Their evidence left little doubt that each of the two hemispheres is specialized for certain functions, just as Dax, Broca, Jackson, and Pavlov had surmised. In 1981, Sperry won the Nobel Prize for Physiology or Medicine for his explorations of hemispheric differences.

As the number of asymmetry investigations grew exponentially under the Nobel wreath, and evidence from disparate domains began to converge, cognitive scientists learned that the left hemisphere tends toward analytical or sequential processing, while the right is more holistic. This generalization, however, may operate in practice only when the two hemispheres are experimentally or surgically forced to work independently of each other, something they are not likely to do inside normal skulls under everyday conditions. Several other highly publicized findings rest on soft ground as well. For example, music is lateralized to the right hemisphere only among non-musicians; individuals who are trained to hear music in an analytical manner, as most professional musicians are, usually show left hemisphere dominance for it.[8] Likewise, the notion that language is the exclusive province of the left hemisphere is not correct. In fact, the right hemisphere displays many important linguistic capabilities, including vocabulary, figurative interpretation, contextual integration, understanding of idioms and proverbs, story comprehension, use of prosodic tone, indirect requests, and linguistic humor.[9] It is not able to speak, but speech is only one facet of language.

Left hemisphere dominance, whether defined neurologically or culturally, is also questioned today. From a neurological viewpoint, right hemisphere functioning is dispersed across larger areas of cerebral tissue, whereas left hemisphere functioning seems more tightly localized to small regions of the brain.[10] Thus, there is little structural reason to avow left hemisphere dominance. From a cultural standpoint, the importance of one function over another (like giving directions verbally or by drawing a map) is little more than a matter of social value judgment. The right hemisphere is different from the left, but it is not necessarily worse or less important.

## LATERALIZATION METHODOLOGY

Before embarking on a thorough discussion of hemispheric differences in the encoding and retrieval of human memories, a quick sweep of relevant methodologies is needed. Too often both professionals and amateurs accept the results of hemispheric differences research without a fundamental understanding of how the research is done. Because the field is awash in stereotyped assumptions and extensive exceptions, it cries out for critical understanding. I certainly do not pretend to provide comprehensive coverage of all methodologies; readers who wish to become more familiar with them will find extensive sources cited in this chapter's notes. Here, we take only a peek inside the laboratory door.

Medical advances now allow many people to survive brain injury that would have killed them as little as twenty years ago. In addition, surgical techniques such as the commisurotomy have been developed to treat severe neurological diseases. These advances have saved many lives and as a by-product have supplied scientists with some intriguing populations to study. Investigations of hemispheric differences today are conducted on three populations: people who have experienced natural brain damage by injury or disease; people who have experienced surgical modifications to their brains such as commisurotomy, lobectomy, or hemispherectomy; and normal subjects who volunteer to participate in experimental studies of cognitive behavior. Although a very small number of split-brain subjects produced the most sensational results of hemispheric differences and were therefore heavily publicized, they have now become a historically unique cohort. With the advent of new drugs that are more effective and less invasive than brain surgery, commisurotomy is no longer needed. Thus, the split-brain patients living today are likely to be the last.[11]

Over this matrix of three populations is superimposed a variety of experimental procedures. These include the creation of brain images such as the positron emission tomography (PET) and functional magnetic resonance imaging (fMRI) scans, both of which are capable of showing not only the physical structure of the human brain but its active functioning as well. The PET is the most common scan used in the field of memory research, a field that accounts for the largest number of studies relating PET scans to cognitive function during the late 1990s. This technique requires the injection of a radioactive tracer into the blood. The tracer binds onto glucose, then shows up on a computer screen as a measure of blood flow going into certain areas of the brain. By comparing the amount of blood flow in a specific neuroanatomical region while the subject performs different cognitive tasks, we can see which functions are mediated most strongly by certain regions of the brain.

Less frequently, event-related potentials (ERPs) are measured by tracking the electrical activity of the brain with an electroencephelograph (EEG) machine. Brain waves are then averaged by computer so that consistent patterns can be seen. The changes in brain waves that occur when a stimulus is presented allow us to observe potential differences between the two hemispheres in electrical activity while the brain processes that stimulus. Direct electrical activation of brain tissue is also used occasionally, though much less often than in Wilder Penfield's era. To refresh your memory, a neurosurgeon preparing to operate stimulates certain areas electrically to determine which portion of a patient's brain tissue supports particular capacities such as speech. Because human brain tissue contains no pain receptors, patients undergoing this procedure remain fully conscious and can therefore respond to the surgeon's touch. Aphasic arrest, the temporary inability to speak, occurs when electrical stimulation is applied to a speech region of the brain, acting as a warning to the surgeon: Don't cut here! It also provides researchers with information about regional specialization for certain cognitive functions. More commonly, neurosurgeons now use the Wada test—named after its creator, Juhn Wada—to determine which hemisphere handles specific functions for a particular individual. The patient is injected with a barbiturate drug (usually sodium amobarbital) directly into either the left or right carotid artery, causing the majority of one hemisphere to become temporarily anesthetized while the other remains wide awake. For the next two minutes, while one hemisphere is under anesthesia, tests are conducted to determine what functions the patient can still perform.

Most experiments with split-brain patients make use of lateralized stimulus presentation. The most common variant of this method is to present visual images (such as shapes, words, or drawings) to only one side of the brain by placing each image to either the left or right side of the subject's central view. Neural pathways lead from one side of each retina to the opposite hemisphere of the brain, so a stimulus presented on the left side of the viewing area will enter the patient's right visual half-field and arrive for processing in the left hemisphere. Because the split-brain patient's corpus callosum is cut, the information cannot be transferred in the normal fashion to the right hemisphere. It can get to the right hemisphere through subcortical transfer; in other words, there are other connecting points between the two hemispheres that are still intact even in the surgically split brain. However, subcortical transfer is neither as rapid nor as effective a means of hemispheric communication as the normal route through the corpus callosum. In addition, experimenters must regulate stimulus presentation to avoid reception by the undesired visual half-field. This is usually done by presenting stimuli more rapidly than an inadvertent eye movement can be made, or by controlling visual presentation with a computer that tracks eye movements and blacks out the stimulus whenever it falls on a portion of the eye that transmits information to the undesired hemisphere.

Because two surgically split hemispheres cannot communicate by normal means, the responses of split-brain patients to lateralized stimuli often form stark examples of specialized processing. For example, the fact that the typical right hemisphere cannot speak means that a split-brain patient who sees a word presented to the left visual half-field is unable to name it aloud. If asked, she reports that she has not seen any stimulus at all because, indeed, no stimulus was presented to the hemisphere that can speak. She can, however, point with her left hand at a picture or drawing that depicts the meaning of the word. In this way we know that the right hemisphere understands vocabulary but simply cannot pronounce words in speech. The patient's right hand will be unable to point to the picture depicting the word's meaning because the right hand is governed by the left hemisphere, which remains unaware that any word was presented.

Normal subjects undergo a similar procedure of lateralized presentation in hemispheric difference experiments. The most critical distinction between lateralization experiments done with normal subjects and those done with split-brain patients is that normal subjects have intact corpus callosa that quickly transfer any information arriving in one hemisphere to the other. For this reason, normal subjects are often encouraged to respond to lateralized stimuli as quickly as possible so that response times can be measured. A difference in hemispheric processing might emerge, for example, when a normal subject is significantly faster at reading aloud a word presented very briefly to the right visual half-field and left hemisphere than when the same word is presented equally briefly to the left visual half-field and right hemisphere. Differences of this sort are on the order of a few milliseconds—a tiny span of time but one that can be stable enough to produce statistical significance. Such differences imply that the normal left hemisphere is better able to name words aloud, and hence does so faster than the right hemisphere.

Clinical observation is the oldest method of inferring hemispheric specialization. Brain injuries and diseases leave many individuals with dysfunctions that, if linked to a particular region of brain damage, suggest neuroanatomical location of function. Such dysfunctions are often quite specific in nature so that one narrow ability is impaired while hundreds of others operate unhindered. A panoply of these rare and specific deficits is now known, usually falling into general categories of amnesias (memory disorders), aphasias (language disorders), or agnosias (perceptual disorders). Case studies include individuals whose brain damage left every mental function intact except the individuals' ability to find their way around their own homes or to recognize themselves in the mirror. Linking the region of brain damage to the behavioral deficit is one way that cognitive scientists piece together the puzzle of hemispheric differences.

## NOTABLE EXCEPTIONS

Several cautions must be added to the matrix of populations and methodologies. Clinical observation provides spellbinding case studies of how the brain can go awry, but it is important to realize that these instances are extremely rare. Although we might attempt to make generalizations about the brain damage that can cause an inability to recognize one's own face, for example, only a tiny handful of people worldwide have ever experienced this disorder. In addition, individuals with similar location and extent of brain injury often display radically dissimilar cognitive deficits. More confusing still, accidents and diseases frequently cause diffuse damage to the brain so that the precise localization of an injury is not possible. Regions of the brain that are not damaged in an accident often deteriorate due to a lack of input from the areas that were damaged. The miracles of brain regeneration recapture many patients' quality of life, but they wreak havoc on clinical observation: The brain compensates for injury by vast and speedy reorganization; new regions take over functions that were previously mediated by damaged areas. If performed at a very young age, surgically removing an entire hemisphere—fully half of the human brain—can result in neural reorganization that allows for normal adult functioning.[12]

Alternative methods that rely on brain scans or normal subjects are not foolproof, either. Although in contemporary society we are tempted to assume that the hard science of PET scans or ERP studies must contain the patina of truth, in fact they are as riddled with methodological potholes as softer techniques. PET scans for most real-world cognitive activities, for example, display the bright colors of increased blood flow all over the brain, like a big light bulb turning on. The safest inference would be, quite simply, that one's brain is working—a conclusion that could be reached with far less fanfare and expense, and one that would not encourage the public to assume that a major scientific breakthrough had occurred. These techniques have their uses, but they are not an experimenter's panacea.

The primary exceptions in research on cerebral asymmetry are those of sex and handedness. Right-handed males are the most likely people to be represented accurately by findings on hemispheric differences. On average, male brains tend to be more strongly lateralized for specific functions, while female brains usually display greater information transfer between hemispheres as well as less stringent localization. Female brains are more likely to be bilateral in function; in other words, both hemispheres of the female brain tend to work together on a particular task. This is not to say that the female brain is somehow more cooperative or collaborative—as the pundits will undoubtedly have it—but that it is more redundant than the male brain, perhaps as an evolutionary advantage for the production and care of offspring.

Differences in handedness are even stronger than those for sex. For about 95 percent of right-handers, speech is lateralized more strongly to the left hemisphere than to the right. This is true for only 70 percent of left-handers. The remaining portion of the population, which has not been studied much, displays either right hemisphere dominance for speech or bilateral representation.[13] Furthermore, determinations of handedness are not as straightforward as they might seem. Many individuals write with their right hands but play sports, open doors, and brush their teeth with their left hands. The effects of handedness are so strong that these ostensible "right-handers" are almost always excused from participation in hemispheric difference experiments.

With a better understanding of the difficulties inherent in hemispheric differences research, some observers may be tempted to throw their arms up in despair. If the field is fraught with this much complexity, why bother? But no method of inquiry—scientific or otherwise—is airtight. And no topic worth knowing is without its confusions. A PET scan is not perfect; a split-brain patient is only one unique individual; a normal subject may devise a strategy to fool the experimenter; and an amnesic's brain may defy our best suppositions. Taken in isolation, each of these studies can provide only a speck of information. But considered as a group, compared intelligently, and used to drive further inquiry, a set of disparate investigations can provide tremendous knowledge.

With converging evidence from several different methodologies and populations, we reduce the likelihood of error. If, for example, a number of individuals with damage to the right prefrontal cortex have trouble retrieving episodic memories, we look for converging evidence that blood flow to the same area increases significantly when normal subjects retrieve episodic memories. If split-brain patients cannot understand visual maps presented to their left hemispheres, we seek converging evidence that right hemisphere–damaged individuals have the same trouble and that normal subjects require more time to identify a location on maps presented laterally to only the right visual half-field. When results are consistent, each form of evidence bolsters the other. Inconsistent results serve as a warning of perils ahead.

## DISTRIBUTED STORAGE

Although some of the processes used to form and retrieve memories are mediated separately by the two halves of the brain, stored memory traces are scattered throughout the cortex of both left and right hemispheres. Knowledge of memory's distributed nature dates back to 1950 when Karl Lashley concluded after twenty years of research that ablating specific regions of laboratory rats' brains did not impair their memories for mazes.[14] Penfield's experiments on human memory traces led to the same conclusion: Areas of brain tissue that seemed to elicit certain memories when electrically stimulated could be surgically removed without destroying those supposed memories.[15] To Penfield, who hoped he had localized entire recollections to an area the size of a pinpoint, this discovery represented "the slaying of a beautiful hypothesis by an ugly fact."[16]

Contemporary investigations show that even the amount or location of hippocampal tissue that is removed does not affect patients' abilities to recall visual designs.[17] Patterns of memory disturbance exhibited by head-injured amnesics and Alzheimer's patients add to the converging evidence of distributed storage: Amnesia from localized head injuries impairs the ability to create or retrieve memories, but it seldom harms previously stored traces. For this reason, old memories eventually return to most amnesic individuals as their injuries heal. In contrast, Alzheimer's disease inflicts widespread damage to neurons throughout the cortex and therefore produces an irretrievable loss of previously stored memories. As the disease worsens, Alzheimer's patients lose an ever growing number of their own recollections in terms of semantic memory for facts, lexical memory for vocabulary, and episodic memory for autobiographical events. These remembrances never return.

An intriguing question for the next step of converging evidence is whether systemic chemical disturbances extending throughout the brain affect memory storage in a distributed manner as well. Estrogen and thyroid imbalances, for example, are each believed to harm memory for vocabulary, but exactly how the impairment occurs remains unknown. For that matter, we do not yet know whether these malfunctions occur because the chemical imbalances influence large areas of brain tissue simultaneously or because their impacts are localized to particular memory structures like the hippocampus.

Assertions that each hemisphere contains the engrams of different types of experiences, every one stored as a whole memory, are false despite their disturbing recurrence in the popular media. According to this fallacy, logical experience is stored in the left hemisphere and holistic experience in the right. To put it another way, according to this belief, your memory of da Vinci's Mona Lisa would be stored in the right hemisphere because it is art, while your memory of Tolstoy's *Anna Karenina* is preserved in the left hemisphere because it is language. Even at face value, these sorts of assertions are absurd: What memorable experience could be represented in its entirety as purely logical or completely holistic, strictly art or thoroughly literature?

A finer screen is needed. Although whole memories are not stored in one hemisphere or the other by virtue of some arbitrary social categorization, it is true that memory storage is linked to the location of perceptual processing.[18] For example, the neurons that are first activated when we perceive a stranger's face are the same neurons that will be activated again when we remember that face. We also know that perceptual processing differs across the two hemispheres. For most right-handed male subjects, the neurons likely to be activated in perceiving an unfamiliar face reside in the posterior area of the right hemisphere; hence, the memory of that face—if it is remembered at all—is likely to remain in the right hemisphere. The stranger's voiced remarks, however, are more likely to be perceived and preserved among the neurons of the left temporal lobe. The complete memory, including many different aspects of the face and voice as they were perceived in one fleeting instant, are distributed throughout both hemispheres in this fashion.[19] The medial temporal lobe system, which is comprised of the hippocampus and adjacent areas, serves to bind together these widely dispersed neurons so that they can be activated simultaneously to produce the entire memory.[20] In addition, neurons near the original place of activation may form convergence zones that integrate related fragments of an activated memory into a coherent experience.[21] After the binding or consolidation process is finished so that such an experience is firmly established in long-term memory, the medial temporal lobe system is not needed to produce conscious recollection.

## RIGHT HEMISPHERE REMEMBRANCE

Differences in processing, then, do lead to hemispheric specialization for certain types of experiences that linger within the memory trace. Cognitive neuropsychologist Dahlia Zaidel has gone as far as suggesting that there are two long-term memory systems, one located in each hemisphere. By this proposal, both hemispheres are exposed to the same events, but each one processes the event differently, thereby creating differences in memory. As evidence for this belief, Zaidel considers the standard methods of organizing information that are used in long-term semantic memory. The disconnected right hemisphere has the memory capacity to sort objects into categories, handle objects in a manner consistent with their purpose, and recognize personal belongings. It contains enough semantic knowledge to classify photographs of beloved family members and respected authority figures into a positive category, while placing photographs of Hitler, Stalin, or Ku Klux Klan costumes into a negative category. The right hemisphere of a split brain is also faster than the left hemisphere at standard semantic memory tasks, such as identifying typical exemplars of a category (a robin as a bird, for example), whereas the left hemisphere is faster than the right at identifying atypical exemplars (a penguin as a bird). The same pattern of results appears in normal subjects undergoing lateralized presentation experiments, suggesting that an intact brain under special laboratory conditions uses each hemisphere independently in similar fashion.[22]

Clinical observations offer even more intriguing cases of hemispheric differences in memory. Hughlings Jackson was the first to suggest that visual recognition of locations, people, and objects was subserved primarily by the right hemisphere. Several early reports of brain damage involved people whose topographical memory was disturbed by an injury to the right hemisphere. One patient was unable to find her way around her own neighborhood; another failed to distinguish his own home from other homes; a third could not use a map or recognize local buildings and streets. In each case, other forms of memory were intact, along with normal capacities for intelligence and language.[23] Over many decades, a number of such patients have been identified, the majority of them suffering from right hemisphere lesions. Converging evidence from split-brain patients shows that they, too, suffer from poor topographical memory even when both hemispheres are allowed to function under normal conditions.

The right hemisphere outperforms the left in memory for faces as well. Scores of studies conducted on normal subjects and split-brain patients have demonstrated the right hemisphere's penchant for processing and recognizing faces.[24] Upon seeking converging evidence from brain-damaged patients, we find convincing verification. Prosopagnosia, the inability to recognize familiar faces, requires right hemisphere damage, although a few scientists believe it is linked most prominently with bilateral injury. This rare deficit occurs despite the ability to describe a familiar face verbally. Thus, a prosopagnosic can say that his father has blue eyes, a high forehead, a long nose, high cheekbones, and an angular jaw, but when presented with the face itself—or a photograph of it—he is unable to identify the face as his father's. Worse yet, to stand in front of the mirror unable to recognize one's own face, while able to recognize almost all known objects and places, is a deficit of staggering specialization that remains unexplained. Interestingly, the more generalized disorder of visual agnosia, in which all sorts of objects can be seen and described by a patient but not recognized or identified, seems to require left hemisphere damage. Thus, Jackson's theory of right hemisphere memory functions appears to be correct with respect to people and places, but not objects.

The right hemisphere excels at many key aspects of visual memory, but it is less flexible than the left in recognizing incongruous or unexpected scenes. In one study, Zaidel asked normal subjects to study a series of atypical scenes, like a picture of a mailbox standing inside a living room. Later, the scenes were presented laterally, to either the right or left visual half-field, along with a number of distractor scenes that the subjects had never viewed. Upon exposure to each picture, subjects were to decide whether the scene had been viewed earlier or not. Results showed that memory was significantly improved when the scenes were exposed in the right visual half-field, which connects to the left cerebral hemisphere.[25] The fact that normal expectations had been violated in these pictures caused the right hemisphere to perform poorly. In keeping with this explanation, a follow-up experiment showed that normal subjects had stronger memories of surrealistic paintings done by artists René Magritte and Salvador Dali when recognition was limited to the left hemisphere.[26]

A similar demonstration of right hemisphere reliance on the conventional expectations of top-down processing comes from a study in which each hemisphere was presented with artificially disorganized faces. Experimenters created the stimuli by rearranging the normal position of the nose, eyes, and mouth in simple facial drawings. Split-brain patients were unable to recognize the disorganized features accurately when these stimuli were presented only to the right hemisphere. Errors yielded a systematic bias in that the split-brain patients pointed to the area in each drawing where a nose or eyes should have been, but not to the area where they actually were. Presentation of the same stimuli to the left hemisphere yielded accurate results. Normal subjects who participated in a similar version of this experiment produced the same pattern of data.[27] Considered together, these various experiments conducted on differing populations indicate that the right hemisphere is inferior to the left in its memory for incongruous visual scenes and faces that violate standard assumptions.

## VERIDICALITY: RIGHT OR LEFT?

The right hemisphere's rigidity in visual memory has led some cognitive scientists to speculate that it may produce more veridical memories as well. That is, if the right hemisphere processes incoming material in a literal and inflexible manner, and if it stores and retrieves certain aspects of remembered experiences according to such processes, then those parts of a given memory handled by the right hemisphere might be especially trustworthy as an accurate record of an initial event. This speculation has become the source of current debate. Along with his colleagues, Michael Gazzaniga, a cognitive neuroscientist at Dartmouth College, has recently spoken in favor of more veridical right hemisphere memory. This argument emanates from his theory of the left hemisphere as an interpreter.

Gazzaniga has insisted since 1978 that the left hemisphere is responsible for interpreting incoming stimulation. As primary evidence he offers the results of experiments conducted on split-brain patients. In one of these studies, Gazzaniga displayed one picture of a common object, then an array of pictures containing one scene that matched the common object. For example, in one trial, the disconnected left hemisphere was shown a picture of a chicken's foot, and the patient then pointed with the right hand to a picture of a chicken head, choosing the correct match from the array. The disconnected right hemisphere was shown a picture of snow, then pointed with the left hand to the matching picture of a snow shovel. Both hemispheres, although disconnected from each other, were able to match the two scenes correctly. Gazzaniga then asked the patient to explain verbally why he had pointed to the chicken head and the snow shovel. The patient responded immediately that the chicken foot goes with the chicken head, and the shovel is needed to clean out the chicken shed. His left hemisphere had created a plausible interpretation for what otherwise would have been inexplicable behavior.[28] Gazzaniga offers two related anecdotes in the form of split-brain patients who either laughed or left the room upon reading the word "laugh" or "walk" presented only to the right hemisphere. When asked why they were laughing or leaving, their left hemispheres provided easy explanations that neglected the presentation of the written commands.

This evidence for the theory of a left hemisphere interpreter is troubling in several ways. First of all, it is limited to a very small number of split-brain patients, with little converging verification from other populations. Gazzaniga states that examples of left hemisphere interpretation like these are "rich and . . . easy to elicit,"[29] but he does not supply many of them for public perusal. Second, in at least four books published over a period of twenty years, Gazzaniga presses for acceptance of his left hemisphere interpreter theory but offers no greater evidence in 1992 than he did in 1978. The same three examples (the chicken/shovel, the laugh, the walk) are offered repeatedly, without alluding to follow-up studies or extensions of the original research. This is quite unusual in cognitive science. Normally, a pet theory that returns to the printed page again and again is accompanied by an increasingly solid body of empirical evidence. Third, a psychological literature search turned up no publication in which Gazzaniga tests his own interpretation of the chicken/shovel experiment by offering the right hemisphere an opportunity to explain the pointing behavior. Such a test could not be done verbally, but it could be conducted with interpretive pictures or drawings to which the left hand might simply point. When given a chance, perhaps the right hemisphere can create an equally plausible interpretation of the chicken head and the snow shovel.

Gazzaniga's theory has slightly stronger footing in the results of a few other studies. One shows that the left hemisphere can make simple inferences about an event from two otherwise unrelated components. For example, when given information indicating water and a pan, the left hemisphere infers the act of boiling. When the same information is given to the right hemisphere, it is not able to make the inference accurately.[30] Another investigation demonstrates that the left hemisphere relies on inference even when doing so causes errors in memory. Two split-brain patients watched a photographic sequence of a common scene, then received lateralized presentations of pictures that were either consistent or inconsistent with that scene.

The left hemisphere produced more false alarms on the basis of consistency. In other words, it was more likely to incorrectly recognize a picture as part of the original scene if the picture was consistent with the idea of the original scene. By contrast, the right hemisphere was more accurate in selecting pictures that had actually been shown in the original scene, regardless of whether they were consistent with it. This difference was substantial: The right hemisphere displayed 63 percent accuracy on this visual recognition task, while the left lingered at only 33 percent accuracy.[31] Thus, the left hemisphere was prone to inferences based on previous experience and mental expectations. Such inferences can be helpful in understanding one's environment in daily life, but they can also be wrong.

A study published in 1995 went even further in asserting that the right hemisphere is superior to the left in creating accurate memories. Here, the results of one split-brain patient were presented, demonstrating greater accuracy by the right hemisphere than the left hemisphere in recognizing visual forms, visual faces, and written words.[32] On the basis of these results, along with evidence from other laboratories, Gazzaniga and his colleagues argue that the left hemisphere stores those aspects of an event that it processes, plus all the inferences that it adds. The right side of the brain also stores what it has processed from an event, but it does not include stereotypes and inferences that might be relevant to the material. This leaves the right hemisphere with an impoverished but veridical trace of the portions of an entire memory that it handled. While this theory may be true, the 1995 study has been roundly criticized by experts in the field. These scientists argue that the descriptions of previous investigations upon which Gazzaniga and his colleagues rest their suppositions are flatly inaccurate and that any remaining shreds of evidence "rest primarily on data from a single, albeit unique, patient."[33] Based on their review of the available evidence, Gazzaniga's critics maintain with vigor that right hemisphere processing is known to include its own types of inferences and interpretations. Such interpretations may indeed differ from those produced by the left hemisphere, but they exist nonetheless, attenuating any supposed veridicality of right hemisphere memory.

All in all, whether the right hemisphere really does produce more accurate memories remains unknown at this time. On the basis of her own studies, Zaidel argues that the right hemisphere is more likely than the left to accept conventional, rigid standards, which themselves could alter mnemonic authenticity. The opposing argument, presented by Gazzaniga and his colleagues, suffers from limited generality and a number of mis-stated assertions. Future exploration, converging from various domains, may eventually show that the left hemisphere is indeed the brain's primary interpreter. If so, it will be as prone to inferential errors as it is to interpretive aid. We may also find in time that the features of an event stored in the right hemisphere are more literal than those stored in the left. But for now, solid conclusions simply cannot be determined on the basis of scant evidence that is hotly disputed. Unfortunately, responsible psychotherapists and their clients will have to wait for cognitive scientists to wrestle this issue to the mat.

## EMOTIONAL MEMORY IN THE RIGHT HEMISPHERE

The right hemisphere is as well known for its prowess in visual recognition as for its superior ability to handle emotion. Compared to individuals with left hemisphere damage, patients who have suffered damage to the right side of the brain often display flat affect and perform poorly when asked to comprehend or express emotional language, facial expression, nonverbal cartoons, or jokes in story form. They also recall significantly less information from emotional stories and do not exhibit the usual bias favoring recall of pleasant over unpleasant memories. When asked to generate autobiographical memories to cue words, right-hemisphere-damaged patients are less specific and less emotional in their memories than are normal subjects.[34] This result holds true regardless of whether the cue words are emotional or neutral in nature. Some memory researchers have postulated that people with right hemisphere lesions may be unable to use emotional features of state-dependent recall because they do not experience the emotion that re-membering a past episode would normally induce.

As the relationship between emotion and cognition is investigated more deeply in coming years, our understanding of the role each hemisphere plays will be enlightened. Recent findings, still in need of replication, suggest that the right hemisphere may process emotion in a manner that is largely subcortical and autonomic, whereas the left hemisphere concentrates on controlling emotion via cortical activation.[35] If so, research using split-brain patients—whose subcortical connections are intact—should be instructive. Furthermore, explorations of classical fear conditioning have been proffered as corroboration of the right hemisphere's ability to mediate autonomic responses such as the increased heart and respiration rates that often accompany emotional episodes. For example, greater electroencephalographic (EEG) and electromyelographic (EMG) responses occur when emotional words are shown to the right hemisphere than when the same words are shown to the left hemisphere. In addition, heart rate is affected more strongly when emotionally disturbing film clips are presented to the right rather than the left half of the brain. Measurements of event-related potentials (ERPs) and skin conductance, upon seeing a facial drawing that was associated through classical conditioning techniques with mild electric shock, are also stronger in the right hemisphere than in the left.[36] These autonomic responses could have a strong effect on memory via the chemical underpinning that stress hormones provide to long-term potentiation in neurons of the hippocampus and amygdala.

A number of seemingly unrelated factors, when considered as a whole, suggest a potential role for the right hemisphere in the creation, storage, or retrieval of traumatic memories. First, we are certain of right hemisphere superiority for emotional memory. Second, several research programs have elicited strong suspicions that the right hemisphere is more powerful than the left in controlling autonomic responses. Third, the right hemisphere may use processes that are more automatic than the left. This supposition is founded on long-standing evidence that left hemisphere damage causes poor intentional learning, while right hemisphere damage causes poor incidental learning.[37] Intentional learning, in which we consciously decide to remember something, requires mental control and concerted effort. Incidental learning, in which we remember something without intent, is an automatic process that includes no conscious control. There is little chance that most individuals choose to expend effort at consciously remembering a severe trauma; rather, most expend their effort in trying to forget. Fourth, there is some evidence that the right hemisphere is better than the left at certain types of implicit priming. Although conceptual word priming (in which the word "table" primes a related concept like "chair") occurs in both hemispheres along roughly the same time course,[38] stem-completion priming (in which the word "table" primes completion of the stem "tab__") is best in the right hemisphere.[39]

These four points have fueled speculations that traumatic memory is linked to the right hemisphere. Unfortunately, solid empirical evidence for this claim is not available. Although one or two studies have been done, even the scientists who designed and conducted them offer descriptive articles that are peppered with cautionary statements. For example, one preliminary study indicated that subjects with a history of childhood trauma displayed left hemisphere dominance while recalling neutral memories, but a nonsignificant trend toward right hemisphere dominance while recalling traumatic memories. Normal subjects, included as controls, favored neither hemisphere while recalling any type of memory. But even the researchers themselves pointed out that they had only the barest minimum of subjects (10) per condition on which to conduct reliable statistical tests, that the ERP method they used to measure hemispheric dominance is sometimes faulty, and that the primary difference of interest was not statistically significant by psychological standards.[40] Too often, studies that are marred by methodological flaws of this sort are accepted as plausible evidence leading to clinical application that can be quite damaging. Such studies should be seen not as failures but as provocative suggestions that warrant more investigation. Although a number of practitioners presently assume right hemisphere involvement in traumatic memory, there is as yet no solid evidence favoring their assumption.

Another potential feature of right hemisphere memory is its apparent superiority in creating and preserving personal identity. Diana Van Lancker, professor of neurology at the University of Southern California, argues that the right hemisphere is especially important in the realm of personal relevance and familiarity. She points out that right hemisphere damage causes prosopagnosia, which is limited to familiar faces, and phonagnosia, an inability to recognize familiar voices, but damage to both hemispheres is usually required to produce agnosias that leave an individual unable to recognize faces and voices seen only once or twice. Similar deficits linked to right hemisphere lesions include Capgras syndrome, in which a patient believes that her own friends and family members are imposters, and reduplicative paramnesia, in which a patient believes that he exists in two physical locations at the same time, including his own home. Van Lancker notes as well that aphasics whose right hemispheres are intact are often able to use the names of familiar people and places with ease, yet they remain unable to master other common words of equally high frequency.[41] Further investigation is needed before we know whether the right hemisphere is specialized to integrate autobiographical memories into personal identity.

## LATERALIZATION OF EPISODIC MEMORY

The most recent cerebral asymmetry to be discovered in memory is a difference in encoding and retrieval that is the focus of current investigation in

Endel Tulving's laboratory at the University of Toronto. On the basis of PET scans, Tulving and his colleagues have found that the right prefrontal cortex handles the retrieval of episodic memories, while the left prefrontal cortex retrieves information from semantic memory and encodes novel features of it into episodic memory. Strong evidence has already been marshaled in support of this theory, known as HERA (Hemispheric Encoding/Retrieval Asymmetry). With respect to activation on the left side, as seen in increased blood flow during semantic retrieval and episodic encoding tasks, eighteen of twenty-one analyzed experiments produced the expected results. These eighteen, furthermore, comprised a wide array of experimental tasks and methods, although most of them were verbal. Activation on the right side was obtained in thirty out of thirty-two recent studies employing episodic retrieval tasks for words, faces, scenes, line drawings, and even odors. The increased blood flow in this area appeared in both recall and recognition, across several different intervals of delay.[42]

Tulving and his associates are careful to point out that other regions of the brain also appear to enjoy increased blood flow during the encoding and retrieval of episodic memories. Their research thus far has been limited to a close inspection of the right and left areas of prefrontal cortex, a relatively small amount of potentially involved brain tissue. Still, when a total of fifty-three recent PET studies have been inspected by members of a laboratory so well respected in the field of memory scholarship, and forty-eight of those studies fit the theory, we have good cause to take heed. The research presently testing HERA involves a closer look at other brain regions to see whether episodic encoding and retrieval can be linked, respectively, to left and right hemispheres in areas other than the prefrontal cortex.[43]

Converging evidence from normal subjects, split-brain patients, and individuals who have suffered brain damage shows that important hemispheric differences do exist among the many functions of human remembrance. But communication between hemispheres is also critical in producing normal recollection: Although split-brain patients are able to function in daily life much more effectively than before their surgeries, they do endure various deficits. Malfunctions of everyday memory rank among the most serious. Split-brain patients tend to retain their previous motor skills and procedural knowledge but suffer very poor memory for "current events, appointments, placement of common articles, [and] parked car location" which does not improve over time.[44] In addition, their ability to remember the sequence and primacy of main points in a book or film is severely impaired. Because of this difficulty in story comprehension, most split-brain patients avoid reading, watching television, or seeing films. Such deficits should not be surprising; almost every task in our daily repertoires, such as cooking a meal or comforting a child, requires a combination of analytical and holistic processes.

Each of us has one full brain that contains two hemispheres working together in integrated fashion twenty-four hours a day. Despite this obvious fact, our society encourages us to emphasize differences in a separatist and reductionist manner that merely furthers the old mind/body/spirit dichotomy. Often, the very people who protest such artificial divisions are simultaneously first in line to embrace "right brain" psychologies. Dahlia Zaidel suggested separate meaning systems in right and left hemispheres, Roger Sperry argued for separate streams of consciousness, and psychologist Robert Ornstein believes that hemispheric differences are neurological evidence for the "traditional dualisms of intellect versus intuition, science versus art, and logical versus mysterious."[45] Following the authors of a noted hemispheric difference book, I like to call it "dichotomania."[46]

# CHAPTER 10

# False Memories

*Ten thousand different things that come from your memory or imagination—and you do not know which is which, which was true, which is false.*

—Amy Tan

Contrary to the video camera metaphor, human memory is a dynamic process of unrelenting construction that starts with the initial stage of perceiving an event and ends only after retrieving it even unconsciously for the last time. In other words, Mnemosyne is not a noun; she's a verb. This assembly of remembrance is seen in the laboratory and on the street, in free recall and limited recognition, in normal subjects and amnesic patients, in recollections of fictional stories, tedious word lists, musical songs, visual forms, and personal experiences. To paraphrase Virginia Woolf, if memory is a bowl, it stands upon the never-ending operation of building recollections that shape our self-concepts. What we remember is as much a function of who we are as of what we experience. And, ultimately, who we are is equally dependent on what we remember.

This constructive view of memory has been growing steadily on the trellis of experimental psychology for several decades, blossoming recently into a profuse arrangement that decorates a path different from the one many memory scholars would have predicted as recently as twenty years ago. As the paradigm has shifted away from assumptions of passive reproduction toward an increasingly active form of reconstruction, our methods and inquiries have changed accordingly. Given such a constructivist view, it is hardly surprising that the details of vivid, confidently held memories are sometimes wrong. But can a vivid, confidently held memory be wrong in its entirety? Can its very core, along with all its details, be completely fallacious?

Promising new investigations undertaken since 1994 are quite persuasive in demonstrating that it can. Anecdotal evidence is even easier to find—after all, estimates suggest that as many as 3.7 million Americans may remember being abducted by alien life forms.[1] A growing mass of adults insists that they consciously recall episodes that occurred during infancy, an ability known to be impossible, or that they remember incidents in past lives, even though there is ample reason to suspect that humans have only one life. Paradoxically, many who recall past lives balk at the philosophy of reincarnation, but their experiences are compelling enough that some explanation must be created. Are these people just a bunch of crackpots and liars? No. Most of them are honest individuals who have undergone odd episodes that can be explained by normal functions of the human brain and mind. The trouble is that they are ignorant of those functions. We humans need to assign meaning to the events of our lives, a need that can easily surpass the social desire to behave with logic. If we are ignorant of a body of knowledge that accounts for bizarre phenomena, we create an explanation of our own to justify the experience, if to no one but ourselves. The explanation's accuracy remains secondary to its ability to assign meaning.

The functions of the human mind that allow us to create false memories without realizing we have done so have now been explored in disparate ways by many independent research teams. While it is true that a few researchers may appear biased in their desire to collect data that will corroborate personal agendas on either side of the recovered memory debate, most of them explore the field objectively, holding a genuine belief in the capacity of science and scholarship to address these politically heated issues. There is no lingering uncertainty that strong memories can be fabricated without conscious awareness. This chapter considers the evidence in some detail, including demonstrations of false recall and recognition across the domains of semantic, episodic, and autobiographical memory. How a fictitious recollection can be constructed should be a critical query for all mental health practitioners who rely in part on their clients' reminiscence when providing psychological therapy.

## CONSTRUCTIVE PROCESSING

The earliest empirical demonstration of reconstructive processes in memory probably rests with Frederic Bartlett's research published in 1932. His subjects listened to culturally specific stories that engendered patterns of recollective error signifying the use of top-down inference. Subjects forgot important pieces of the narrative that didn't fit their cultural expectations, they added explanations that did not exist, and they revised the tale to match their own knowledge. The resulting recollections bore little resemblance to the original story. With these findings as his basis, Bartlett concluded that memory for rote materials like nonsense syllables and word lists was reproductive, whereas memory for complex stimuli like stories and personal events was reconstructive.[2] The distinction—now considered incorrect—has dogged experimental psychologists ever since.

Scientists following in Bartlett's footsteps confirmed the existence of constructive error in sentences, drawings, stories, photographs, and films. Its manifestations were mild, however, and usually limited to mistakes in recognizing the exact words of a previously presented sentence or the pattern in a series of photographic slides, but nevertheless knowing the gist of sentence and slide. It wasn't until later that studies of the misinformation effect in eyewitness testimony clinched the possibility that people could create memories of details that simply weren't there—"details" as large as a nonexistent barn. Still, the memories that participants produced were merely erroneous, not wholly counterfeit.[3]

Although most of the misinformation research creates illusory beliefs in the recognition of details, some of it considers memory for core actions in an event. For example, one group of children watched a videotape showing a girl visiting a neighbor's pond, a pond she had been told not to visit. The neighbor reprimands her verbally for the violation and sends her home. Upon returning home, the girl reports to her parents that the neighbor hit her, an action that the videotape clearly shows he did not do. Nevertheless, almost 30 percent of the subjects said they remembered that the man did hit her at the pond.[4] Confidence remains high in most misinformation studies, with subjects not only supplying high confidence ratings on paper-and-pencil tests but also betting money on their incorrect recollections.[5]

People's memories for their own actions can be mistaken as well. Voting behavior, for example, is notoriously overestimated, with as many as 25 percent to 30 percent of respondents saying they voted when in fact they did not. Of course, this effect is partly determined by social pressure: Few upstanding citizens wish to admit publicly that they didn't vote in an election. But the effect is also mediated by faulty memory. Over a six-month period, the percentage of sampled voters who said they voted when they really didn't increased from 16 percent to 40 percent. The 24-point increase is unlikely to have been caused solely by social demands.[6]

## ILLUSORY INTRUSIONS

Until 1994, most demonstrations of illusory memory were limited to recognition rather than recall tests. People often reported, upon seeing or hearing a given stimulus item, that it was previously presented when in fact it had never appeared. Fewer indications existed that subjects would pull false information entirely from their own minds in a standard recall test, believing all the while in the veracity of the recollection. Yet even when memorizing materials as trivial as lists of words, people tend to make two types of errors: omissions, in which they forget that a word has indeed been presented, and intrusions, in which they recall words that have not been presented. The latter error has formed one major prong of the false memory research being conducted today. The other prong focuses on autobiographical memories of personal events.

Memory psychologist Henry Roediger, along with one of his former graduate students, Kathleen McDermott, recently rediscovered a systematic pattern of false memory in the recall of word lists. (The original discovery was made by James Deese of Johns Hopkins University in 1959, but it attracted so little attention that it was virtually forgotten for the next thirty-five years.[7]) The effect is robust enough that you can try it on a friend in about thirty seconds under completely uncontrolled circumstances, and it will probably work. Tell your friend that you are going to read aloud a series of words to be remembered. When you are finished reading the words, the friend should immediately repeat them back to you, in any order. Read the words in a clear voice at the rate of roughly one word every 1.5 seconds. Here is the list: thread, pin, eye, sewing, sharp, point, pricked, thimble, haystack, pain, hurt, injection.[8]

In Roediger and McDermott's experiment, 40 percent of the subjects falsely recalled the word "needle" as being presented in the list of words. Perhaps your friend made the same error. Fully 84 percent of the subjects falsely recognized "needle" when asked to look at a long list of words and to determine which ones had been presented originally. This elevated rate of false recognition nearly matched the correct recognition rate for words that had indeed been presented, which hovered at 86 percent. In other words, subjects were as willing to say that "needle" had been presented as they were that "thread," "pin," and the other original stimuli had been presented. When asked to rate their confidence that unpresented words like "needle" were on the original list, these participants bestowed the highest possible confidence rating on more than half (58 percent) of their false recognitions.[9]

Other stimulus lists, each containing about a dozen words related to an unpresented associate like "needle," were presented to many college students, with the same result occurring reliably. The size of the effect is easily increased by adding a few more related words to the list; for example, when subjects were given fifteen related words instead of twelve, false recall shot up to 55 percent and false recognition soared to 93 percent. Although it is not terribly unusual for people to misrecall a word, the circumstances under which this effect transpires are astonishing. First, it persists when subjects are specifically warned not to guess. Second, it weathers the complete lack of any retention interval; that is, subjects make this systematic error even when they are permitted to recall the word list immediately following its presentation. Third, it survives under measures of both recall memory and recognition memory. Fourth, it occurs after the presentation of a very short list of words, short enough to be remembered fairly well. Fifth, it endures under conditions of intentional learning; participants in these studies know that they will be asked to prove their memories for the stimulus words after each list has been presented. Sixth, it remains unweakened when experimenters tell subjects point-blank not to make the common error of mistaking an associated word for one that was presented in the list. Seventh, it perseveres in graduate students of psychology who know about the effect and strive to avoid it. And eighth, subjects of all types frequently argue when debriefed that the experimenter must have made a mistake because there is no doubt that the nonexistent associate was indeed presented.[10] One group of participants in a follow-up study categorically refused to believe that the associates had not been presented even after hearing a tape recording of the original list.[11]

Such undeniable certainty in the face of totally false recollection caused Roediger and McDermott to take their study a step further, asking subjects to categorize their responses to each unpresented associate. Do you explicitly "remember" the associate being presented in the sense of having a mental image of the presentation moment, they asked, or do you feel you "know" the associate because it seems familiar and therefore must have been presented?[12] Subjects' answers to these questions were startling. In most other tests of recognition memory, subjects assign a "know" rating to items they have falsely recognized. Contrary to these expectations, Roediger and McDermott found that nearly three-quarters (72 percent) of falsely recalled associates like "needle" received a "remember" rating. Equally high levels of explicit memory (73 percent) were obtained for the falsely recognized associates. These subjects consciously remembered an experience that never happened.[13]

Follow-up studies in other laboratories have substantiated the salience of these explicit recollections. When the original words are read aloud using two different voices, participants claim 87 percent of the time to "remember" rather than "know" which voice was used in the supposed presentation of a nonexistent associate.[14] When participants hear some words on the original list but see others, they "remember" whether the unpresented associate was delivered visually or auditorily.[15] Similarly, they "remember" explicitly the position of an associate's supposed presentation in the list.[16] Results are not altered in any way when subjects are told ahead of time that they will have to justify their "remember" and "know" responses with reasonable explanation.[17] These counterfeit memories, then, are accompanied by sturdy feelings of confidence and explicit recollections of presentation that are unparalleled in previous work.

Roediger and his collaborators have also applied the distinction between "remembering" and "knowing" to the misinformation effect in eyewitness testimony. In this case, subjects who observed photographic slides of a simulated crime were then presented with misinformation in the form of a written narrative about the slides. Incorrect memory on the basis of misinformation occurred for about one-third of the subjects even though these experimenters measured accuracy with a recall test rather than the standard recognition test, which typically exposes misinformation. Even more intriguing, the subjects claimed to explicitly "remember" the moment that false information was presented in the photographic slides although in fact it had been presented in the written narrative. When misinformation was repeated through consecutive memory tests so that subjects were retrieving it again and again, their false explicit memories only grew stronger.[18]

As every political campaign manager knows, repeating a statement leads people to believe it. Psychological research since the 1960s verifies that repetition increases the perception of truth as well as the degree of preference for most stimuli.[19] Repetition also enhances both true and false memories. Studies of the misinformation effect in eyewitness testimony and the false recall effect in memory for word associates validate this assertion. After people watched the simulation of a burglary on videotape, the same misinformation repeated to them three times was more likely to produce false memory than was misinformation presented only once. To provide a concrete example, after watching a five-minute videotape in which the main character, a burglar, was clearly not wearing gloves, subjects are told he was wearing gloves. Not only do they accept this misinformation once but they go on to accept it three times in succession, all the while establishing a stronger memory of the nonexistent gloves. Repetition also increased subjects' confidence ratings in the misinformation. And, paradoxically, it boosted their claims to "remember" explicitly the moment at which the misinformation had been provided, while it simultaneously strengthened their belief in the accuracy of the misinformation. These repetition effects lasted through a range of retention intervals, ranging from immediate testing to a one-week delay.[20]

False memories of unpresented word associates are also susceptible to repetition at the time of testing. We might think that people who are asked to listen to lists of word associates repeatedly, recalling the words from their memories each time, would become more accurate. Shouldn't they eventually figure out that "needle" was never presented? Instead, the number of both correct and false memories climbs with repeated testing. By the end of the series, unpresented associates are more likely than ever to intrude into subjects' recollections. And when a final free recall test is taken two days after original presentation of the lists, unpresented associates like "needle" are recalled significantly more often than are the words like "thread" that had actually been presented in list form.[21] In other words, with repetition, false memory became more robust than true memory. Furthermore, and contrary to what we would predict from a century's research on true memories, the two-day delay caused no decrease in people's false recollections. In virtually every other experimental memory paradigm, time reduces memory's accuracy, and stimulus repetition increases it.

A clever extension of the research on word associates requires subjects to hear a story in which the main character carries out a common activity, such as washing a car. The story mentions some of the tasks related to the activity, like turning on the hose or scrubbing the bugs off the headlights, but it fails to mention others, like dipping a sponge into a bucket of soapy water. As long as the unpresented actions fit with a general schema—what we would expect to occur during the activity of washing a car—subjects falsely recognized many of them. In addition, 20 percent of the falsely recognized actions received "remember" rather than "know" ratings, indicating that subjects did not merely assume that a plausible nonexistent action must have occurred but explicitly remembered hearing about it in the story.[22]

## FALSE MEMORY FOR AUTOBIOGRAPHICAL EVENTS

False memory is readily apparent with respect to associated words, misinformation in eyewitness testimony, and schema-based actions. But these forms of illusory remembrance are a far cry from personal reminiscences of one's own life history. As such, they are of less consequence to the typical psychotherapist and might at first glance be waved away with some annoyance as largely irrelevant to the practitioner's problems. I offer them nonetheless because they supply a worthy underpinning to the second prong of current research: confident, detailed recollections of complex personal events that never happened. Here, we move away from the trivial memorization of associated word lists in a stuffy laboratory and toward a more ecologically valid exploration of autobiographical creation in real life.

With his colleagues, Stephen Ceci, a developmental psychologist at Cornell University, pioneered the research on false autobiographical memory when his long-standing investigations of children's susceptibility to suggestion led to an inquiry of just how wild a story a child might accept. In one study he asked preschoolers to tell him about the time they got a hand caught in a mousetrap and had to have the trap removed at the hospital. According to their parents, none of the children had ever experienced such an event. The request was repeated over the course of ten interviews, until more than half of the children not only agreed that the mousetrap story was true but went further to supply complex—and totally false—details as to how, when, and where the event took place.[23] One boy explained that "my brother Colin was trying to get Blowtorch [an action figure] from me, and I wouldn't let him take it from me, so he pushed me into the wood pile where the mousetrap was. And then my finger got caught in it. And then we went to the hospital, and my mommy, daddy, and Colin drove me there, to the hospital in our van, because it was far away. And the doctor put a bandage on this finger [indicating]."[24] The only portion of the story that was supplied to the child was the suggestion that his hand was stuck in a mousetrap, which had to be removed at a hospital. Some of the children in this study later insisted to their own parents that the event really had happened.

In a later variation, Ceci and his collaborators showed that ten interviews' worth of encouragement were not needed. They read aloud a list of true and false events to a group of children, asking them to say whether each event had truly occurred. In the very first session, 44 percent of the three- and four-year-old subjects remembered at least one false event as having happened. The percentage of older children reporting false memories for at least one false event (25 percent) was lower but still formidable.[25] In further work, Ceci found that children are most likely to accept emotionally neutral events as true, and least likely to accept emotionally negative events as true, with false memory for emotionally positive events falling in the middle.[26] This does not mean, of course, that children never create false memories of negative events; ample substantiation through legal proceedings and experimental psychology shows that they do.

Given the immaturity of memory at preschool age, these results aren't particularly shocking, but they certainly should give pause to psychotherapists, law enforcement officials, and parents who ask children to tell them the truth about a given event. It is now obvious that children's memories can be fallacious, not just in the details of an episode but in the very gist of the situation itself. A child can easily believe that something happened when in fact it never did. But is everyone this suggestible? Can the same sort of false memory for autobiographical events be observed in mature, reasonable adults? Absolutely.

Elizabeth Loftus, a cognitive psychologist at the University of Washington whose ground-breaking research in eyewitness testimony during the 1970s and 1980s turned psychology's attention to constructive processes in memory, has developed a method of testing false memories in adults. Basically, it involves presenting four childhood events to an adult subject, three of which the subject's parent provides as true, and a fourth which is created by the experimenters and verified as false by the parent. Subjects are asked to describe all four events. To be counted as a false memory, an event must be described in details that were never presented. In other words, it is not enough for a subject to merely state that he remembers the event occurring; he must provide a detailed description of it. The first case study in which Loftus attempted this method occurred when a teenage boy was told by his brother that he had been lost at age five in a shopping mall. In fact, the teenager had never been lost in a mall. After writing about the incident every day for five days, along with three other events that were true, the teenage subject remembered more and more details about the mall escapade. He remembered the feeling of being frightened upon realizing he was lost, he described the store he was lost in, he recalled the scolding he received when found, and he remembered what the man who found him looked like. The man was wearing a blue flannel shirt, he said, seemed old, was partially bald, and wore glasses. He rated the clarity of this memory near the top of the rating scale, at a level higher than two of the three true memories received. When debriefed, he was asked to guess which of the four memories was false. He chose one of his true personal experiences.[27]

Another subject who experienced the same procedure remembered the older woman who found her, recalled that the woman was wearing a long skirt, recalled the woman's questions as to whether she was lost and what her name was, and remembered the woman taking her to the security office in the mall. Upon being reunited with her parents, she remembered crying— even though she knew she had not cried while lost. This subject was so convinced of the truth of her entirely fictitious illusion that she telephoned each of her parents after the debriefing to ask whether she had indeed never been lost in a mall.[28]

On the basis of these preliminary case studies, well-controlled research has now been conducted to determine whether a sizable percentage of adults recalls inauthentic autobiographical events. One of the earliest experiments showed that 29 percent of adult subjects recalled being lost in a mall even though it had never happened. Although the "remember" or "know" distinction was not used, several of the subjects remarked that they genuinely experienced the recollection as if it were happening again: "I totally remember walking around in those dressing rooms and my mom not being in the section she said she'd be in."[29] In all of these cases, it is important to realize how little of the event was supplied by the experimenter, and how much by the subject. Experimenters in these studies said nothing more than that the individual had been lost in a mall at age five. Everything else was constructed in the mind and supplied to conscious awareness with all the vitality of confident personal knowledge.

Because being lost in a mall is quite plausible, other psychologists have wondered whether false memories could include more unusual events. One study produced a false memory rate of 20 percent among adults who were told they had once been hospitalized with an ear infection. The rate rose to 25 percent when subjects were interviewed three times and false events included spilling punch at a wedding, evacuating a store whose overhead sprinklers activated, or releasing the parking brake in a car that rolled into some object. These researchers also manipulated the age at which the bogus episode was said to occur—either 2 years, 4 years, or 10 years—but the false memory rate was not altered accordingly.[30]

Elaborate detail was again produced in these experiences of fallacious reminiscence. For instance, one subject was told, "When you were five you went to the wedding of a friend of the family and at the reception you were running around with some other kids, bumped into the table holding the punch bowl, and spilled the punch on the parents of the bride." Here's what she made of that: "The people I spilled punch on, I picture them to be a heavyset man, not like fat but like tall and big kind big beer belly, and I picture him having a dark suit on, like greyish dark and like having greyish dark hair and balding on top, and . . . uh I picture him with a wide square face and I just picture him getting up and being kind of irritated or mad, then the woman, I see her in a light colored dress that has like flowers on it, I think I see flowers on it and stuff, and I see like a big red punch thing down the front of them, can see that. Her hair hadn't turned grey yet, it was still dark, it was brown. . . . They were near a tree. . . . Like the table was a round table with a couple of chairs sitting around it and they were under the shade of a tree . . . there were some drinks on the table. . . . I like bumped the table and the glasses tipped over on them."[31] The subject's parents verified that the event had never happened.

False autobiographical memories such as these have now been demonstrated in preschool children, teenagers, college students, and middle-aged adults. Typically, about one-fourth of the subjects in a false memory experiment claim to remember a fabricated event, which they describe in great detail. Research thus far shows that men and women seem equally susceptible to the effect. In almost all of the experiments, subjects are told ahead of time that accuracy is very important; in many studies they are told that the primary goal of the research is to test the accuracy of their childhood memories. Undoubtedly, the social demands of the testing situation have an effect: A close relative and an authoritative experimenter conspire to increase a false event's credulity, with the relative implying that it really did happen. In addition, repeated questions and encouragement to remember creates the need for a memory, a need that is then only too easily filled by a willing brain. Of course, with the exception of the authoritative experimenter, exactly these social factors come to bear on our memories in everyday life. Is there any one of us who has never experienced a family gathering at which an elder asked with surprise, "Don't you remember that?" combined with some piece of a story like "You were up in the treehouse when the plank broke, and then . . . "

Although some of these fictional events can be considered negative (being hospitalized, releasing a brake, spilling punch, getting lost), none of them fulfills the definition of traumatic. To my knowledge only one experiment has been conducted so far in which the researchers attempted to implant in adults the false memory of an act that some might consider bodily shameful or embarrassing. That study compared the likelihood that subjects would construct a false memory of being lost in a mall as opposed to a false memory of receiving a rectal enema. The manipulation produced no conclusive results. This study is mentioned only because its results have been presented elsewhere as if they were definitive despite the fact that they are unreliable by the experimenters' own admission. In fact, no statistically significant difference in false memory rates was obtained between the two conditions. Because the difference was not significant, it cannot be generalized in any reliable way to individuals other than those particular subjects who were tested. Furthermore, the data from the standard condition, in which some subjects thought they had been lost in a mall, do not resemble the data obtained by other psychologists, casting doubt on the methodology of the entire experiment.[32] We need further investigations of this type, ones in which reliable results are obtained in one direction or the other before we deliver them to an unsuspecting public.

Anecdotes of erroneous memory for traumatic events are easy to find in the popular and professional literature. Too often, though, they are rendered in a manner that implies more knowledge about false memory for trauma than we actually have. Take, for example, the true story of a Texas woman who, along with her teenage daughter, was bound, blindfolded, held at gunpoint, raped, and sodomized. With absolute conviction, she later identified a man she knew as the perpetrator of this violent scene. A few weeks after he had been sentenced to fifty years in prison without evidence beyond the victim's eyewitness identification, another man confessed to the crime, providing detailed information that no one but the real rapist could have known. The victim, even when shown a videotape of the real rapist and hearing his voice again, refused to believe that his confession was true. She was thoroughly convinced that the innocent acquaintance had committed the crime.[33]

A more famous anecdote comes from Jean Piaget, the Swiss developmental psychologist. He wrote about his own memory of being kidnapped from a baby carriage at age two. The narrative is replete with vivid details about the scene, including the particular street on which the kidnapping occurred, the straps fastened around Piaget's young body, his nurse's attempts to defend him, and the scratches she received on her face. All the details were false. At age fifteen Piaget discovered that his nurse had made up the story to endear herself to his parents as a brave protectress. In more recent years, children's memories of a sniper attack at their school playground were explored, only to find that even the children who were nowhere near the school during the event held distinct memories of it.[34] These anecdotes, while provocative, are fairly weak indicators of wholly fallacious recollection for traumatic experiences, in my opinion. Far more inspection is needed, but, obviously, ethical principles prevent lost-in-the-mall experiments from being applied to truly traumatic memories.

## HOW FALSE MEMORIES ARE CREATED

Inquiry from many quarters employing various methods to study the construction of nontraumatic illusions leaves no doubt that meticulous memories can be completely false from core to surface. But precisely how such memories are created, and why they feel so certain to us, remains vague at this time. Top contenders in the flood of potential explanations include implicit associative responses, failures in source monitoring, faulty metamemory, schematic reconstruction, and social desirability bias. If false memories are like most other psychological phenomena, we will eventually learn that they are caused by a combination of many such factors.

Implicit associative responses have been evoked to explain false recall and recognition of unpresented associates in related word lists since Deese's era. According to this supposition, as each word on a list is first heard, the set of neurons that represent it are automatically activated. When several related neural networks are activated by the presentation of words like "thread," "pin," "sewing," and "sharp," activation spreads to any other neural network that is connected through semantic relationship and frequent usage.

Picture a small bubble of neurons that physically represents the mental experience of the concept "thread," another bubble linked to the mental experience of "pin," and so on. Each bubble lights up when its word is presented. The bubbles are connected to each other because of the semantic relationships among the entire set of words. At some point, when enough connected bubbles have turned on, any node representing a closely related but unpresented word (like "needle") will be activated even though it was never actually presented.[35] This concept of spreading activation is based on a perennial cognitive theory of mental representation.[36]

Neural activation can occur without conscious awareness of content; in fact, most cognitive processing takes place at a level of automatic neural activation that remains below the threshold of consciousness. We are conscious of only a tiny fraction of the activities occurring inside our minds at any given time. Thus, it is perfectly plausible that the concept of an unpresented word like "needle" could be activated without our knowing. At the time of retrieval, the brain can distinguish between neural networks that have been recently activated and those that have not. However, it may have trouble discriminating between a neural network that has been activated by external stimulation and a neural network that has been activated to an equivalent degree by internal spreading.

The same spreading activation that occurs at the time of initial presentation and encoding may also occur when a word list is retrieved. In other words, recalling other words on the list may activate the node for the unpresented associate, which then suddenly seems to have been presented earlier. Why else, subjects sometimes ask, would it have come to mind? The retrieval explanation fits with our knowledge that unpresented associates are usually recalled in the middle or at the end of the retrieved word series; subjects in these experiments almost never produce an unpresented associate at the beginning of their recall. The fact that repetition aids false memory for words is also compatible with the notion of spreading activation. Quite possibly, implicit associative responses account for false word recall by virtue of their operation at both the encoding and retrieval stages. If encoding and retrieval occur repeatedly, the process has that much more opportunity to function.

Why people frequently claim not merely to "know" but to "remember" the explicit presentation of an invisible associate is harder to explain. Perhaps those associates did enter conscious awareness after being activated by internal spreading.[37] The conscious memory of the concept might then fool us into believing that the word was really presented. This kind of error is typical of a failure in what cognitive scientists call source or reality monitoring.[38] We've already seen that source amnesia is a common problem in which people—unconsciously—cannot remember the actual source of a piece of information and hence fill the gap with what seems to be the most plausible source. The misinformation effect in eyewitness testimony is thought to arise from source amnesia: People fail to remember whether a piece of information came from their original view of a crime or from a brief comment during later interrogation. They assume the former incorrectly.

Source monitoring is almost certain to play a similar role in creating illusory reminiscences. Various details that an individual has reconstructed into one memory may have originated from different sources that are now forgotten. Actual sources often include dreams, television scenes, film clips, and people or situations other than those we consciously credit. Former President Ronald Reagan spoke publicly on at least three occasions about the historical World War II commander who received a posthumous Congressional Medal of Honor for remaining with his airplane when it was shot down over Europe, facing his own death while calming a young wounded soldier with the words, "Never mind, son, we'll ride it down together." In fact, the episode was a purely fictional scene from the movie "A Wing and a Prayer" filmed in 1944.[39] Researchers who specialize in studying source amnesia report that people even misattribute pure imagination to accurate memory, frequently confusing an imagined event with a real one. Most of us, at one time or another, have probably wondered whether we actually did some task we planned to do or merely imagined doing it. Later, the confusion dissipates, and a memory solidifies, leaving the uncertainty behind. Whether that memory is true or false can be very difficult to determine.

Imaginary thoughts occur to people in a variety of ways. Sometimes we simply daydream, other times we think more purposefully about what might have been or what might come in the future. Normal neurological phenomena can exacerbate these imaginary thoughts and experiences. For example, brief sensory hallucinations are common under conditions of sleep deprivation, prolonged stress, hunger or malnutrition, and even during the everyday acts of falling asleep and waking up.[40] The fact that claims of alien abduction are often connected with sleep or long drives is a telling point. I once watched a gigantic circus elephant lumber across an Oregon highway on a thirty-six-hour drive, but I do not believe that the elephant abducted me. Of course, had I been steeped in the *National Enquirer*'s true stories of elephant abduction, the outcome might have been quite different. As two leaders in the field of false memory research have said, the source of abduction memories "might be intracranial rather than extraterrestrial."[41] All humor aside, people who believe they have been abducted by aliens are suffering partly from source amnesia.

Increasing attention is now devoted to psychological research on normal source monitoring. How do people typically tell the difference between real and imagined events? How do we discriminate between neural activation from external experience and the same activation from internal operations? The answers, not yet fully determined, suggest that people usually monitor their autobiographical recollections for perceptual details or inferential reasoning through the activity of the frontal lobe.[42] Memories that are more complex, contain extensive implications, seem more intense, and are mulled over frequently in mental thought tend to be classified as imaginary. Inferential reasoning based on logic and past experience is also a common ingredient of ersatz remembrances: "I wouldn't have been there at all unless . . ." By contrast, memories that contain perceptual details of sight, sound, smell, or taste, and for which a particular location or setting can be identified, tend to be considered by the monitoring individual as likely to be true.[43] Unfortunately, as we have seen, perceptual details are readily available in both incorrect and wholly counterfeit memories. They serve only to boost the degree of confidence the individual holds for the reality of the event. Even under prime circumstances, then, monitoring is not perfect. When fatigue, hunger, sleep, or stress are added to the mix, all cognitive processes—including reality and source monitoring—are hindered.

A neuropsychological clue to the localization of source monitoring comes from brain-damaged patients with frontal lobe lesions who display extreme source amnesia without other concurrent memory problems.[44] These patients, whether damaged in the right or left frontal lobe, have severe difficulty recalling or recognizing the source of information that they remember. In addition, such patients tend to confabulate, spinning long, bizarre stories about events that never occurred. Logic is often thrown to the winds in these tales, with patients protesting vehemently that an event occurred even though it could not possibly have happened. Usually, confabulation is limited to autobiographical memory for events and may itself be linked to the deficit in source monitoring. That the frontal lobes may be used to evaluate the accuracy or relevance of information coming from memory is a possibility that Tulving's HERA model takes into account. A number of wide-ranging cognitive and neurological experiments buttress that theory.[45]

People's beliefs about how memory works, or metamemory, are also partly responsible for recollective illusions. In both clinical practice and experimental inquiry, examples teem in which clients, patients, and subjects assume that any event that comes to them as a memory must be real. How, they ask, could it be stored in memory if it never happened? Such assumptions lead most people to pay little attention to source monitoring; they assume that any mental image unaccompanied by conscious creation must be a memory. They also assume that every memory is real. They know that a recollection can be flawed in its trivial details but may not realize that a memory can be completely false. Those who contend that vivid detail is the hallmark of truth are likely to experience even more falsehood. And people who believe that human memory is nothing more or less than the video camera of life are highly unlikely to suspect that a recollection is wrong. Without applying vigilant skepticism to the processes of our own minds, the potential errors inherent in spreading activation, source monitoring, schematic reconstruction, and social demands are given free rein to trample any remnants of veracity.

Experimental evidence confirms that faulty metamemory can have profound effects.[46] In one study, college students were asked to describe their earliest recollections. They were warned to be accurate in providing true personal memories that did not sprout from family stories or photographs. As we would expect from an understanding of the physical maturation that occurs during infancy and early childhood, the age of the earliest memory report was an event that had occurred when subjects were, on average, 3.7 years old. After this phase of the study had been completed, the subjects were given one piece of false information about metamemory: They were told that most adults, if they try hard, can remember experiencing their second birthday. With nothing more than this, the proportion of subjects who described their second birthdays shot up from zero to 60 percent. With more encouragement, 33 percent of all subjects reported events that occurred prior to the age of 1 year, and the mean age of the earliest memory report plummeted from 3.7 years to 1.6 years.[47]

Event schemata are also critical contributors to fallacious memory. We all hold schemata in our minds for typical activities, including, for instance, the knowledge we have of what usually happens when we dine at a restaurant. The sequence of events forms a restaurant schema in which a hostess or maître d' seats us, we look at a menu and choose our meals, the waiter or waitress takes the order and some time later brings our food, we eat, we request a check and pay the bill, we leave. The schema affords some flexibility—we can order wine before or after selecting our meal, or not at all—but it also provides a firm scaffolding for the entire experience. In studies that implant false memories for autobiographical events, such as spilling punch at a wedding, participants summon a relevant schema and use it to mentally explore the fake event. Thoughts of what usually happens at weddings are combined with suggestions of what was said to have happened when attending a specific wedding, creating the kind of example mentioned earlier in which a college student falsely recalled bumping into a table and spilling glasses of punch on people wearing nice clothes. Clearly, that individual used schematic knowledge of weddings to derive appropriate descriptions: a man wearing a dark gray suit, his wife in a pale flowered dress, a round table under the shade of a tree. These descriptions aren't true at all, but they certainly fit the scene better than, for example, a biker wearing nothing but leather chaps. If the schema had not been used to fashion the memory, the subject's recollection would be less plausible on the surface and therefore more conducive to accurate source monitoring.[48]

Neurologically, schematic reconstruction could occur when information from an internal schema causes certain neural networks to become activated along with the networks representing the false information provided by the experimenter. Simultaneous activation of this kind is likely to bind the various networks together into one memory, which is then consolidated over time by the hippocampus. Later, when retrieving the memory, all of the networks are activated at once, with no distinction between those that came from the schema and those that came from the experimenter. Still, schematic reconstruction isn't all bad. Most of the time, the activation of a schema helps us to understand and respond rapidly to ongoing events in our environments. It may aid our memories as well. For instance, the fact that it is easier to alter some feature of a generally true memory than it is to implant a completely false memory is partly due to internal schemata. Memory can cling to a framework that already exists more readily than it can swing free across the vastness of an empty mind. Empirically, several research teams have provided independent evidence that people really are more likely to create false memories of events for which they have readily available schemata. For example, 24 percent of Catholic subjects accepted a false memory related to Communion, whereas  no Jewish subjects were so persuaded. Opposite results appeared when the false event was related to the Jewish practice of Shabbat.[49] Of course, schematic knowledge need not derive from direct personal experience. Schemata that define the typical sequence of events in being hospitalized, for example, are known by many people who have never been admitted to a hospital. Most schemata can be developed through vicarious experience with a friend or relative, literary accounts both fictional and historical, newspaper reports, television or cinema, and word of mouth.

All false memory research, from associated word lists to full-blown autobiographical events, relies to some extent on social demand. Social psychology has a long history of testimony on this score; even people who proudly call themselves independent thinkers often try to conform, to fit in, to please. In studies of fictitious autobiographical recollection, both the experimenter and a parent or close relative tell the subjects that certain events took place when they were younger. Very few subjects argue that their parents must be wrong about what happened during their early childhood years; after all, how many of us would trust our own memories of being five years old more than our parents' fully mature remembrances of that time?[50]

Whether false memories for events that occurred during adulthood can be implanted is an intriguing empirical question presently under consideration in several laboratories. Studies do indicate that the misinformation effect in eyewitness testimony is stronger when incorrect details are supplied by authoritative individuals or by a majority of individuals. In addition to the social effects of authority, majority, conformity, and obedience in everyday living, the social demands of the experimental laboratory have also been studied in great detail, altering many research methodologies to avoid the strong effects that are inherent in most subjects' desires to produce results that they think the experimenter wants.[51] Bogus memories cannot be blamed solely on social demands, but in experimentation—as in real life—people do sometimes alter their beliefs according to perceived social expectations.

## TRUE OR FALSE: TELLING THE DIFFERENCE

Psychologists today know that stalwart memories can be entirely fallacious, and we understand at least some of the factors contributing to their creation. This knowledge will aid both clinical practitioners and experimental scientists, and, if adequately explained to the public, will help to build a more accurate collective metamemory in American society. What is perhaps most disconcerting is the agreement among virtually all scholars who conduct research in false memory that we have no way of discriminating reliably between memories that are authentic and those that are counterfeit. In one part of Stephen Ceci's study of the mousetrap event, a group of experts was asked to determine from a videotape which of the children's memories was real and which was not. The experts included psychologists who conduct research on memory illusions, psychotherapists in active practice, and police interrogators—all of whom had professional expertise in working with young children. Not one of them was able to discern the true memories from the false ones.[52] Many were fooled by the ornate complexity of narrative detail offered by the children while describing the ersatz experience of having a hand caught in a mousetrap. People believe so fervently in their own false memories that observers sense no fraudulence accompanying the tale. Even neuroscientists employing PET scans have failed to observe significant differences in brain activity during true and false recognition.[53]

One team of researchers wrote in 1994 when false memory research was in its infancy: "We would all be better off if we faced the hard truth which is that, at the moment, we do not have the means for reliably distinguishing true memories about the past from false ones."[54] Since then a great deal of intense investigation has taken place, allowing us to sharpen our understanding and hone more pointed hypotheses to test. But as this book goes to press scientists from yet another laboratory have concluded that "differentiating between recovered true memories and created false memories . . . does not appear possible at this juncture. . . . We have not been able to identify any obvious distinctions in the verbal reports individuals provide. . . . [T]he confidence participants displayed in the recovered true memories and the created false memories was nearly identical."[55] We may never be able to develop a reliable means of discrimination.

Two critical points remain to be mentioned concerning false memories: that the majority of individuals do not remember false events often and that false remembrance holds some positive connotations. Although false recognition reaches rates of 80 percent and 90 percent under the right circumstances, the standard rate of fallacious episodic recall obtained across a variety of procedures and laboratories rarely exceeds 25 percent, or one in four. While this percentage of illusion is much higher than our socially flawed metamemories of the video camera metaphor might have assumed, it hardly suggests that we routinely fabricate the important events of our lives. We should not lose sight of the converse proportion: three-quarters of the time individuals do not fall prey, even under social pressure, to the creation of a completely fictitious memory. Furthermore, the research thus far is limited to implanting false memories of childhood events; as yet there is little empirical indication that counterfeit remembrance can be implanted for events that occurred during adulthood. In addition, individual differences are sure to play a critical role; we have already seen that people who have an accurate understanding of Mnemosyne's mercurial nature are less likely to be fooled by her ploys.

The fluctuation of memory at all stages from initial encoding to final retrieval has its pitfalls, but it is exactly that property which allows us to adapt to change—and therefore act intelligently—on a regular basis. If our memories were more accurate and less susceptible to suggestion, they would also be more rigid, incapable of molding themselves to the moment. Mnemonic alterations that seem distressing in the context of a desire for absolute truth are precisely the processes that help us learn new concepts, develop meaningful bonds, define ourselves at the deepest levels, and provide fresh opportunities for psychological growth.

# CHAPTER 11

# Enhancing Retrieval

*Instead of remembering here a scene and there a sound, I shall fit a plug into the wall; and listen in to the past. I shall turn up August 1890.*

—**Virginia Woolf**

If it were possible to switch on memory like a radio, retrieval enhancement techniques would be moot. But remembering the past is much more difficult than selecting a spot on the dial and cranking the volume up. Our minds are beset with the signal equivalent of static and interference, received through an occasionally feeble antenna. Fortunately, experimental psychology offers a panoply of techniques that can improve the human ability to reconstruct the contents of our memories. While experimental psychologists do not pretend to know how to elicit every memory accurately, we can volunteer practical suggestions based on a century of empirical research. Moreover, further knowledge is gained every day through scientific inquiry. By keeping apprised of the burgeoning literature, practitioners can consistently upgrade the quality of care they provide.

An understanding of how memory works is critical for jurors and judges, teachers and students, politicians and voters, friends and family, but especially for psychotherapists and their troubled clients. Most psychological practitioners ask clients for personal information from the past and consider the responses consequential even if they do not deem the process a form of "memory recovery." Added to that, approximately three-quarters of licensed clinical psychologists report using formal recovery techniques to improve their clients' retrieval for a variety of reasons.[1] Unfortunately, many of those techniques are unsupported by empirical investigation, uninformed by basic principles of memory scholarship, and highly controversial even within the clinical arena. Better methods are available to any psychotherapist whose decisions rest on a solid foundation of knowledge about the capacity for human remembrance.

Before describing general axioms and specific procedures that can procure accurate recall and recognition, several caveats are in order. In keeping with the concise nature of this guide, no effort has been made to create an exhaustive list of retrieval techniques. Superficial coverage of many potential methods is avoided in favor of deeper treatment for the best few. In addition, techniques that aid in the retrieval of forgotten or partial memories are favored over those that are used to process existing recollections. Eye movement desensitization and reprocessing (EMDR), for example, focuses on existing memories of past trauma and is therefore excluded.[2] Those methods that are included here can be applied as prototypes to many different situations, and the reasons for their efficacy will provide a background that therapists can use to evaluate other techniques. As research on retrieval enhancement continues, I hope that entire volumes will be written describing the methods by which we all can learn to elicit solid recollections of autobiographical histories.

My evaluation of the techniques described in this chapter is based solely on their ability to advance accurate retrieval. Some of the techniques are used in other important ways as well. Hypnosis is a strong case in point: It is a very poor method of memory recovery, yet it may be extremely effective as a form of therapy for other purposes. It is certainly not my place to tell practitioners which therapies to use in the treatment of any client's mental disorder or personal problems. As a cognitive scientist, however, I am qualified to proffer knowledge on aspects of human memory that clinicians may face.

In discussing suggestibility and memory construction, I am not accusing anyone—practitioners, clients, or researchers—of intentionally lying or misleading. Suggestion has at times been employed with the intent of implanting a false memory; Pierre Janet, for example, reported instances in which a client's evil history was purposely replaced with a more mundane one.[3] However, I seriously doubt that clinicians spend their time carrying out such practices today. Pointing out that memory is always constructive, often overconfident, and occasionally inaccurate is completely different from saying that rememberers lie. Likewise, pondering the opportunity for unintended suggestion in the clinical context is in no way similar to denouncing therapists as malevolent. That such wild misinterpretation occurs so frequently today is a sad commentary on the bitter relationship between clinical and experimental psychology, the subject of the final chapter of this book.

The last caveat is the most important one: *There is no magic bullet!* In other words, although we can improve retrieval accuracy by virtue of the principles and techniques discussed here, no method is capable of generating purely accurate memories. Readers should be aware by now that a purely accurate memory is as rare as snow on a summer beach. Many methods of enhancing retrieval boost the amount of authentic material remembered at the cost of simultaneously raising the amount of inauthentic material remembered. Worse yet, we have no means by which to determine the authenticity of any memory other than external corroboration. Despite occasional reports to the contrary, no feature of memory is a reliable gauge of veracity—not level of detail, depth of emotion, apparent honesty, disbelief in horrible reminiscences, consistency, articulate description, willingness to engage in confrontation, or confidence.[4] Such ostensible indicators tell us only what we already know—that people believe genuinely and deeply in their own remembrance regardless of whether it is historically true. In fact, the detail, vividness, and raw emotion that accompany such staunch belief lead precisely to the difficulty in distinguishing false memories from true.

## IS RETRIEVAL ENHANCEMENT NECESSARY?

The critical issue of whether psychotherapy requires historical truth is one that deserves concentrated scrutiny from mental health practitioners of all ilks. Perhaps the question must be answered anew with each individual and each problem, depending on how the remembered material might be used in the future by the clinician and by the client. Narrative story may be adequate for some purposes; factual accuracy may be necessary for others. Although the psychotherapist's talents should not be wasted playing detective, some awareness of which features of a recollection are likely to be true and which false would seem to inform both therapist and client for, respectively, the work to be done and the life to be lived. One of the earliest considerations in applying techniques for enhanced retrieval, then, is whether and in what way a client will benefit by remembering certain events of her past. Is such remembrance in the client's best interest? The answer holds monumental consequence because, as some psychologists have argued, "memory recovery therapy is analogous to a powerful medicine that may be helpful to victims of a disease but that can cause great harm when given to people who do not have that disease."[5]

Once the question of memory's necessity has been answered to the therapist's satisfaction, the most appropriate method of enhancing retrieval must be selected for each individual. Naturally, different people in different situations with different goals respond best to different techniques. Judicious choice is necessary because the effects of suggestibility are magnified with simultaneous application of multiple retrieval enhancement techniques.


## METAMEMORY

The first method to be discussed, metamemory, is effective with a wide variety of people and should be considered a standard tool in the black bag. Curious clients who like to learn and who can accept ambiguities and contradictions are most likely to profit from greater knowledge about how memory works. At the same time, however, no client should be permitted to maintain incorrect assumptions about her own memory. If, for example, a client believes—as most laypeople do—that memory is like a radio or video camera, or that everything remembered must be true, the psychotherapist has a responsibility to gently revise the misinformation. Failing to do so leaves clients with incorrect knowledge about memory that will sabotage future attempts at meaningful retrieval.

Metamemory may be improved directly or indirectly. Teaching a client directly about the vulnerability, unreliability, and dynamic nature of human memory can be highly valuable when done prior to retrieval, and it takes only a brief period of time. For instance, practitioners who use bibliotherapy might recommend that clients read a concise article on standard principles of human memory. Clients who are encouraged to use retrieval enhancement techniques without a general understanding of how memory works are likely to assume that their brains have preserved historically accurate details of the past and that the only difficulty with memory is in retrieving those perfect details. Anything remembered is therefore assumed to be true. Very few people are aware that the memory of any event is altered meaningfully at every stage: perception, encoding, consolidation, storage, and retrieval. In addition, what happens before the event and what happens after it change the memory by virtue of what cognitive scientists call proactive and retroactive interference. Merely retrieving a memory—consciously or unconsciously, explicitly or implicitly—also changes it. Thus, a memory trace in the mind is never static; it does not remain the same from year to year or even from day to day. These facts surprise most people who are not familiar with Mnemosyne's customs. Because vigilance aids in source and reality monitoring, training a watchful eye on memory helps us to distinguish between remembered reality and imagined fantasy, and to determine the source of a particular bit of information, thereby rendering it less prone to inaccuracy. Vigilance is increased through knowledge of how memory works.

Direct aids to metamemory also include informing clients that features such as vividness, detail, and confidence are not reliable clues to veracity. They should be aware that even a completely counterfeit memory can be as vivid, detailed, and certain as one that is entirely true. Empirical investigations of false remembrance often show, in fact, that people spontaneously offer their incorrect assumptions about metamemory as evidence that an event must have occurred. Such comments include "Well, I remembered it, so it must be true," "I must have been in denial to avoid recalling my birth until now," and "Gee, I must have repressed that."[6] Psychotherapists point out similar examples, reporting that they are commonly told by their clients, "I wish someone would just hypnotize me so I'd know what happened."[7] One psychiatrist mentioned that his patients frequently requested amytal interviews under the assumption that these would produce memories of sexual abuse, which in turn would explain their adult problems.[8] We will consider the use of hypnosis and amytal interviews as memory enhancement techniques later in this chapter; for now, the point is not what effects these procedures actually have on memory but what effects uninformed clients incorrectly assume they have. The distasteful reality is that unsubstantiated speculations of infant memory and repression are more familiar to most Americans today than are the known facts of forgetting.

Indirect lessons in metamemory can be even more powerful than direct transmission. Often, such lessons are provided entirely without the therapist's awareness. Silence in the face of misinformation is perhaps the easiest error to make. Repeated encouragement to try harder to remember something merely reinforces the client's underlying assumption that the malicious Mnemosyne is holding the golden trace captive. But never fear—

victory is ours if only we fight tenaciously in our war with the gods. It's a thinly disguised blend of the Protestant work ethic: Any problem can be overcome if only we work harder than ever before. Working hard does increase retrieval, but unfortunately most of the recollection that comes from such labor is false.[9]

Techniques of remembering that are used during hypnosis also provide indirect—and incorrect—lessons in metamemory. Hypnotists frequently use instructions that are not compatible with the manner in which memory actually operates: "Now you will remember everything . . .", "You will see a perfectly clear image of the event . . .", "It will now be easy to remember . . ." These commands are both instructive and informative to hypnotized clients, and the fact that they are intoned during the trance merely boosts their suggestive power. The television technique, in which a hypnotist advises a client to zoom in on a detail, slow down a motion image, or freeze a frame, emanates plainly from the video camera metaphor. It teaches clients that memory saves every pristine detail of every event we have experienced. The mental film may then be rewound or fast-forwarded to a particular location and played, slowed, speeded, or stopped at any time. A moment's thought clarifies that we cannot possibly "zoom in" on an image that was perceived originally from afar, but individuals under hypnosis are encouraged to follow orders without thought. Psychologists writing more than fifteen years ago argued that the television technique of enhancing memory is nothing more than a "powerful and indirect suggestion to hallucinate," especially when used in conjunction with hypnosis.[10]

Accurate metamemory is useful not only for clients and patients in therapeutic settings but also for the psychotherapists themselves. All of us, including scientists whose entire careers have been devoted to the study of human memory, are prone to overconfidence in our own recollections. A practitioner's memories of a previous therapeutic session with a particular client, for example, are flavored by the events in his own life as well as the occurrences that transpired before and after the meeting in question. The practitioner's engram, like everyone's, develops dynamically over time. In addition, confirmatory bias affects us all in making decisions. Recent explorations have verified that psychotherapists are prone to confirmatory bias during client assessment. They pay more attention to signs and symptoms that would confirm their expectations about the client's difficulty than they do to signs and symptoms that would disconfirm those expectations. Memory for the evidence on which a psychological assessment is founded is therefore biased in the direction of confirmation rather than disconfirmation. The important but ignored disconfirming symptoms are soon forgotten entirely, to the client's potential detriment.[11]

## SOCIAL INTERACTION

In addition to sharing knowledge about memory itself, psychological practitioners can aid their clients in recollecting the past by considering the emotional and linguistic aspects of social interaction. The implicit rules of social discourse change from one context to another—most of us would interact differently at an elegant cocktail party than at a rodeo, for example. The discourse of the psychotherapeutic clinic is no exception; it, too, has customs of social interaction that may unconsciously baffle new clients. Furthermore, the psychological problems that patients may have could exacerbate the possibility that they will misinterpret social context. Psycholinguistic research shows that standard social conversation is based on certain principles: We assume that partners in a conversation will take turns in expected sequence, remain cooperative and truthful, give and receive similar amounts of information, keep utterances relevant to the topic, and try to clarify rather than confuse.[12] Certain types of interruptions are accepted at specific junctures in a conversation but rejected at others. Furthermore, we see authoritative figures as believable sources of important information.

As we gain prowess in verbal interaction, we recognize exceptions to these rules, and we learn how to wield conversational power to modify the speaking partner's social position. We also learn the effects of our statements at an emotional level, soon realizing that the simplest utterance can lead to embarrassment, sadness, or anger that was never intended. Yet no matter how proficient we become at conversation in known contexts, all of us are vulnerable to the uncertainty of new settings in which the standard rules of familiar discourse are suddenly broken. An attorney who is a masterful speaker in the courtroom may be reduced to muddled phrases at her therapist's office, not only because she may be experiencing psychological difficulties but also because she is unfamiliar with the new discourse context.

Such disparities in discourse can lead to memory malfunctions, both intentional and unintentional. People's expectations, beliefs, and coping strategies play a strong role in retrieval. Upon sharing some kernel of remembered information, we are faced with the possibility that the listener will react with scornful laughter or shocked disbelief, that we will be seen as stupid or selfish or, in the mental health setting, sick. Ambivalence about an issue may prevent us from reporting what we remember about it. In therapy, clients are likely to perceive the psychological practitioner as an expert who knows everything, who may interpret a forgetful or confused response as a sign of the simple mind. In addition, a disturbed individual is likely to have little motivation to remember certain events, a desire to avoid what he fears will become further failure or humiliation, and a host of ingrained defenses that hinder accurate retrieval.

Attention to these emotional and linguistic features of social discourse can help people produce more accurate memories of personal events. To test this claim, one pair of experimenters created an intervention that significantly reduced subjects' errors in remembering the details of previous episodes. To achieve the strongest possible manipulation, the subjects in this experiment were children and the interviewers were adults, but the same principles can be applied effectively to the social interaction between adult clients and their professional clinicians. The experiment began with an uncomfortable argument in which schoolchildren had been given markers that belonged to a teacher who entered the classroom in anger, demanding to have his markers returned immediately. In clear possession of the markers, the children felt actively involved as participants in the argument and did not realize that it was part of an experiment.

Two weeks after the event occurred, research assistants taught half of the children about the social discourse of a forensic interview. The subjects who received this special training were told that some questions might be misleading, that they should provide information only if they were certain of it, that the adult interviewer had not been present at the event and therefore would not know much about it, that they were not expected to know all the answers, and that it was all right to admit lack of knowledge. Research assistants also explained why witnesses in forensic interviews sometimes answer incorrectly or without knowledge, and they emphasized that an error could cause an innocent person to be punished. Further, the assistants tried to raise subjects' levels of assertiveness by supplying phrases to think about during the interview, such as "I can do it." The subjects then practiced answering leading questions, receiving praise whenever they challenged the interviewer's version of an event or admitted that they didn't know an answer. A control group spent the same amount of time in training but received much less explicit instruction. They were told to try hard to remember what had happened and to do their best in the interview. They also answered practice questions, but no feedback was provided concerning their responses. Results of the ensuing interviews showed that explicit instruction in the conversational expectations of memory interrogation yielded a 26 percent reduction in the number of errors subjects made when asked misleading questions.[13]

When applying such results to psychotherapeutic practice, we might be tempted to argue that an intelligent adult need not receive such childish instruction. But in an unfamiliar setting an intelligent adult may need exactly such instruction and may be even more prone than a child to the desire not to seem stupid. Both children and adults are reassured by knowing the basic structure of any new social situation, especially when their normal functioning is disturbed in even a slight way. Explaining to a client what she should and should not expect from psychotherapy is standard; this technique merely carries that practice a little further to provide the client with a view of how therapeutic sessions differ from standard social conversations. In addition to advancing accurate remembrance through emotional and linguistic features of the interaction, this procedure can help practitioners establish the rapport and relieve the situational anxiety that will otherwise hinder meaningful recollection.[14]

## QUESTIONING

Retrieval can be enhanced even more specifically by tailoring the questions that are asked as an interview proceeds.[15] Obviously, a prefabricated series of questions that remains fixed in order and content, regardless of the client's responses, is both patronizing and ineffective. Instead, questions should build on the client's answers and should be grouped according to the client's implicit categories. Open-ended questions (for example, "What happened that day?") produce the highest levels of mnemonic accuracy.[16] As questions become more narrow in scope, the effects of suggestibility increase while accuracy decreases. Although narrow questions are occasionally necessary, they should be asked only after encouraging free recall of the entire event through a few open-ended questions and a lot of quiet listening. Even subtle reinforcement, such as smiling or nodding in response to some answers, encourages the client to guess and solidifies retrieval errors in both the therapist's and the client's mind.[17] And as already discussed in previous chapters of this book, leading questions can be formed unintentionally by changing only one word, with dramatic consequences. One research team recently discovered that the nightly dreams of psychological clients are affected significantly by the wording of their therapists' queries. Clients who were asked to notice whether they were alone in their dreams reported significantly fewer people than did those who were asked to notice whether they were accompanied by other individuals in their dreams.[18] Neutral wording is a challenge to achieve, but it is most likely to result in authentic memories.

Although rememberers often express annoyance at the practice, they should be asked to describe their exhaustive recollection of an entire episode a second time.[19] This procedure usually results in more information, although it can increase guessing and confabulation. Therapists can reduce the extent of these problems by making their requests for repeated recall as direct, open-ended, and nonexpectant as possible, and by reminding clients that it is normal to forget certain aspects of an important experience. The correlation between accuracy and confidence can be improved if clients are given the opportunity to watch themselves recount an experience on videotape.[20] We sometimes see and hear our uncertainty from a distance more clearly than we feel it at close range.

Because human memory runs the gamut of expressive forms, recall should not be limited to verbal narrative. Rough sketches, floor plans, clay sculptures, simple architectural models, and demonstrations of movement may all help to increase retrieval. Furthermore, these modes of expression help clients describe the memory in ways that the therapist will fully grasp. Because no experience is purely verbal, no retrieval mode that is purely verbal will suffice as a thorough characterization of the experience. Contrary to popular assumption, however, nonverbal methods of expression are as prone to memory error as are methods that rely primarily on verbal accounts.

Distancing and pacing techniques are also useful during the questioning period. Novelist Isabel Allende alludes to the simultaneity of memory in language more eloquent than I can summon: "In the long, silent hours, I am trampled by memories, all happening in one instant, as if my entire life were a single, unfathomable image. The child and girl I was, the woman I am, the old woman I shall be, are all water in the same rushing torrent. My memory is like a Mexican mural in which all times are simultaneous."[21] To better comprehend the mural, at least in the linear chronological terms that characterize contemporary American psychology, a client with a traumatic memory whose emotions must be temporarily subdued may be encouraged to separate it into small pieces that can be considered in isolation. Integration is attempted only after the isolated fractions of the memory have been fully exposed. Distancing by virtue of perspective is also useful: Suggest that the client describe the event without being part of it, as if watching from above or from some other participant's perspective. Using the past tense and third person in a verbal narrative may also reduce the emotion felt during early discussions of a difficult experience.

## CONTEXT REINSTATEMENT

Reinstating the context in which an event originally took place usually helps people remember what happened. A broad array of contextual cues may be reinstated within the physical environment, such as geographic area, building, room or outdoor location, furniture, time of day, lighting, temperature, weather conditions, and season of the year. If certain sounds—music, conversation, nearby construction—or aromas seem to be part of the memory, reinstating them is likely to help as well. In addition to its positive effects as a relaxant, music has helped a number of Alzheimer's patients remember autobiographical events from the distant past.[22] Similarly, tape-recorded battle sounds have been used successfully in helping combat veterans recall war trauma.[23] Reinstating one's original mood at the time of an event can also act as a retrieval cue. The most effective procedure for reinstating mood temporarily is the continuous music technique.

Therapists can make use of this technique by asking their clients to conjure up positive or negative thoughts (depending on the particular mood to be induced) while they listen to music that matches the desired mood. To induce sadness, popular musical selections include Barber's *Adagio for Strings*, Mahler's *Adagietto*, and Rachmaninoff's adagio from *Piano Concerto No. 2*. Happy selections often include portions of Vivaldi's *The Four Seasons* as well as *Eine Kleine Nachtmusik* by Mozart. Of course, many other types of music would be suitable, and some might aid in inducing more complicated moods such as fear or anger. Clients should continue to generate mood-related thoughts and listen to the music until they have reached the desired level of mood, as ascertained by a ratings grid that is easy to use. Reaching the desired level through the continuous music technique takes an average of fifteen to twenty minutes for pleasant or unpleasant moods, although some individuals require as few as five minutes or as many as sixty. Once the appropriate mood level is obtained, the music should continue to play while the client attempts to recall.[24]

Context reinstatement can even operate somatically; that is, reproducing the same bodily feelings that originally occurred during a specific event can help a patient recall that event—through the neurons in her brain, of course. In general, the most reminiscent blend of context reinstatement is both external and internal. One study that blended context reinstatement in this way boosted retrieval accuracy from 40 percent to 60 percent when seventy-two subjects were tested five months after observing a staged vandalism.[25]

## THE COGNITIVE INTERVIEW

One of the most effective forms of retrieval enhancement is the cognitive interview. Developed by psychologists Ron Fisher and Ed Geiselman, the cognitive interview combines specific aspects of metamemory, discourse analysis, questioning techniques, and context reinstatement to create a concrete technique that really works. The original procedure was developed during the early 1980s using standard knowledge from cognitive psychology, but it has undergone several improvements since then. It is one of the few retrieval enhancement procedures available today that substantially increases the amount of episodic information remembered without simultaneously boosting the guesses and confabulation that cause mnemonic error. Although the cognitive interview has been applied most frequently in forensic settings of police investigation, it can be very effective for retrieval enhancement in the clinical context.[26]

According to Fisher and Geiselman, two basic principles of human memory govern the cognitive interview: encoding specificity, in which the probability of recall increases with greater relationship between retrieval cue and memory trace, and alternate paths, in which several different retrieval paths lead to the same trace. In general, the procedure begins with the interviewer developing a sense of rapport with the witness. The interview takes place in a quiet location without interruption, and the witness is encouraged to maintain a relaxed but alert position. In keeping with the importance of metamemory, the technique is described to the witness in advance with the help of a printed page that remains in plain view throughout the session. In this manner the witness can refer to the planned sequence of remembrance at any time. Overall, the witness is told to expect five stages: an introduction in which the technique is explained, an opportunity for free recall based on a small number of open-ended questions, a probing stage in which more specific questions are asked, a review of the narrative to be sure the interviewer understands what the witness has described and to provide the witness with a second opportunity to recall, and the conclusion during which the interviewer offers to listen to any other information the witness would like to provide.

As part of the introduction, the witness is told explicitly not to fabricate or guess when responding to the interviewer's questions. Detail is also requested directly even if the witness assumes a detail is not relevant to the interview. During the first recall stage, the witness is asked to mentally reinstate the context of the event and to report everything, even bits and pieces of memory that may seem irrelevant or disorganized. The event is recounted in a variety of sequences (backward, forward, or from a particular moment in time) and from a number of perspectives (side, front, above, or as seen by another person). Nonverbal expression is encouraged, so a witness may draw a map or act out a movement to describe it more accurately. Throughout the interview, but especially while initial recall occurs, any form of distraction or interference is avoided. Ringing telephones and knocks on the door serve only to hinder memory. Preventing distraction also means that the interviewer must remain quiet and attentive, must listen without interrupting, and must resist the temptation to fill silent pauses—a feat that any psychotherapist knows can be quite difficult. The witness and not the interviewer is in charge of directing the flow of information. Digressions and tangents are accepted silently; this is not the time for a would-be Jack Webb to halt a rememberer with that notorious warning: "Just the facts, ma'am!" We don't always know what the facts might be until after we have heard everything a witness or client remembers.

During the third stage, the interviewer asks specific questions that delve more deeply into certain aspects of the witness's earlier narrative. These probes are categorized to focus on one feature of the memory at a time. For example, if a witness is describing someone's face, she may be asked whether the face had a high forehead or a sharp chin, but she should not be asked at that time what clothes the person was wearing. If what seems to be a digression was relayed during the initial recall period, the probing stage allows the interviewer to ask what relevance that information may have had or why the witness mentioned it. During the probing period, the witness is also asked to consider general features of a particular stimulus, such as whether a forgotten name is short or long, common or uncommon, what letter of the alphabet it begins with, and how many syllables it has. Tip-of-the-tongue research shows that people often know the answers to such questions even though they cannot remember the name itself.[27] Furthermore, thinking about these features frequently serves to activate the neural network that represents the previously forgotten name.

Training for the cognitive interview is usually conducted in an intensive two-day workshop. Through hands-on experience, questioners can practice their new skills under the supervision of a qualified cognitive interviewer, and benefit from specific suggestions that apply to certain situations. Tests of the cognitive interview's effectiveness under well-controlled laboratory conditions and real-life observations produce astounding results. Compared to the standard police interview of a witness's memory for an event, the cognitive interview increases the amount of accurate information remembered by 96 percent, with no concomitant increase in error.[28] Moreover, this enormous effect is consistent; independent researchers testing a wide variety of adult and childhood populations obtain the same pattern of results repeatedly. Although I would never equate psychotherapy with police interrogation, this forensic technique of retrieval is ripe for widespread application to current clinical needs. No other method of retrieval enhancement known today produces such impressive results.

## TESTING

Although wholly false memories are much less common than partially incorrect remembrances, certain forms of psychological testing may be useful to therapists in identifying clients who are especially prone to illusions of recollection. The Dissociative Experiences Scale (DES) and the Creative Imagination Scale (CIS) both correlate positively with the unwitting creation of mnemonic illusions.[29] The DES measures an individual's tendency toward the disintegration of various facets of memory, cognition, and personality; the CIS focuses on the ability to create mental images, the vividness of those images, and hypnotizability. People who are able to imagine an event well, who are easily hypnotized, and who can separate various aspects of consciousness are most likely to experience counterfeit or largely inaccurate memories. The Gudjonsson Suggestibility Scale (GSS), which measures susceptibility to leading questions and pressure during interviews, may be useful as well, although I am unaware of research verifying its efficacy in this arena.[30] Information gleaned from these psychological tests can help the therapist select methods of retrieval enhancement that are least likely to augment unintended fabrication in specific clients.

Some mental disorders can alter memory profoundly, though not always in the direction we would expect. One recent study demonstrates, contrary to common folklore, that depressive patients are less likely to confabulate than normal healthy controls. The researchers who conducted the study speculate that the clinical depression experienced among their patients served to make their minds less imaginative.[31] With a less creative imagination and less vivid imagery, the powers of reality monitoring may have less work to do in discriminating between real stimuli and imagined ones. Cognitive scientists have also proposed that people who experience the most heightened degrees of suggestibility (approximately 20 percent of the adult American population) and hypnotizability (10–20 percent of the population) are most likely to experience false memory as well as false forgetting, or amnesia.[32] In other words, their ability to forget what happened during a historically authentic episode may be accompanied by an ability to remember what did not happen. This intriguing speculation still requires empirical verification. In general, testing patients to determine their levels of dissociability, imagery, depression, suggestibility, and hypnotizability may be a useful aid to therapeutic decisions about memory.

## SUGGESTIBILITY

The largest obstacle to effective retrieval improvement is suggestibility. Most people—including highly trained clinicians, respected experimental psychologists, savvy clients, and bright research subjects—grossly underestimate the degree to which human beings are swayed by mild suggestion. But in reality the briefest murmur is often interpreted as a cue and the tiniest nod as reinforcement, regardless of the perceiver's intelligence, social class, educational level, or income. Suggestion affects us all because it is a critical aid to mental performance that allows us to disambiguate, categorize, and control incoming information at a rapid pace. Without it we would lumber along in our fast-lane high-tech world at the mental equivalent of a maimed slug trying to outpace a forest fire.

The potential influence of psychological suggestion can be assessed partly by considering placebo effects. Under the most stringent conditions of laboratory experimentation, the standard placebo effect ranges between 55 percent and 60 percent for treatments running the gamut from powerful pharmaceutical medications to simple psychotherapeutic techniques.[33] In other words, more than half of the effect of a potent painkiller or therapeutic intervention is merely one's mind accepting the suggestion that we ought to begin feeling better soon. In natural settings without strict experimental controls, the placebo effect looms even larger. Classic experiments have for decades made their indelible mark on psychology through the demonstration of basic human suggestibility. Who hasn't heard of Milgram's (1963) obedience experiments in which 65 percent of adult subjects deliver electric shocks labeled as highly dangerous at 450 volts while confederates howl in pain?[34] Or of Asch's compliance research showing that intelligent people follow an absurd majority decision that a two-inch line is longer than a three-inch line?[35] How about Rosenthal and Jacobson's famous finding that students whose intelligence scores are falsely exaggerated to their teachers outperform smarter classmates by the end of the school year?[36] Or Orne's subjects who wish so deeply to please an unknown experimenter that they continue to calculate two thousand pages of addition problems by hand until the experimenter gives up five and a half hours later?[37]

Social pressure is a strong force in every setting, not the least of which is the psychotherapeutic session. The ingredients of wholly or partly fallacious recollection often derive from unintended suggestion. Any snippet of experience, whether from a book, television, radio, conversation, thought, film, or dream, can be incorporated unknowingly into a true or false memory. Source amnesia for these individual snippets allows them free rein. One woman even identified her rapist as a man who had been on live television at the time; she saw his face on television and linked it incorrectly to her own rape.[38] Methods of retrieval enhancement that encourage clients to look through family photographs or watch films of traumatic events merely offer the bogus details of unconscious fabrication. Extremely high rates of false recognition that are obtained in empirical studies, rates frequently approaching 90 percent, provide even greater reason to avoid such practices. It is perilously easy for anyone to recognize an isolated stimulus as part of an authentic memory when in fact it is not. When the episode to be remembered occurred many years ago, the haze of time exacerbates the problem even further. And memories from early childhood are filled with fuzzy holes arising from a coupling of the time that has passed and the physiological immaturity of the young brain. The fact that we usually remain unaware of these holes gives them even greater opportunity to fool us. Add a subtle suggestion or two as putty, and we'd never know the difference.

We have already seen that repetition and plausibility can increase a client's willingness to believe in wholly false or partially incorrect memories. In addition, rapport, motive, social proof, commitment, and authority all play starring roles in social influence.[39] Rapport exacerbates suggestibility, rendering us particularly prone to the suggestions of people whom we know well and like. Thus, greater understanding between clinician and client leads to greater likelihood that the clinician's questions and comments will infiltrate the client's memory. Motive is also known to alter the consequences of influence. One investigation showed that leading questions were significantly more likely to yield erroneous answers when they emanated from people who were perceived as having no reason to mislead.[40] Once again, then, the therapist's efforts to gain a client's trust backfires in the development of an increasingly pungent atmosphere of suggestion. Of course, I am not advising a reduction in rapport or a rise in vulgar ulterior motives to reduce inaccurate retrieval; rather, I am advocating an awareness of the powerful effects that rapport and motive can have in the practitioner's ability to shape a patient's recollection through unintended suggestion. This awareness is critical because many people assume that achieving greater rapport and trust with another individual lessens the power of suggestion. Exactly the opposite is true.

The principle of social proof occurs whenever the evidence with which we unconsciously justify a belief or action is merely the fact that others agree. Therefore, if my psychotherapist seems to believe that I have been neglected in the past, I am more likely to believe it myself. It is the client's perception of the therapist's belief, and not the therapist's actual belief, that produces the suggestive effect. The principle of social proof is just as malignant when people misinterpret the convictions they assume others hold as it is when they comprehend those convictions accurately. Public commitment to any position can also create a situation in which people want to change their minds but feel they cannot do so without appearing indecisive or unstable. A person who suspects silently that a particular event may have happened is more likely to conduct a vigilant form of unconscious reality monitoring than a person who has publicly committed herself to the event by telling someone else that it occurred.

Mental health practitioners hold tremendous authority in the eyes of their clients. The therapist may easily be viewed as the client's last hope, as a knowledgeable savant who guides confused men and women safely through all of life's distressing difficulties. This kind of perceived su-

premacy causes a radical rise in people's willingness to comply with perceived expectations, mnemonic and otherwise. Standard misinformation effects in eyewitness testimony research are significantly reduced when an
individual with little apparent authority presents the misleading information.[41] To compound the effects of authority, clients pay a high price, finan-
cially and emotionally, for a therapist's advice and are therefore inclined to
follow it closely.

Powerful unintended suggestion can be very subtle. A slight nod of the
head, a shifting forward in one's seat, rapt attention—all of these are signals
that clients will unconsciously attempt to imbue with meaning. Obviously,
the clinician cannot remain stone-faced and silent throughout a psychotherapeutic session, but an attempt to demonstrate equal interest in various ver-
balizations will reduce unintended influence. Privately analyzing videos or
audiotaped recordings of previous sessions is also helpful in allowing a
practitioner to uncover implicit suggestions that he has made unwittingly.
Many therapists report surprise at the extent to which their comments are
suggestive—but only after they have listened to them outside of the therapeutic setting.

In a recent investigation of people's awareness of the leading nature of
their own comments, adults were provided with inaccurate information
about an event and then were asked to interview children who had observed the event. The adults were told point-blank that it was very important to remain as objective and unbiased as possible in questioning the
children. When the interviews were analyzed later, 30 percent of the questions asked were blatantly leading despite the adults' genuine attempts to
avoid such questions.[42] Suggestibility is something that none of us can eliminate; whether aware of it or not, each of us is influenced by others' suggestions, and each of us influences others by our suggestions. However, we
must take suggestibility effects into serious account when attempting to understand key memories that people describe.

## HYPNOSIS

The effects of suggestibility on memory are primary culprits in certain methods of retrieval enhancement that are as popular as they are dangerous.
Hypnosis is a perfect example. Survey research that was still in press in 1998
shows that as many as 34 percent of psychological practitioners today use
hypnosis as a technique to establish historical truth through memory.[43]

When respondents were limited only to practicing clinical psychologists with doctorate degrees, the use of hypnosis for memory enhancement was roughly the same, 32 percent.[44] The results of a 1992 survey, presented in the first chapter of this book, demonstrated strikingly incorrect convictions about hypnotic remembering among one thousand degreed psychotherapists. Specifically, 75 percent believe that hypnosis increases the amount of information retrieved, 54 percent believe that hypnosis can recover memories of one's own birth, 47 percent believe that hypnosis increases the accuracy of traumatic memory, and 43 percent believe that hypnosis increases the accuracy of all memories.[45] Despite the sweeping popularity of hypnosis as a retrieval enhancement technique, empirical research from both clinical and experimental bastions of psychology has demonstrated that it does not work.

Normal degrees of suggestibility are vastly increased under hypnotic conditions, to the extent that physical pain can be blocked more effectively by hypnotic suggestion than by morphine injection.[46] Because of this increased suggestibility, memories that are retrieved under hypnosis are especially prone to errors that persist after the hypnotic interview has ended. The capacity for false memories among highly hypnotizable people, whether under hypnosis or not, has been part of the psychological literature since at least 1888.[47] After research in the area was revived during the 1970s, one article followed another demonstrating the perils of applying hypnosis to recollection. Volumes of empirical research now show that hypnosis elevates the production of fallacious recollection at least as much as—and sometimes more than—it increases the production of authentic remembrance. Concomitantly, it boosts confidence by a statistically significant margin, regardless of whether the remembered information is true or false. This surge in confidence is especially robust among individuals who are highly hypnotizable, exactly the population that may be most likely to experience psychogenic amnesia and false memory in the first place. Hypnosis raises the level of the standard misinformation effect so that the same misleading questions result in an even greater number of erroneous beliefs than usual.[48]

Hypnosis operates in the same way on emotional, stressful, and arousing memories as it does on all others, but the personal cost of fabricating a traumatic memory is much higher than the price of creating a benign one. It also amplifies vivid imagery so that false details seem especially vibrant and compelling.[49] In one study, twenty-seven hypnotized individuals were asked whether they had heard loud noises several nights previously. After the hypnotic interview concluded, thirteen of the twenty-seven normal adults stated that they had actually heard the noises on that previous night. When debriefed, six adamantly refused to believe that the noises had merely been suggested during hypnosis. Many of them reported extreme auditory vividness as one reason for their absolute trust in the false event.[50] The results of this study shed some light on the power of hypnotic suggestion: Asking only one brief question caused half of the entire sample to create an illusory memory and believe in it.

The social features of hypnosis also lend error to reminiscences that emerge from the trance. Hypnosis is an inherently social interaction between two people who wish to please each other, thereby increasing the dangers of suggestibility. At the same time, critical evaluation is forbidden during the hypnotic interview, reducing the vigilance that is needed in monitoring memories. The fact that many people believe hypnosis will aid recall causes them to overestimate the accuracy of hypnotically induced memories and, therefore, believe even more zealously in their supposed authenticity.[51] Furthermore, hypnosis is known to increase people's willingness to guess. In one investigation, neither hypnotized nor control subjects were able to recall a number seen earlier on a criminal's shirt. Only 20 percent of the nonhypnotized subjects were willing to guess the number, compared with 90 percent of hypnotized individuals.[52] And many of the guided memory instructions used under hypnosis, such as the television technique, magnify people's assumptions that petrified engrams are held forever, like fossils waiting to be plucked from the recesses of the mind.

Neither laboratory studies nor naturalistic observations demonstrate any consistent effect of hypnosis on accurate retrieval improvement. Studies that test memory for word lists or pictures show no improvement under hypnotic conditions. More important, investigations that employ meaningful real-world stimuli such as personal events produce the same zero effect, as do studies in which the material to be remembered is emotional, stressful, incidental, or consequential. To describe only one study from literally hundreds of potential examples, subjects who watched an eight-minute film showing accidents in a woodworking shop were later tested for their memories of the events under either normal or hypnotized conditions. The accidents ranged from woodworkers whose fingers became caught in the machinery to an incident in which a man was impaled and killed by a projectile of wood flying from a circular saw. Hypnosis did not aid recall in any way, either when used after a short or a long retention interval.[53]

Quite clearly, then, hypnosis is of no use as a retrieval enhancement technique. Not only does it fail to improve memory of authentic events, but it also inserts serious mistakes that are then imbued with hypnotic overconfidence that can persevere for a lifetime. Considering multitudes of data from studies of hypnotically induced retrieval, a 1997 review concludes that "the answer to the question of whether hypnosis should be used to recover historically accurate memories in psychotherapy is 'no.'"[54] The reason for this conclusion is summed up by a practicing hypnotherapist who advocates memory recovery: "This complex interplay between memory and hypnosis can create memory distortion, and there is no way to distinguish this from true recall without corroboration. . . . Clients under hypnosis are highly suggestible and their 'memories' can be altered by unwitting suggestions or leading questions."[55] The American Medical Association, the International Society of Hypnosis, the Society for Clinical and Experimental Hypnosis, and the American Society of Clinical Hypnosis have all published stern warnings that hypnosis should not be used in memory retrieval.[56] And as is well known, American courts of law ruled long ago that memories retrieved under hypnosis are inadmissible as evidence. This decision is based on the Frye rule, in which admissibility is determined by virtue of a scientific procedure's general acceptance as a reliable tool within the scientific community.[57] If hypnotically induced memories are not good enough for the courts, they certainly should not be good enough for desperate clients who need help in coping with genuine traumas.

Techniques of hypnotic memory enhancement often include the highly questionable practice of age regression. In fact, age regression merely creates unrecognized falsehoods. Though often used in conjunction with hypnosis, age regression alone is enough to engender bogus reminiscences. A recent investigation that compared the effects of age regression with and without hypnosis obtained startling results. Subjects who underwent age regression during hypnosis reported infant memories at an average rate of 70 percent. Worse yet, the subjects who experienced age regression *without* hypnosis reported memories from the cradle at an average rate of 95 percent! Half of the subjects in both conditions claimed with certainty that these impossible memories had to be real.[58]

## AMYTAL INTERVIEWS

The amytal interview is sometimes used in hopes of eliciting historical truth about the past, but it actually serves only to increase the effects of suggestion while simultaneously hindering normal cognitive processes. Sodium amytal is a barbiturate that produces relaxation and a desire to talk when injected very slowly into the bloodstream. In the 1920s it was dubbed "truth serum" by newspaper reporters seeking a sensational headline. A practicing psychiatrist recently reviewed the medical literature on amytal interviews, covering a period of sixty-five years, and reported that "not a single investigator who had actually conducted amytal interviews endorsed this procedure as a means of recovering accurate memories of past events."[59]

Sodium amytal's ability to elicit new memories is the same as that of a placebo; in other words, if you waved your arms over a believer's head, he'd remember at about the same rate. However, the drug does have strong effects unmatched by placebos: It dramatically increases the incidence of confabulation, misattribution, distortion, misinterpretation, and misquotes. These are not minor errors, either. One patient, for example, mixed up his first wife with his second wife. Other patients insisted that they had children who did not exist, that their living children did not exist, and that they would kill individuals who were already dead. In every case the information was supplied in a supremely confident manner that required external verification to determine that the statements were false. People under the influence of amytal lie and withhold information just as easily as they might without the drug, but more often they report erroneous memories based on mild suggestions from the interviewer. The primary effects of sodium amytal, rather than producing accurate memories, are "confusion, bewilderment, inability to assay and select thought, impoverishment of vocabulary, automatic rather than reasoned responses, disturbed memory, distorted sequence of chronology, and loss of discrimination between what is real and what is illusory."[60] In other words, a clinician who uses the amytal interview to recover memories will achieve much the same result—at significantly less expense and harm to the patient—by reading a fantasy novel.

## JOURNALING, HEMISPHERIC EXPRESSION, IMAGERY, AND GROUPS

A few other methods that are occasionally used to improve recall deserve some attention as well. Journaling can be helpful in memory retrieval, but only if it is conducted very judiciously. If clients are asked to write about their memories, they should write once in a careful and disciplined manner about specific aspects of a known episode. This technique reduces—but certainly does not eliminate—the likelihood of false details being incorporated into the memory. Free writing in stream-of-consciousness mode produces no more authentic information than free verbal description would, and it is quite liable to cause unintended fabrication. Similarly, pressing a client to make the writing "more real" by reading it aloud serves merely to enhance false memories and therefore should be avoided. Real memories don't need to be made more real. Furthermore, writing freely and repeatedly about the same event, a technique mentioned in chapter 10, is precisely the method by which experimenters caused research subjects to fashion bogus recollections of being lost in a mall.

Hemispheric expression, imagery, and group therapy are techniques that may be effective for other psychological purposes, but they simply do not belong in the therapist's arsenal of retrieval enhancement procedures. There is no evidence that certain memories are stored in only one cerebral hemisphere or that they can be retrieved only through the use of that hemisphere. For that reason it is foolish and professionally irresponsible to suggest that a client use a hemispherically nondominant means of expression for the purpose of recalling an unusual event. Confabulation occurs as easily when drawing with the left hand as when drawing with the right. A variety of verbal and nonverbal modes of expression can be useful in memory retrieval, but not because of hemispheric differences.

Typical imagery techniques involve asking a client to close his eyes, relax, and create imaginary scenarios; asking a client to supply a fictitious end to a story; or asking a client to imagine reliving the sensory details of a known event. Several experimental psychologists believe that these practices generate a dissociative state of consciousness in which suggestibility is increased, thereby raising the likelihood of mistaken recollection.[61] In one false memory experiment, subjects were told of four events that had happened during their childhoods. As usual, three of the events were real, but the fourth had been created by the experimenter. Half of the subjects who initially failed to recall an event were led through a guided imagery protocol intended to boost retrieval, whereas the other half were merely told to think about the event quietly. Subjects in this control condition produced false memories of the bogus events about 12 percent of the time. By comparison, subjects who experienced the guided imagery technique produced false memories 36 percent of the time. This rate of error is higher than any yet obtained in false memory research.[62]

Memory recovery in group settings is highly problematic. No matter how careful group members try to be, tremendous social pressure is exerted to remember similar events through the effects of repetition, public commitment, social proof, desire to conform, and social modeling. As we have seen, these factors enhance the formation of false memories while failing to elicit true ones. The false recollection then becomes firmly established in a person's mind, interfering with subsequent retrieval of related memories that may be true. Psychotherapeutic retrieval of personal memories should always take place in individual sessions. Such action is one of the easiest ways to cope with the stubborn persistence of suggestive misremembering.

A sizable array of retrieval enhancement techniques is known to be effective, and many more are being tested at this time. The responsible psychotherapist can choose from these procedures those that are most compatible with a particular client's needs and apply them in disparate ways. Methods that are most effective include direct and indirect knowledge in the form of accurate metamemory, attention to emotional and linguistic factors in social remembering, effective questioning procedures, physical and mental context reinstatement, the inclusion of nonverbal modes of expression, and early psychological testing for imagery, hypnotizability, dissociability, and suggestibility levels. The cognitive interview is an excellent proven means by which clinicians may elicit greater information from their clients, information that may help in designing an intelligent plan of psychotherapy. Understanding and accepting the power of suggestion is also critical in providing clients with a form of memory recovery that maximally reduces the potential for harm. Although suggestibility cannot be eliminated, mental health practitioners should certainly be aware of the many ways in which memory is altered by standard social effects, including authority, social proof, and public commitment. In addition, lesser-known factors such as repetition, rapport, motive, and plausibility must be taken into consideration. Perhaps most important with respect to suggestibility is the knowledge that both clients and therapists are likely to underestimate the power of such social pressures.

The fundamental problem with retrieval enhancement in the psychotherapeutic setting is that most techniques that encourage recovery of true memories simultaneously encourage the creation of false memories. Once elicited, there is no way to tell the difference. As we have seen, inauthentic recollections can be shockingly vivid, tormentingly emotional, ornately detailed, and tremendously certain. No method of memory enhancement is foolproof, but clinicians can at least choose those that are safest and most effective.

# CHAPTER 12

# Bridging the Canyon

*Solitude had made a selection in her memory and had burned the dimming piles of nostalgic waste that life had accumulated in her heart, and had purified, magnified, and eternalized the others, the most bitter ones.*

—Gabriel García Márquez

One hundred years of empirical research proves human memory to be malleable, dynamic, and easily altered by external forces. Although the various features of a reminiscence are usually correct, some of them are not. These incorrect bits and pieces may reside among the trivial details of a memory, or they may live within the most integral parts of the core experience. The confidence with which we believe our own remembrances seldom correlates with accuracy, partly because memories are constructed and thereby distorted to some degree. Physiological immaturity of the brain prior to about three years of age precludes lasting memory of autobiographical events from infancy and very early childhood. Emotion and mood alter the ability to remember, while trauma seems to result in a flood of neurotransmitters that occasionally exhaust memory but more often fortify it. These facts hold true for both explicit and implicit forms of remembrance, as well as for semantic, episodic, procedural, and autobiographical memory systems. Although mnemonic malleability leads most often to inaccurate features that the mind supplies to fill unconscious gaps in an authentic event, entire memories can also be wholly false.

Evidence supporting these claims comes from neurology, psychiatry, clinical psychology, experimental psychology, and the interdisciplinary area of cognitive science. A broad assortment of methodologies has been employed to explore human memory, including clinical case studies, neurological testing, experimental research paradigms, nonexperimental laboratory studies, surgical alterations, brain scans, simulations, and naturalistic observations. The population experiencing these methods is comprised of normals and amnesics, the elderly and the young, police officers and jurors, college subjects and psychological clients. Together, such inquiries yield converging evidence that memory works exactly as described throughout this book. Readers need not take my word for any of these claims about memory; the original studies supporting them are fully documented in the endnotes so that readers can more easily delve into the memory literature on their own. I hope that skeptics will read the empirical research and arrive at their own conclusions.

With many common assumptions about memory refuted in this book, we may wonder how so much misinformation has entered professional and popular psychology. Talk show hosts and unqualified authors of best-selling self-help books are often the first to be blamed, but others of us hold greater responsibility. I have lamented the role of American culture and media on several occasions, but they, too, are secondary factors. In fact, the problem rests squarely within psychology itself. The discipline has become an overburdened collection of scattered topics stuffed with internal contradictions. This unwieldy load has pushed us to the verge of utter balkanization into a number of disciplines that rarely pretend to inform each other at all. As the clinical and experimental sides of the psychological canyon continue to pull farther apart, and as the quality of both endeavors drops accordingly, we must ask where contemporary psychology is going and whether we will still want to be psychologists when it gets there.

The repressed memory battles of the 1990s mirror these larger problems within our discipline. These battles were characterized by instant accusation, a knee-jerk reaction that reflects deep, long-standing hostility between clinical and experimental camps. Some people pointed their fingers at therapists, arguing that practitioners have abandoned their responsibility to remain up-to-date in every aspect of psychological knowledge that is crucial to their clients, most of which is readily available in any college library. Leaders of the American Psychological Association caught some flack for the breach of licensure and formal education they condone. If the right to practice the sophisticated art and science of psychotherapy is offered indiscriminately, without regard for education, training, or licensure, then we should not be surprised at the harm that results. Academic psychologists contributed to the problem by encouraging students to believe that courses in personality, counseling, and abnormal psychology are rightfully divorced from the study of human perception, language, thought, and memory. Experimental psychologists are also guilty. We have remained cozy and quiet within our artificial laboratories, describing our research in prose so labored that it has become unreadable; we have seldom lifted an eyelid to see how our work might be applied to real-world tragedies of personal desperation. And, paradoxically, for all its talk of interdisciplinary devotion, the new wave of cognitive science has pulled experimental psychology even further from clinical concerns.

It was the climate of psychology for the last hundred years, not the weather pattern over the past ten, that motivated us to blame rather than solve. True collaboration on topics of clinical and experimental interest had been so scarce for so long that little consideration was afforded to the possibility of cooperating to share knowledge concerning recovered memories. By the time psychologists on both sides stopped blaming each other and began to suggest cooperation, most of the players had become enraged enough to refuse.[1] For too long we have allowed separation to eternalize our most bitter experiences.

Both experimental and clinical psychology, along with their respective clientele, can benefit from mutual efforts to solve these perennial problems. With that belief in mind, this final chapter offers a brief historical excursion through the chasm that has always divided psychology, followed by suggestions for change. Memory stars as one example of the many topics that practitioners and researchers could have studied together to greater fruition. Although we now know a great deal more about human memory than we did a century ago, all of us have more to learn. Many critical questions remain unanswered at this time, especially with respect to the very topics that psychotherapists may find most important. The science and scholarship needed to answer those questions will travel in a direction and with a force that depends almost entirely on the future relationship between clinical and experimental psychology. If that relationship continues to be marred by bitter power disputes, the two areas will never supply each other with the knowledge necessary to move forward. More specifically, the fire of recent memory debates will either burn down the opportunity for better research or illuminate the path to greater knowledge. You and I must choose between those futures.

## THE CHASM IS BORN

Isolation between clinical and experimental pursuits dates to the very beginning of the discipline. Upon founding psychology in 1879, Wilhelm Wundt maintained his vision of a purely experimental science. His reasons for this focus were threefold. First, the study and treatment of mental disorders had long been the province of psychiatrists, who worked in mental asylums, and neurologists, who saw uninstitutionalized patients. There was no need for a third group of professionals to offer the same services that were already accommodated by these medical physicians. Second, the value of science could not be underestimated following two centuries of enlightenment philosophy. To become successful, any new discipline during the 1800s almost had to be advertised as a scientific enterprise. Naturally, this emphasis on science dictated the types of problems that would be studied and the methods that would be used. Some scholars now complain that science has stunted psychology's growth, but most would agree that it served the new discipline well in the 1880s. Had any method or topic been fair game from the start, early psychologists would have been overwhelmed by the colossal sweep of human behavior to be investigated. Third, by focusing on science, Wundt and his colleagues were able to distinguish the new discipline from paranormal and spiritual studies—which at that time were occasionally referred to as "psychological." The Society for Psychical Research, along with its flagship journal, was also well known in the late nineteenth century, served by common paradigms of inquiry that included gazing into crystal balls and analyzing automatic handwriting.[2] Wundt wanted to be certain that the new psychology would not be mistaken for nonscientific dabbling in occult practices.[3]

Some of Wundt's students, including Hugo Münsterberg and G. Stanley Hall, believed that pure psychology should be applied but only as a secondary goal. Their belief was grounded in the assumption that all application would have to rest firmly on a bed of pure scientific research. Others, such as Edward Titchener and Wundt himself, argued against any form of application. Thus, whether psychology should be applied in any way was a source of debate from the start.[4] That the possibility of applying psychology to neurological or psychiatric needs was never even mentioned during the discipline's youth is a very telling omission. Clearly, psychology was to be an experimental science. It might be applied in limited ways, but it certainly had nothing to do with the diagnosis, study, or treatment of mental dysfunction.

Lightner Witmer, who received his Ph.D. in experimental psychology from Wundt, is credited with the founding of what he dubbed "clinical psychology." The intended field bears little resemblance to what we call clinical psychology today. Witmer's first client was a dyslexic, whom he helped through experimental research on reading processes. From that point on, the clinical applications that Witmer and his students offered were strictly educational and were provided mostly to children who suffered from learning disorders or speech impediments. In keeping with this bent, Witmer described the new field as closely linked to sociology and pedagogy. He never conducted any form of psychotherapy, and his published articles criticized methods of psychological application that were not purely scientific. Once clinical psychology had been established under these guidelines, the few psychologists who worked in clinics did little more than administer psychological tests. Most of the tests assessed intelligence levels, and any "treatment" that was applied took the form of academic instruction. Until Witmer reached his seventies, agreement reigned among both pure and applied psychologists that the treatment of disease—mental or physical—belonged to medicine.[5]

Psychoanalysis began to rise in popularity during the early 1900s. Sigmund Freud, M.D., a neurologist, first arrived in the United States in 1909 to deliver a series of lectures on psychoanalytic theory at Clark University. The lectures were heard by those with medical curiosity but were considered irrelevant to psychology. Accordingly, psychoanalysis remained part of medicine for at least its first forty years (roughly 1900 to 1940). As greater pressure was exerted to admit psychoanalysis to the discipline of psychology, the finest psychologists of the time belittled it extensively. Robert Woodworth argued that psychoanalytic theory revealed nothing more than Freud's own "deep-seated wish for a career of unbridled lust." John Watson referred to it as "voodooism." Christine Ladd-Franklin remarked with ponderous doom that "unless means can speedily be found to prevent its spread . . . the prognosis for civilization is unfavorable."[6] James McKeen Cattell chastised a colleague publicly for merely mentioning Freud's name at a meeting of the American Psychological Association.[7] Psychologists of the time saw Freudian theory as unscientific and unpsychological. If the medical field of neurology wished to accept it, that was fine, but it certainly wasn't psychology.

By 1940 psychoanalysis had become popular with the general public, most of whom assumed incorrectly that it was part of psychology. To this day, if my experience with thousands of introductory psychology students is any indication, most people are certain that Sigmund Freud—not Wilhelm Wundt—is the founder of psychology. In line with this incorrect belief, most also assume that all of psychology is clinical and that the entire discipline revolves around the treatment of mental disorders and personal problems. To put it in their parlance, every psychologist is a shrink. It was the force of public sentiment toward Freud as well as the need for psychotherapy at the end of World War II that created the existence of clinical psychology as we know it today. One scholar from that era remarked, "History has bequeathed us one type of psychology and society is insisting that we produce, in addition, a second type."[8]

## CREATING CLINICAL PSYCHOLOGY

Upon returning from World War II around 1945, 80 percent of war veterans requested some form of psychological counseling to help them assimilate into American society. This spawned a sudden demand for practitioners, more than the existing ranks of neurologists and psychiatrists could supply on a moment's notice. In response to that need, the Veterans Administration began to fund a program in which psychologists were trained as psychotherapists. Their decision caused rancor among medical providers, who ever since have been embroiled with clinical psychologists in a power struggle over the treatment of the mentally ill. Clinical psychologists have wrested from psychiatrists in the ensuing fifty years the right to admit and discharge patients from mental institutions, the right to serve as expert witnesses answering psychiatric questions in courts of law, the right to be paid for their services by insurance companies, and the right to be certified as practitioners by individual states.[9] The last battle, for the right to prescribe and administer medication, is still being fought today. Not surprisingly, hostility grew between the American Psychological Association and American Psychiatric Association, leading practitioners of all types to become defensive about their talents and training.[10] In addition, because so many war veterans needed help so quickly, psychotherapies flourished at a rate that quickly outpaced scientific research. Soon an increasing number of therapeutic techniques were in use that had never been tested for efficacy or grounded in psychological science.

When the Veterans Administration decided to fund training for clinical psychologists, it turned to the American Psychological Association (APA) for several critical decisions. Would the training programs include both research and practice? If so, would the two components be equally balanced, or would one be emphasized over the other? If practice was to be the primary focus, would clinicians also be expected to churn out publishable research? What exactly was the proper role of scientific research in psychological practice? In what ways would the training of clinical psychologists differ from that of psychiatrists? Would the M.D. or the Ph.D. serve as the primary model for training in clinical psychology? Or should a new degree be developed? To this day a wide array of opinions exists among practitioners regarding the answers to these questions, and tremendous ambivalence lingers about the proper role of science, and even the role of scholarship, nonscientific research, and knowledge construction, in clinical psychology.

To answer these questions, the APA held a national conference in Boulder, Colorado, in 1949. The scientist/practitioner model was fashioned as the appropriate goal for all clinical psychologists, with scientific training given higher billing than professional service.[11] Hence, the Ph.D. would be required for providers of psychological therapy, and original research that contributed to knowledge in psychological science was expected from them. Although some clinical psychologists today manage to maintain strong reputations as both scientific researchers and applied clinicians, the Boulder scientist/practitioner model was viewed with skepticism from the start. Some psychologists argue that it is nothing more than "a rhetorical device"; others insist that the intent behind it "has never been fully realized."[12] Moreover, as the amount of new information relevant to human behavior expands each year, I wonder whether it is fair to expect practitioners to excel simultaneously at two very challenging occupations. Perhaps this 1949 expectation is no longer realistic.

Clinicians were way ahead of me on this score. As early as 1968 the first Psy.D. was offered without APA approval. This professional degree was developed with the belief that scientific training is not needed in clinical work. Proponents pointed to the M.D., in which holders of the degree usually do either medical research or medical practice but not both. The rationale, then, seemed to be based on an assumption that psychotherapy would be provided by clinical psychologists, but it would be developed and tested by experimental psychologists. That this assumption has never seen the light of reality did not prevent the APA from approving the Psy.D. in 1973. Twenty years later, more than forty institutions offered it, and a growing number of psychology students reveled in their freedom from the rigors of original research.[13] Unfortunately, this retreat from scientific training sometimes went as far as to free students not only from conducting their own basic investigations but also from understanding the strengths and weaknesses of relevant research done by others.

## THE AMERICAN PSYCHOLOGICAL ASSOCIATION

The APA itself developed along the same lines of historical division that characterize clinical and experimental psychology. When it was founded in 1892 by thirty-one experimental psychologists, the original goal of the APA was "to promote psychology as a science."[14] By 1917 applied psychologists were so disgruntled with the emphasis on pure science that they resigned from the association and founded their own society, the American Association of Clinical Psychologists. These individuals wanted the APA to offer greater recognition to clinical pursuits—which at the time were characterized by treating learning disorders and testing intelligence—and to enforce certification of such clinical work. The APA capitulated two years later, offering a special division within its ranks for clinical psychologists and enforcing a certification process to ensure that psychological testing was done by qualified practitioners. Sadly, the certification that clinicians fought so hard to win was abandoned in only eight years.

Twice thereafter, in 1930 and again in 1937, psychological practitioners became so embittered at the experimental focus of the APA that they pulled out and set up their own organizations. In an ill-fated attempt to solve this continuing problem, the APA agreed during the 1940s—just as World War II brought dramatic need for psychotherapy—to drop its long-standing requirement that all members had to publish original research. In addition, a number of separate divisions were created within the organization, and its goal was changed: "to advance psychology as a science, as a profession, and a means of promoting human welfare."[15] All in all, despite its origins as a purely scientific discipline, psychology was pulled inexorably toward the need for practical application. In addition, although that need for application was born in the form of educational social work and pedagogical training, it was attracted to psychopathology and psychotherapy like teenagers to a telephone. By 1985 roughly three-quarters of all APA members were clinical practitioners. Experimental psychologists felt that their very discipline had been stolen from them piece by piece.[16]

Many experimentalists now believed that the APA had abdicated their needs. In 1959 the first group of experimental psychologists formed their own organization, the Psychonomic Society. In 1987 resentment had matured to such a degree that an effort to reorganize the APA to provide greater recognition to experimental psychology resulted in acrimonious arguments that were never resolved.[17] Many experimental psychologists left the APA at that time and created the American Psychological Society (APS), which began with five hundred angry charter members and grew to fifteen thousand by 1994. Today the APS enjoys loyal support from psychological scientists in all areas of psychology, accompanied by a few who study clinical psychopathology and counseling techniques.[18] In return, the new organization seeks out the federal funding and national attention for psychological science that the APA had refused to pursue.

A glance at some descriptive statistics for growth of the discipline as a whole may also explain why many psychologists who teach and conduct research, but do not practice any form of therapy, might feel they have been spurned. From 1960 to 1979, psychology in general grew by 435 percent, a whopping figure for any field. Partitioning that growth by area shows that from 1966 to 1980 the number of clinical psychologists increased on average each year by 8 percent, counseling psychologists by 13 percent, and school psychologists by 18 percent. The growth rate for experimental psychologists—an umbrella term that traditionally includes developmental, social, cognitive, organizational, physiological, comparative, health, and sport psychologists at a minimum—was 1 percent per year. By 1980 experimental psychologists—all of whom must have doctorates—comprised only 14 percent of all the Ph.D.s in psychology.[19] It is little wonder, then, that the APA has acted in favor of its majority population. Simultaneously, these numbers explain why many psychological scientists feel that their contributions are largely ignored within their own discipline. If we add to that mind-set the nasty skirmishes over repressed memory that have cropped up in recent years between experimental and clinical camps, we should not be surprised at the acrid results. Unless we make radical changes now, we can expect the same sort of counterproductive rancor to continue to darken psychology's future.

## INCREASING SEGREGATION

A prominent textbook of psychology's history in America, copyrighted in 1987, specified several mechanisms that the author believed were integrating the discipline at that time.[20] These mechanisms included the strength of one national association for all psychologists, the existence of academic departments that collect all the subfields of psychology under one rubric, and the publication of books that combine review articles from multiple topic areas, such as the *Annual Review of Psychology*. By now, all three of these mechanisms have been weakened, and several opposing factors are at work. Psychologists are served today by two very separate national associations plus a host of smaller organizations that cater to fragmented subfields. A growing number of American colleges and universities now have cognitive science, neuroscience, or human development departments that are completely separate from their psychology departments. While professors of clinical psychology remain within traditional departments of psychology, some also having small private practices, experimental psychologists of all sorts are more likely to be assigned to the new groupings. The *Annual Review of Psychology* still exists but is now accompanied by related review publications such as the *Annual Review of Neuroscience*.

Factors that push the canyon walls farther apart also include the intensity of recent quarrels between experimental and clinical psychologists. The repressed memory battles are an ideal example; they represent one of the few areas of psychological knowledge over which scientists and therapists have communicated at all during the past few decades, and they are characterized on both sides by vituperative assaults that prohibit rational thought and careful listening. Furthermore, as the amount of new information to be digested in psychology has soared beyond human capacity, different subfields have come to delineate their boundaries more forcefully. This has exacerbated disparities in language style, terminology, and mode of training to the degree that psychologists of varying specialties can barely speak with one another even when they want to. By the same token, the amount of information to be understood is now so vast that few individuals have the time to learn more than what they need to perform adequately within their own bailiwick. A therapist who wishes to genuinely understand all that is known about autobiographical memory will have to abandon his clients for a substantial period of time in order to learn it. Likewise, the cognitive scientist who wants to delve into psychotherapy is going to be hard-pressed to keep up with her teaching, research, and service requirements.

The term "cognitive science" has become increasingly popular among young experimental psychologists who do not conduct the kind of interdisciplinary scholarship that defines the field. One reason for this shift is that any link to "psychology" creates instant confusion about the type of work that the cognitive scientist does. Furthermore, if the headings in American bookstores are any indication, popular psychology is moving fervently toward new age philosophy, self-help, relationships, and spiritual enlightenment. Wundt would be horrified. Books on these topics are placed in close proximity to one another, usually in the same physical location that was previously reserved for "psychology." They wear colorful dust jackets and catchy titles. Meanwhile, dusty tomes about the human mind and brain are herded into a storage bin many yards away. A growing number of trade bookstores no longer use "psychology" as a heading for any portion of their collection.

The trend of isolation marches on in other ways as well. A recent volume on the future of psychology in the twenty-first century contains not a single chapter and barely a single word about the future of psychotherapy, clinical diagnosis, or psychological treatment. The book is touted as a "wide-ranging work" intended for "anyone with a professional or personal interest in psychology."[21] Where, then, is the view of psychology's future as seen by practitioners? Moreover, as recent critiques of science gain prominence, a number of psychotherapists have openly devalued methods of scientific inquiry despite their proven utility in generating knowledge about both normal and psychopathological minds. If science is worthless in psychology, then psychological scientists are, too.

## INCOMPATIBLE EPISTEMOLOGIES

At a superficial level, the history of the split between clinical and experimental psychology can be traced to the philosophical dualism of separation between mind and body, soul and matter, reason and emotion—a dualism for which René Descartes often takes the heat but which largely belongs to Plato. In more recent centuries, this traditional schism has been played out in the debate between humanists and scientists, creating sharply disparate worldviews among members of the one profession we call psychology. These differences in worldview lead naturally to incompatible epistemologies, a common problem between separate disciplines but rare within one. Yet, in truth, the clinical and experimental sides of psychology have become as isolated from one another—in languages, expectations, goals, purposes, assumptions, and ways of knowing—as art and chemistry are. When we ask an artist and a chemist to describe what constitutes acceptable evidence, how theory differs from fact, how knowledge is constructed within their fields, we expect to receive different responses. The answers are every bit as conflicting when we ask experimental psychologists and clinical psychologists the same questions.

Issues of epistemology may seem esoteric in daily life, but in fact they are quite critical. Suppose for a moment that you are diagnosed with a brain tumor. When you sign consent forms allowing a neurosurgeon to slice into your brain, do you believe that he has no empirical evidence on which to base his surgery? That he believes science is worthless? As the scalpel quivers over living human tissue, is it enough for him to have a theory? Is it enough for him to have read one case study in the literature? Five? Most of us would probably expect the neurosurgeon to have a much stronger basis on which to carry out his treatment, one that has undergone rigorous tests on a large and representative sample of the population over a significant period of time. We would probably refuse his plan for treatment if it were not based on such evidence. The same standards of care should be applied to psychotherapy, which can have lifelong effects as profound as those of brain surgery. To lower the bar is to devalue our own work.

Nonetheless, some mental health practitioners tend to rely on clinical case studies as sole support for their treatment decisions. If a technique has produced successful results for one or two clients, it is used on others with the hope—not the belief or knowledge—that it might work again. If the technique is known to cause no harm and if other proven techniques cannot be used or have not worked, then this practice might be acceptable. However, concern is justified when untested techniques are applied as substitutions for proven therapies. Certainly, case studies are a valuable method of inquiry, especially in preliminary stages of investigation. In fact, they are very helpful in pointing the way to important questions and beliefs that can then be tested under strict conditions. But much more can be known if we combine case studies with controlled comparisons that rule out alternative explanations for psychotherapeutic results. As one practitioner has opined,

"We want to know, not if it worked once, but if it is *generally* effective, at least for a certain kind of problem and patient."[22]

The relationship of theory to fact is another area of psychological knowledge construction that yields different opinions among practitioners and scientists. Experimental psychologists see theories as speculative possibilities—pipe dreams—that need to be tested. Many practitioners view theories as factual knowledge that can be applied to real-world problems. For example, Terr's theory of Type I and Type II trauma is frequently mentioned as fact in the clinical literature despite the lack of empirical support for its accuracy. Theory comes first, and testing either never occurs or is assumed to take place during therapeutic application. By contrast, many memory scientists refuse to theorize or, if pressed, develop fragmented mini-theories that explain only one or two narrow facets of a paradigmatic result. Here, data comes first, with theory held in abeyance until a layer of promising results provides a safety net. Both approaches are troubling.

Laboratory research cannot promise answers or applications, but it can usually offer information that will be helpful. The history of science across a varied array of disciplines—chemistry, physics, astronomy, biology—has borne out repeatedly the fact that pure research leads to applications that were entirely unexpected at the time the original studies were conducted. Research on word priming was considered boring, abstract, and meaningless by the vast majority of humanity until, years later, it was suddenly related to implicit memory, traumatic remembrance, and illusions of reminiscence. Even some of us who conducted the early priming research are surprised that it now plays a primary role in explaining how false beliefs may be created by activating associated ideas that are unconsciously injected into a memorial narrative. No one can count the apples in a seed.[23]

Obviously, laboratory research has its downfalls, just as case reports do. The study of traumatic memory is a good example of knowledge that must rely on clinical case studies to a greater extent than most scholars would prefer. We cannot intentionally traumatize human beings just to see how their memories will respond. However, the fact that laboratory research has one slate of strengths and stumbling blocks, while case studies have another, is all the more reason to combine methods in an effort to learn more about the topic at hand. Moreover, all research is conducted by human beings who make mistakes, so any one set of results can be faulty despite the best of intentions. This, too, is a good reason to rest therapeutic decisions on results that have been produced consistently by different investigators. Furthermore, scientific evidence pertinent to psychotherapy is not limited to tests of efficacy. General evidence of the way a system—such as the episodic memory system—operates under normal conditions can aid both clinical and experimental psychologists.

Criticisms of science are omnipresent within the recovered memory battles. Unfortunately, it is almost always a mythical caricature of science that is critiqued rather than science itself. No psychological scientist I know truly believes that science has the capacity to produce universal truth, that science is entirely pure and objective, that science is the sole god of inquiry in the intellectual universe, or that science will bring us immutable laws of mentality that apply wholesale to every human being on the planet. These assumptions are rubbish. If science is to be attacked, let it be attacked for what it is, not for what nonscientists might assume it is. Science, in fact, is rife with disagreement and controversy, it is biased by political needs and personal desires, it is incapable of addressing certain questions that are critical to life as we know it, and it is amenable to error.[24] It is also one of our best tools in the search for knowledge, and we need to use every tool we have.

The historical schism between clinical and experimental psychology, combined with conflicting epistemologies and criticisms of science, has created a relentless circle of confrontation between therapists and scientists. Cognitive scientists and experimental psychologists have long suspected that practitioners do not read, understand, or value our contributions to psychological knowledge. This suspicion lessens our willingness to conduct research in areas of clinical application. Had psychological scientists believed that clinicians wanted their knowledge, we would have amassed considerably more information about autobiographical and traumatic remembrance long before the late 1980s when the recovered memory hell broke loose. Partly because clinical desire for scientific knowledge was not apparent, many experimenters concentrated on other areas of research, areas for which their contributions were more likely to be recognized and appreciated. Unfortunately, this led to the publication of more research that seemed irrelevant to clinical needs, hence pushing clinicians even farther away. Thus, when practitioners did read experimental journals, they were indeed faced with extraneous mumbo-jumbo bearing little relationship to the kind of information they wanted. And while a researcher has time to inspect a psychological phenomenon thoroughly, the clinician may not. When a desperate client pleads for help, the therapist cannot respond by saying that the results of an impending study might provide some answers in six months. When therapists complain today that they have read some of the research on memory but that it does not answer their most important questions, they are pointing to a section of the vicious circle I have described. Upon viewing the whole curve, practitioners may begin to understand why there is not as much memory research of the type they would prefer, and researchers might begin to want to conduct the types of investigations that are sorely needed.

The outlook for psychology appears bleak unless we change the status quo. For that reason, I would like to suggest a few changes. I have been immersed in academia long enough to know that these suggestions will not be accepted and applied; indeed, that is not my intention in offering them. Rather, I hope that they will provide a platform from which many individuals in psychological professions will enter active conversation about the specific ways in which all of us will alter psychology's future. From that conversation we can develop better ideas to be implemented for improvement. Such ideas will never bring the two sides of the psychological canyon together, but they may help create a footbridge of communication.

## SUGGESTIONS FOR CHANGE

As a rudimentary starting point, we must stop accusing each other. One clinician recently remarked that the 1990s controversy over memory has been "a tale of villains, disbelievers, accusers, victims, scapegoats, charges, and blame."[25] Sometimes the story has become so vile as to imply that every memory recovery critic is a sexual abuser, while every therapist is intentionally implanting false memories of a horrendous past. What constructive purpose does such angry rhetoric serve? The only effect it has is to undermine any hope of mutual cooperation. To move forward successfully we need intelligent scholarly discussion, not cruel ad hominem attacks.

A corollary to braking pointless accusation is to seek out and kill false dichotomies and stereotypes. It should come as no surprise that experimenters are as offended at being dubbed "control freaks" as therapists are at being called "touchy-feely." Scientists and practitioners, like everyone else, are individuals. Each of us varies in our beliefs and hopes, our assumptions and practices, our opinions about memory and psychology, our knowledge base. The fact that I can be categorized as a "scientist" and you as a "practitioner" should not be used to engender offensive stereotypes. During the course of writing this book, I've communicated with therapists who worry that they may have suggested false memories, and I've communicated with experimental psychologists who suspect that trauma might break all the known rules of standard remembering and forgetting. Likewise, not all psychological scientists believe that science is the only—or even the best—method for the study of certain aspects of memory, and not all clinicians are willing to base their therapeutic actions on case studies alone.

Some false dichotomies are hard to identify without concerted effort. For example, the ersatz distinction between "quantitative" and "qualitative" methods of psychological research merely increases the distance between clinicians and experimenters. Good scholarly inquiry leads to solid knowledge; solid knowledge demands a combination of research techniques along with a willingness to mix and match methods in the most intelligent manner. Another case in point is repression: Those who argue that repression rarely occurs are not necessarily saying that almost every memory can be retrieved. If not repressed, the memory might have been forgotten via normal processes, lost through amnesic failure of psychogenic origin, or impaired by physical damage to the brain. Black and white are easiest to see, but shades of gray will lead us home. Simply put, psychologists need to begin to practice the respect for individualism, diversity, and tolerance that we preach.

We must revise our methods of educating psychology students, both at the undergraduate and graduate levels. Every undergraduate psychology major should be required to pass a selection of basic content courses in both clinical and experimental psychology. In addition, each student should be required to pass methods courses that address a broad selection of research techniques, including scientific and hermeneutic methods of psychological scholarship. Within all courses we need greater focus on content and application than on methods. This is especially true in cognitive psychology where, for example, too many professors organize a course on memory around narrow experimental techniques. People who enroll in a course on memory want to know about memory, not about the Sternberg paradigm. To teach a topic more by paradigmatic style than conceptual substance is like welcoming an avid young reader to a beautiful new library and then forcing her attention away from the contents of the books to the methods by which their spines are pressed. We need to include, in all our courses, examples that appeal to both clinicians and experimenters. In the memory course, then, we might offer knowledge about multiple personality disorder, fugue, and Alzheimer's disease, along with the more traditional serial position curves and levels of processing. These pedagogical alterations should be designed to prevent our undergraduate students from falling into the present trap of separate tracks for either clinical or experimental pursuits.

If a more balanced approach to psychology is provided at the undergraduate level, greater specialization can still occur in graduate programs. Even at the graduate level, however, careful consideration should be given to course requirements. For example, if remembering is an integral part of creating and comprehending the self, and if clinical practice revolves around various aspects of personal self, then a course in human memory should be required of students who plan to become practitioners. Similarly, if graduate students in experimental psychology are planning to conduct research on memory, perhaps they should be required to pass a course on clinical or counseling psychology that will help them understand what sort of research is needed most. At undergraduate, graduate, and postdoctoral levels, clinicians and experimenters should invite each other to participate in their courses and laboratory groups. This cross-fertilization will add to the education that all students may claim, by virtue of discussion that transcends the tight boundaries of a closed subfield.

As part of the need to revise educational practices, psychologists must identify and resolve conflicting definitions in important terminology. The fact that a basic phrase like "short-term memory" refers to two entirely different processes, depending on whether you ask a clinician or an experimenter, is inexcusable. For that matter, it is not even clear that both groups consider short-term memory—or memory as a whole—to be a process at all. These terms, like "cognition," can refer to a thing, an event, or a process. Such incompatible definitions aren't noticed when we wear our disciplinary blinders, but they are obviously a source of bewilderment when we attempt to learn about other areas of psychology. Even within a given field, these distinctions can be important. For example, people who think of memory as a thing may assume that a given reminiscence has one storage location, is static in content, and can easily be retrieved (picked up) or stored (put away). Those who see memory as a process have a wholly different conception of reminiscence as distributed, dynamic, and fluid.

To alter psychological education in the manner I suggest, all of us will have to learn more about the areas outside our own specialization. Experimental psychologists should occasionally read general overviews of the clinical literature, just as practitioners should devote some attention to the experimental literature. While writing this book, I was pleased to find my own stereotyped assumptions about therapists loosen upon reading the clinical literature. Obviously, the scientist/practitioner model is still alive, as evidenced by many admirable articles describing rigorous methodologies, creative new ideas, and trenchant critiques of investigations into various forms of psychotherapy. In addition to reading across the literature, more of us should contribute to it. Specifically, we need more books and articles written by practitioners for experimentalists, and vice versa. The fact that this guide is unusual in its technical exposition of cognitive science to a professional audience is a sad symptom of psychology's ills. Addressing an audience outside one's specialty is indeed challenging, but the potential rewards for both author and reader are rich. I hope that practitioners who find in this book erroneous assumptions about psychotherapy will correct me in a publication of their own that is intended for experimental psychologists and cognitive scientists. In addition, nonacademic therapists might find it fruitful to teach a course every year or two at a local college or university, sharing their knowledge not only with other practitioners in the area but also with local experimental psychologists.

I also suggest that psychologists—academic and professional—get back into the classroom as students, to learn more about the areas of psychology outside their specialization and to sharpen their own counseling or teaching skills. My college implemented a program during the mid-1990s for professors to become master learners in their colleagues' classrooms. Not only did the program meet its primary goal of enhancing undergraduates' education by providing them with a role model for learning, it also succeeded in improving professorial knowledge in both content and pedagogy.[26] The program was used in an interdisciplinary course that largely excludes psychology, but the same principles could be applied to experimental and clinical courses.

Faculty and others can also learn more about psychological areas outside their expertise by simply enrolling in a course. College courses in human memory have been offered annually by most psychology departments for at least two decades; qualified psychotherapists who wish to learn more about human remembrance should take advantage of such opportunities. Similarly, experimental psychologists who plan to contribute to the clinical literature might take a course or two in abnormal psychology once in a while.

With improved educational practices in place to alleviate blind accusations, stereotyped assumptions, and ignorance of the other's knowledge, true collaboration can begin to transpire between clinical and experimental camps. To conduct meaningful research on human memory, cognitive scientists need help from clinicians. Without collaboration we are unlikely to ask the questions or develop the studies that will provide answers that therapists need. In most instances, experimental psychologists and cognitive scientists have had extensive experience in designing, analyzing, and interpreting empirical research. Most psychotherapists have tremendous expertise in assessing, identifying, and correcting the mental disorders and psychological problems their clients experience. Instead of trying to make therapists into part-time researchers, and researchers into part-time therapists, let's work together in teams to take the best advantage of each individual's proficiency.

A few specific programs to encourage such collaboration are presently under way. The National Institute on Drug Abuse recently brought psychological practitioners and scientists together for a series of planned workshops to develop behavioral therapies. The workshops are funded through grants for research that not only tests the efficacy of a given therapy but actively develops new therapies on the basis of known psychological science. The workshop presentations and responses are published in the American Psychological Society's flagship journal so that psychologists at large can become aware of the program and its accomplishments.[27] All of us should insist that our national associations, APA and APS, begin to lobby for more Stage I funding of collaborative efforts between clinical and experimental psychology. In addition, we should demand that our organizations educate national funding sources about meaningful acceptance criteria: Grant proposals in many areas could be approved or denied partly on the basis of their ability to use scientific knowledge to develop new psychotherapies, and vice versa. Local organizations should take notice as well. The Pennsylvania Psychological Association has established a formal network among therapists and scientists that advocates greater collaboration, and it is seeded with dollars from the APA. The Pennsylvania State University psychology department has also set aside money for interdisciplinary research that integrates basic and applied science as a five-year strategic plan.[28]

The needs for education and collaboration are tightly intertwined. Neither will attain success if attempted for only a temporary period of time. The words of one psychologist who has been instrumental in designing the new collaborative programs in Pennsylvania deserve consideration: "The only way for integration truly to occur is through sustained interaction. . . . As a clinical researcher, I need to give basic-research colleagues a thorough introduction into what I know about the pathology and therapies I investigate; what my underlying theoretical questions are; how I pursue those with designs, measures, and methodologies; and how my collaborators' knowledge and methods are potentially relevant to my questions. My collaborators need to give me the same types of information about their research and central questions."[29] Thus, I am not suggesting that we collaborate on occasion or for particular purposes but that we work together with mutual respect and cooperation on a more permanent basis. Whether this suggestion strains the bounds of credibility too strenuously remains to be seen.

With sustained collaboration and mutual education, we will be able to create new methods of conducting research that test clinical hypotheses more powerfully. Empirical investigations of psychotherapeutic techniques present some of the most difficult methodological problems known, problems that do not exist or are less salient in traditional investigations common to experimental psychology. Yet, ironically, we have handed these challenges not to our best scientists but to people who specialize in psychological practice. Furthermore, traditional research methods in experimental psychology focus on the group rather than the individual, tend to generalize rather than specify, and require tight controls that elude ecological validity. These biases—and others—represent significant weaknesses for clinicians, who practice their therapies on individuals handling specific problems in the real world. Rather than complaining about the dearth of useful methods, I suggest that we begin through education and collaboration to make the methods we need. Statistical analyses and research methodologies are not gods; they were created by mortals and can be recreated, rescinded, or replaced at any time.

Even if we assign the hardest of our methodological problems to the best of our researchers, we cannot relinquish the clinician's responsibility to remain knowledgeable about general features of scientific analysis. All psychologists should be capable of critically evaluating a complex research report. Yet some of the recent literature on therapeutic techniques is rife with errors. For example, a review of studies conducted during the 1990s to test eye movement desensitization and reprocessing (EMDR) shows them to be characterized by nonrepresentative samples, no baseline data, nonequivalent control groups, no control for demand and placebo effects, blatant confounding variables, incorrect statistical analyses, nonblind assignment, nonrandom assignment, nonstandardized measures, and inadequate sample size.[30] One research team went as far as to conduct forty separate *t*-tests on one set of data, then used the results to conclude that EMDR is a powerful method for coping with stressful memories![31]

All these flagrant flaws are addressed in standard research methods courses offered to college psychology students in their freshman or sophomore years. There is no excuse for such sloppiness at the professional, postdoctoral level. The comedy of errors is not at all funny when applied directly to the victims of trauma. Furthermore, it means that valuable time has been wasted in testing the true efficacy of a promising technique. The process of working memory interference on which EMDR is unwittingly based is well grounded in psychological science and likely to yield several successful therapeutic techniques.[32] In general, experimenters and practitioners alike should be aware of the fundamental principles of scientific research so that they have the knowledge necessary to assess the research they read. The same knowledge will allow us to root out incompetence among ignorant researchers and irresponsible journal editors who publish studies that are done poorly.

Licensure is an issue I am tempted to avoid, not being a therapist myself, but I enter the fray because issues of certification profoundly affect the general reputation of psychology as well as all experimental and clinical psychologists individually. We live in a society in which licensing is required for physicians, nurses, dentists, schoolteachers, accountants, lawyers, airplane pilots, veterinarians, architects, building contractors, engineers, land surveyors, and hairstylists—to name just a few. We even require licenses for driving, hunting, and fishing.[33] This means that while anyone can legally provide psychotherapy, the most highly trained commercial fisherman cannot toss a line in a stream without a license. Something's wrong here. Why is it acceptable for any untrained, unlicensed individual to meddle actively with the innermost workings of another human mind, while an official imprimatur is required to fill out a tax form, draw the floor plans for a shed, or follow a deer through a forest?

Even more critical than licensing or certification is the need for educational requirements. Individuals who attempt to practice medicine without a medical degree are immediately condemned, but a high school dropout who decides to advertise her services as a "psychotherapist" is in instant business. We cheapen our own discipline—both the experimental and clinical sides of it—when we stand silently on the sidelines and allow anyone to practice psychology on unsuspecting victims. This is not to say that every unlicensed psychotherapist is incompetent or that every licensed clinician is well trained. Neither claim is true. However, it seems absurd that people who have no formal training or accredited education in the vast and complicated field of psychology should be practicing it. Requiring some advanced degree of education in psychology or psychiatry, along with a license to practice it, will boost the discipline's reputation and encourage a higher standard of care for all psychological clients.

The problem of licensure and educational requirements is exacerbated by a public that does not recognize basic distinctions in training among psychiatrists, neurologists, clinical psychologists, counselors, social workers, and other psychotherapists. A depressing number of psychology majors even after graduation from college are still not aware that psychology can be practiced without a degree, a license, or even a passing grade in a high school course. Some of them have not been taught this information; others have disbelieved or quickly forgotten it because the notion is so foreign in an otherwise regulated society. We need to clarify such distinctions by publicizing the amount and type of training that make a strong psychological career. Too many people assume that a good psychotherapist needs nothing more than a sense of compassion and a willingness to dispense casual advice. Practitioners should be incensed at the very idea.

Given all the contradictions within psychology, compounded by the oversimplified misinformation peddled through the media, it's no wonder the public is confused. In a 1969 presidential address to members of the American Psychological Association, cognitive psychologist George Miller advocated giving psychology away. He envisioned a sharing of knowledge with the general public that would serve to educate them about their own minds and brains. A decade later, when popular psychology already bore little resemblance to the real thing and inaccurate self-help books infiltrated the market, psychologist Sigmund Koch reconsidered Miller's advice: "In sum, I believe the most charitable thing we can do is not to give psychology away, but to take it back."[34] Today, twenty years after Koch's advice, psychology is in even deeper trouble. Still, my heart remains with Miller.

To give psychology away responsibly, we must gain greater control over the type of publicity that our work receives. This could be achieved in several ways. First, we need to usurp the position of pop-psych journalists who know very little about psychology. Let's describe our own work to the general public rather than let someone else do the job for us. Contemporary Americans demonstrate sustained curiosity about the human mind and brain, curiosity that can be sated with entertaining but accurate exposition from within. A few individuals are presently contributing to this goal—Howard Gardner, Steven Pinker, William Calvin, Oliver Sacks, and Richard Restak come to mind—but more need to join the endeavor. Second, in writing to a lay audience, and even to each other, we must abandon the supercilious prose and arrogant jargon that marks most psychological literature. We've been a discipline for more than one hundred years now; we do not need to continue pumping ourselves up through an artificial language of exclusion.

Third, we need to strike back when reporters misconstrue psychological knowledge, instead of remaining silently annoyed. Inaccurate newspaper and magazine articles should be met with stern letters or telephone calls from top psychologists demanding a retraction or remediation. We can also help by volunteering to serve on the editorial review boards of such publications. Talk show hosts who supply their own uninformed versions of one-minute psychotherapy to guests, while millions of television viewers watch and learn, should be publicly rebuked for their ignorance. Publishers should be encouraged to employ psychology authors who are respected experts in the fields about which they write. This need not banish from the marketplace books written by outsiders, which can be valuable contributions in their own right. But the author's biography printed on such volumes and the publishers' techniques of advertising them should clarify to readers that someone from outside the topic's circle of expertise is writing. Bookstore managers should be offered intelligent advice concerning their marketing strategies for various types of psychological books. Many of them are happy to consider the effects their prominent displays may have on the public perception of a discipline.

Finally, we must remind our lay audience that real psychology does not fit into soundbites. To understand a psychological subtopic, our audience needs to read not one article but ten, not one book but five. Without such reminders readers fall into the lazy trap of blaming the discipline for offering so little information when in fact the knowledge exists but they simply have not sought it. This book, for example, provides little more than a brief introduction to a tiny slice of the memory literature, a compass to guide readers to greater knowledge. There's a lot more learning left to do if you want to know everything scientists and scholars have discovered about memory.

The changes I have suggested will not come easily. They will require time and effort, attention to issues that we would prefer to ignore, close inspection of personal motives, and the courage to risk secure reputations. They may backfire in ways we cannot predict. They may fail. But surely the notion of saving psychology is worth our consideration. For if each of us donates just one small piece of our time and talent to the joint enterprise, everyone may benefit. I offer this small book to the discipline of psychology in the sincere hope that practitioners, theorists, and scientists will someday join forces in the true spirit of mutual cooperation.

# For Further Reading

Christianson, S. A. (Ed.). (1992). *The handbook of emotion and memory: Research and theory.* Hillsdale, NJ: Erlbaum.

Cowan, N. (Ed.). (1997). *The development of memory in childhood.* Hove East Sussex, England: Psychology Press.

Gruneberg, M., & Morris, P. (Eds.). (1992). *Aspects of memory. Vol. I: The practical aspects.* London: Routledge.

Lynn, S. J., & Payne, D. G. (1997). Memory as the theater of the past. *Current Directions in Psychological Science, 6(3),* 55–83. (special issue, Cambridge University Press.)

Pezdek, K., & Banks, W. P. (Eds.). (1996). *The recovered memory/false memory debate.* San Diego: Academic Press.

Rubin, David C. (Ed.). (1996). *Remembering our past: Studies in autobiographical memory.* New York: Cambridge University Press.

Schacter, D. L. (Ed.). (1995). *Memory distortion: How minds, brains, and societies reconstruct the past.* Cambridge, MA: Harvard University Press.

Schacter, Daniel L. (1996). *Searching for memory: The brain, the mind, and the past.* New York: Basic Books.

Searleman, A., & Herrmann, D. (1994). *Memory from a broader perspective.* New York: McGraw-Hill.

Springer, S., & Deutsch G. (1993). *Left brain, right brain.* New York: W. H. Freeman.

The most relevant journals include:
*Memory*
*Memory & Cognition*
*Cognition and Emotion*
*Applied Cognitive Psychology*
*Consciousness and Cognition*
*Journal of Experimental Psychology: Learning, Memory, and Cognition*
*Journal of Memory and Language*

# Notes

## CHAPTER 1

1. Philosophical claims about memory and self are explored in Hamilton (1995).

2. The power of self memory is discussed in Greenwald and Banaji (1989).

3. The metaphor of chapter headings that I refer to is found in Tulving (1995).

4. The number of American mental health care providers is estimated in Baker (1994).

5. Michael Yapko's survey and its results are published in his 1994 book.

6. Quoted survey statements and results are from pages 50-55 and 231-236 of Yapko (1994).

7. Data concerning memory recovery techniques that are presently in use are supplied in Poole et al. (1995).

8. The quote concerning the safety of memory therapy is on page 434 of Poole et al. (1995).

9. I'm aware of the contradiction in my use of the Pope's maxim that "a little learning is a dangerous thing." T. H. Huxley replied in 1877, "If a little knowledge is dangerous, where is the man who has so much as to be out of danger?"

10. The historian's quote about memory research is from page 41 of Roth (1994).

11. Some of the recent clinical literature to which I refer offers specific applications of memory. For example, altering self-concept through memory is discussed in Nurius (1994). Milestoning is discussed in Lowenthal and Marrazzo (1990). Reminiscence therapy and other applications of memory therapy in the elderly can be explored further in Coleman (1986). Of the several sources available on reconstructive narrative, I recommend Freeman (1993). A more specific book on the topic is Rosen and Kuehlwein (1996). Smith (1994) describes the use of reconstructive narrative among women making the transition to motherhood. Efforts to use memory in self-reconstruction of cancer victims is described in Taylor (1983). Memory distortions and contrivances designed to meet social goals are discussed in Gentry and Herrmann (1990).

## CHAPTER 2

1. An indirect discussion of Chinese concepts of memory is available in Takehiko (1997).

2. Information on Thoth is from Lorimer (1995).

3. Mnemosyne is described briefly in McHenry (1993).

4. Minerva appears in Lorimer (1995).

5. Greek and Roman authors who wrote about memory include Homer, Heraclitus, Aristophanes, Herodotus, Thucydides, Virgil, Lucretius, Plotinus, Plutarch, Tacitus, and, of course, Plato and Aristotle.

6. Plato's (1952a, 1952b) discussions of memory are integrated throughout his writings but appear rather distinctly in *Theaetetus* and *Meno*. Aristotle (1952a, 1952b) presents his views on memory primarily in *De Anima* and *On Memory and Reminiscence*.

7. The quote from Plato is found on page 180 of the *Meno* and is ascribed to Socrates.

8. Searlemann and Herrman (1994) present the information concerning medieval troubadours.

9. Mill and Butler are two of the philosophers who debated Locke's belief that memory and identity were the same. The debate that continues today is considered in Hamilton (1995).

10. In their day, Charcot and Janet were highly respected neurologists who treated a number of patients successfully. Freud, though also holding an M.D. in neurology, might be categorized more accurately as a theorist whose daily experience with real patients was limited.

11. Ebbinghaus's contributions to the century of memory scholarship are discussed in Roediger (1985), a special section of the *Journal of Experimental Psychology: Learning, Memory, and Cognition* that was produced to commemorate the one-hundredth anniversary of his investigations.

12. The quote from Hacking is found on page 198 of his 1995 book.

13. Hacking's description of the soul is on page 208 of his 1995 book.

14. Early research findings in studies of human learning are discussed in Hilgard (1987).

15. Chomsky, Miller, and Neisser—along with Freud, Broca, and Ebinghaus—bestowed far more knowledge on the discipline of psychology than the few items I have identified, In addition, there are many other individuals who count as critical figures in 1880s and 1960s psychology—Charcot, Janet, Ribot, Wundt, and Fechner, as well as Piaget, Bruner, Craik, and Treisman, to name just a few.

16. Skinner's theory of language acquisition was set forth in his 1957 book. Chomsky's (1959) scathing review of the book is often cited as the death knell for behaviorist psychology in America.

17. The cognitive revolution is discussed in greater detail in Baars (1986).

18. A casual survey of twenty-five graduate programs offered in California during 1997 turned up only one behaviorist/learning specialty.

19. The behaviorist who refers to his specialty as ghettoized is Leahey (1991).

20. Neisser's (1976) argument was published in *Cognition and Reality*.

21. Neisser (1982) criticized cognitive research in memory in *Memory Observed: Remembering in Natural Contexts*.

22. The quotes are from pages 5 and 6 of Neisser's (1982) book.

23. The argument against Neisser's call for ecological validity was published by Banaji and Crowder (1989). The infamous Aunt Martha quote appears on page 1187 of that article.

24. Fowler (1991) edited a special issue of *American Psychologist* that was devoted almost entirely to articles written by leading memory scholars detailing the importance of everyday memory and the absurdity of Banaji and Crowder's argument.

25. The quote is on page 42 of Tulving (1991).

26. My definition of cognitive science is based on Gardner's (1985) description of the budding field. His book is an excellent and lively introduction to cognitive science for those who are interested in learning more about the discipline.

27. The practitioner's definition of short-term memory is from Terr (1994).

28. Tulving first argued for a distinction between semantic and episodic memory in Tulving (1972). His argument was stronger and better supported by empirical evidence in Tulving (1983). For a more recent elaboration of episodic memory, see Tulving (1993). Tulving (1993) supplies the quote I have used about "the self's experiences" on page 67.

29. The amnesic K.C. is described in Tulving (1993).

30. The introductory chapter of Rubin (1996) elucidates these components.

31. Proust's infamous recollection based on the aroma and flavor of a madeleine is presented in Proust (1981).

32. Quoted on page 48 of Connor (1989).

## CHAPTER 3

1. The television documentary is Bikel (1995).

2. A review of the studies done on infantile amnesia in the early 1900s can be found in Dudycha and Dudycha (1941). More recent reviews of the many studies that support adult inability to recall events from infancy and early childhood include Kihlstrom and Harackiewicz (1982) as well as Pillemer and White (1989).

3. The fact that people do not recall a sibling's birth unless they were older than four years of age when it occurred is corroborated in Sheingold and Tenney (1982).

4. The quote describing childhood recollection is from page 8 of Salaman (1970).

5. The quote about good guys and bad guys is from page 117 of Kotre (1995).

6. The paraphrase of Proust is suggested on page 94 of Salaman (1970).

7. Evidence of new neurons in an eighty-three-year-old man is presented in Cotman and Nieto-Sampredo (1982). The same article also provides general information about brain development that some readers may find useful.

8. Facts about the poor quality of infant vision are discussed in Matlin and Foley (1992).

9. Average ages of neurological development change depending on the individual and on the particular region of the brain under scrutiny. Pruning, for example, occurs as early as six months of age in the hippocampus but is delayed until after the age of two years in certain parts of the frontal cortex.

10. Research on babies' ability to recognize sounds presented prenatally is presented in DeCasper and Spence (1986).

11. Evidence that babies recognize visual patterns after a two-week delay comes from Fagan (1990).

12. Evidence that six-month-olds remember footkicks is offered by Rovee-Collier and Shyi (1992).

13. Evidence that nine-month-olds will reproduce novel acts is presented in Meltzoff (1995).

14. The deferred imitation paradigm developed by Meltzoff is described in several of his articles. One that addresses most of the important issues is Meltzoff (1995).

15. Evidence that preschoolers remember events from age two is described by Fivush and Hammond (1990).

16. The quote is on page 313 of Howe and Courage (1993).

17. Ibid.

18. The hippocampus is sometimes described as being located in the limbic system. Because the boundaries of the limbic system, and its contents, fluctuate with the prevailing winds of theory, quite a few cognitive scientists now avoid that terminology.

19. H. M. is described in Hilts (1995).

20. The information concerning hippocampal development is from Arnold and Trojanowski (1996a, 1996b). This is a two-part article written by the same authors; it does require knowledge of neuroanatomical vocabulary.

21. According to Arnold and Trojanowski (1996a, 1996b), the protein that is found in large quantities in the hippocampus is known as microtubule-associated protein 5 (MAP5).

22. Lifelong learning may be aided by MAP5, but it is also mediated by a process known as long-term potentiation. Johnson (1991) does a good job of explaining long-term potentiation in fairly plain language.

23. K. C. is described in Tulving (1993).

24. The review of PET scans showing increased activity in the right prefrontal cortex, as well as an asymmetry between hemispheres in encoding and retrieval of episodic memories, is contained in Nyberg, Cabeza, and Tulving (1996).

25. Ibid.

26. Further information on the creation of procedural memories in the basal ganglia is available in Hook, Davis, and Beiser (1994).

27. Theories concerning the evolution of various brain regions are presented in MacLean (1990).

28. One team of theorists who have brought the language argument into recent consideration is Pillemer and White (1989).

29. Piaget's theory of language as a platform for memory is described in Ginsburg and Opper (1979).

30. The proposal that the development of a cognitive sense of self comprises the psychological shift away from infantile amnesia is offered in Howe and Courage (1993).

31. The quote concerning the difficulty of understanding self in infants is found on page 313 of Howe and Courage (1993).

## CHAPTER 4

1. Results showing that 33 percent of psychological practitioners believe in the computer metaphor of memory are presented on pages 51–52 and 231 of Yapko (1994).

2. The quote describing memory as a theater of the past is from page 55 of Lynn and Payne (1997).

3. The *Challenger* study is described in Neisser and Harsch (1992).

4. The *Challenger* disaster is described in Broad (1986).

5. Readers who are interested in Neisser's analysis of John Dean's memory during the Watergate testimony will enjoy reading Neisser (1981).

6. One study demonstrating flashbulb memories' undue proneness to high confidence is described in Weaver (1993).

7. Recall of high school grades was studied by Bahrick, Hall, and Berger (1996).

8. Binet's early research on children's eyewitness memory is described in Ceci and Bruck (1993).

9. Münsterberg's (1908) book is the earliest to focus on eyewitness memory.

10. The idea that words are inappropriate stimuli for investigations of memory is still radical today even though a few of us have been expressing it informally for many years.

11. A 1997 report describes two subjects whose severe amnesia was caused by medical problems in infancy but who nonetheless display normal vocabulary for words, including pronunciation, spelling, and usage. Thus, these children were able to acquire standard spoken language despite their inability to remember anything about episodes. This finding suggests not only a potential dissociation between episodic and semantic memory, but also the possibility of greater independence between language processing and memory than has previously been assumed among most experimental psychologists. For details, see Vargha-Khadem et al. (1997).

12. Estimates of a 5 percent false conviction rate are explained in Radin (1964).

13. The survey showing 73 percent conviction for defendants against which no evidence other than eyewitness identification exists was conducted by Devlin (1973), as cited by Stern and Dunning (1994).

14. The general review of witness and event factors in eyewitness memory is from Fruzzetti et al. (1992).

15. The study showing that subjects produced a mean estimate of two and a half minutes when asked to guess the duration of a thirty-second simulated bank robbery was done by Loftus et al. (1987).

16. Information regarding type of face and existence of weapon is presented in Fruzzetti et al. (1992).

17. The study yielding 29 percent incorrect identification of the thief who stole money from a wallet is described in Stern and Dunning (1994).

18. The study showing 26 percent incorrect answers to the film clip of the man in the threatening crowd was done by Loftus, Levidow, and Duensing (1992).

19. The size of the standard misinformation effect is estimated in Lindsay (1993).

20. Evidence that the misinformation effect occurs in children as well as adults is provided by Molyneaux and Larsen (1992).

21. The early study I've chosen as an example of the misinformation effect was conducted by Loftus and Palmer (1974).

22. The quote that supplies so many examples of the misinformation effect is from page 607 of Loftus et al. (1989). In quoting their passage, I have deleted the citations that the authors provided for each of the individual findings, but they are available in the original article.

23. Many studies demonstrate the confidence with which subjects recall misinformation; one example is Tversky and Tuchin (1989).

24. One of the many reports showing the degree of detail included in misinformed memories is Schooler, Clark, and Loftus (1988).

25. Evidence that misinformation is more easily accepted when presented by an apparently knowledgeable individual is presented in Smith and Ellsworth (1987).

26. Readers who wish to enter the methodological debate on the cause of the misinformation effect might read McCloskey and Zaragoza (1985). This article generated many studies designed to determine whether the misinformation effect is real or is merely some sort of artifact.

27. The fact that the misinformation effect is not an experimental artifact is now settled, for reasons that are amply demonstrated in a review of that literature by Belli and Loftus (1996).

28. Correlation coefficients for the relationship between confidence and accuracy in eyewitness memory were analyzed across thirty-five studies by Bothwell, Deffenbacher, and Brigham (1987).

29. The comparison between percentages of variance in accuracy that are accounted for by confidence in eyewitnesses as opposed to jurors' beliefs is presented in Luus and Wells (1994).

30. The study showing a .75 correlation between confidence and accuracy for information gained by listening to the news was done by Schneider and Laurion (1993).

31. The investigation of subjects' accuracy and confidence at recalling events they had recorded in their diaries was done by Barclay and Wellman (1986).

32. Information concerning memory for event dating, and the fact that time is a poor cue for event recollection, is elaborated in Larsen, Thompson, and Hansen (1996).

33. Ibid.

34. Gabriel García Márquez (1970) applied his words, "an intricate stew of truths and mirages" (page 230), to the concept of reality.

35. Daniel Schacter's notion of fragile power is elaborated in his (1996) book. The quotes I have used are found on page 7.

## CHAPTER 5

1. Wilder Penfield's research is described in Penfield and Perot (1963).

2. Penfield's studies are evaluated critically in Loftus and Loftus (1980).

3. Results showing that the context of previous exposure to facial drawings affects subjects' perceptions of the young woman/old woman illusion are described in Atkinson et al. (1990).

4. Hemispheric differences in the perception of music are discussed in Springer and Deutsch (1993).

5. A standard source for cross-cultural differences in perception, which describes the Müller-Lyer results and many others, is Deregowski (1980).

6. The study comparing the extent of the Müller-Lyer illusion in two groups of Navajo subjects was conducted by Pederson and Wheeler (1993).

7. Nurius (1994) provides brief instruction on enhancing self-esteem with memory.

8. Research using the classic levels of processing paradigm (Craik & Tulving, 1975) shows that deeper processing aids long-term retention.

9. Estimates of the number of synapses in the average human brain are from Shepard and Koch (1990).

10. The connectionist account of neural networks is fully described in Rumelhart, McClelland, and the PDP Research Group (1986). The terminology of synaptic connections is potentially confusing. I refer to neurons being "connected," "linked," and "joined"— even though each synapse is actually characterized by a tiny gap between neurons.

11. Clear introductions to long-term potentiation are hard to find, but readers might wish to try Johnson (1991).

12. Recent advances in neuroscientific research concerning the development of synapses in response to learning experiences are summarized in Swain et al. (1995).

13. The study investigating advertising inferences was done by Searleman and Carter (1988).

14. Conway's theory of autobiographical remembering is presented in Conway (1995).

15. Ibid.

16. Virtually every memory textbook on the market discusses Ebbinghaus's forgetting curves. The details I present here are from Searleman and Herrmann (1994).

17. Evidence that 70% of life events are retained for six months is provided in Wagenaar (1986).

18. Searleman and Herrmann (1994) supply the impressive details concerning the amount of material Ebbinghaus attempted to remember.

19. Theoretical discussion of the importance of event-specific knowledge to autobiographical memory is provided in Conway (1995).

20. The role of sleep in memory consolidation has been investigated by Winson (1985).

21. Schacter's words about the pattern between cue and engram are found on page 71 of his 1996 book.

22. Nyberg, Cabeza, and Tulving (1996) present PET evidence concerning the activation of right and left prefrontal cortex in episodic remembering.

23. The study demonstrating conflicting memory details with multiple retrieval is described in Conway (1995).

24. Research showing that facial expression cues altered memories for tone of voice is described in Schacter (1996).

25. Evidence that multiple choice questions increase erroneous retrieval is discussed in Lipton (1977).

26. Field and observer memories were investigated by Nigro and Neisser (1983).

27. Work showing that emotion can be attenuated by switching from field to observer memories was done by Robinson and Swanson (1993).

28. A great deal of research has been conducted to verify the reality of the misinformation effect since it was questioned by McCloskey and Zaragoza (1985). The ensuing investigations demonstrated that the misinformation effect is indeed a real phenomenon of memory impairment and not merely an artifact of experimental procedures, as summarized by Tversky and Tuchin (1989). A review of twenty-two studies providing further support for the misinformation effect is found in Belli et al. (1992).

29. Richard Semon's theory is described in Semon (1904/1921) and in Semon (1909/1923). His ideas are also discussed briefly in Schacter (1995).

30. Freud presents a constructivist view of memory in Freud (1899/1962).

31. The "War of the Ghosts" experiment was first presented in Bartlett (1932). It has since been described in scores of memory textbooks.


## CHAPTER 6

1. The literature on memory for emotional events and memory that is dependent on mood is rife with confusion as to the distinction between "emotion" and "mood." Although few researchers hold themselves to a consistent separation in meaning, most argue that such separation should exist. Emotions, according to Niedenthal, Setterlund, and Jones (1994), " are phenomenal states that are associated with distinctive expressive displays, eliciting events, and subjective feeling tone" (page 88). However, "Moods are ... more diffuse, often longer lasting, and non-specific in their associated responses" (page 88). Thus, a person might display the specific emotion of anger upon being treated rudely by a colleague but would experience the mood of anger while feeling a general hostility that was unrelated to any particular event. In this chapter, I attempt to maintain the distinction without fanfare, but sometimes the terms could be interchanged with no loss of meaning.

2. The psychologist who was teased for studying such "obvious" phenomena was Gordon Bower, according to page 68 of Eich (1995).

3. The number of manuscripts submitted to *Cognition and Emotion* annually was verified by the journal's editor in a personal communication dated February 25, 1998. The reference to "a genuine interweaving" between cognition and emotion is found on page 271 of Gray (1990).

4. Damasio makes his argument in his 1994 book.

5. Brain structures known to mediate both emotional and cognitive functions include the ventromedial prefrontal cortex, the amygdala, the right somatosensory cortex, and the anterior cingulate cortex. Supporting research and an explanatory review of this information can be found in Damasio (1994) as well as in Gray (1990).

6. Probably no memory is entirely unemotional. The term is used for simplicity.

7. That a consistent positive correlation exists between emotionality and vividness is corroborated in a review by Reisberg and Heuer (1995).

8. The quote concerning rehearsal of emotional memories is on page 172 of Heuer and Reisberg (1992).

9. The quoted statement indicating that detailed emotional memories are most likely to be inaccurate is from page 152 of Heuer and Reisberg (1992). Their article provides a good review of the accuracy and vividness of memory for emotional events.

10. The Easterbrook hypothesis was first presented in Easterbrook (1959).

11. Evidence supporting the Easterbrook hypothesis is presented in Christianson and Safer (1996) as well as many other articles.

12. Heuer and Reisberg (1992) consider evidence on weapon focus.

13. Studies of tunnel memory, showing spatially compact memories of emotional events as if seen through a telephoto lens, are reviewed in Christianson and Safer (1996).

14. Reisberg and Heuer (1995) describe their study comparing errors in readers' comprehension of emotional and unemotional stories.

15. Ibid.

16. The within-subjects study that demonstrates excessive retrieval of negative memories during depression was conducted by Clark and Teasdale (1982).

17. The meta-analysis comparing depressed and normal subjects' recall of positive and negative information was done by Matt, Vazquez, and Campbell (1992).

18. Most of the information presented here on the cognitive biases of depressed and normal individuals in remembering positive and negative events is from work done by Mark Williams. His 1996 and 1992 publications are especially helpful.

19. The example of overgeneral memories provided in response to the cue word "angry" is from Williams and Broadbent (1986).

20. The study showing rates of 70 percent and 40 percent specificity for depressed and control subjects, respectively, was conducted by Williams and Scott (1988).

21. The various populations that tend to experience nonspecific memories are identified in Williams (1996).

22. Williams's theory of mnemonic interlock is presented in Williams (1996).

23. The quote in which Williams argues that overgenerality occurs even after trust has been established in therapy is on page 471 of Williams (1992).

24. Studies showing that specificity aids recovery from depression are discussed in Williams (1996).

25. Evidence that disturbed mothers improved relationships with their children by encoding acts of misbehavior more specifically is described in Williams (1996).

26. Recommendations for anamnestic therapy are described in Williams (1992).

27. The difference in mood congruence that occurs when moods are induced rather than natural is described in Niedenthal, Setterlund, and Jones (1994).

28. Mood incongruence, as evidenced in sad memories among people who had done well on exams or been questioned on sunny days, was first found by Parrott and Sabini (1990).

29. The quoted lists of reasons to inhibit a good mood are offered on page 283 of Parrott (1993).

30. Ibid.

31. The fact that mood congruence is stronger and more reliable than mood dependence is reported by Christianson and Safer (1996).

32. The classic study of mood dependence, in which subjects learned neutral words under happy, sad, afraid, and angry moods, was done by Bower (1981).

33. Bower (1981) developed the emotion network model.

34. The four features of mood-dependent memory that Eich has identified as crucial are fully described in Eich (1995). His brief review is quite helpful in understanding current research on mood-dependent memory.

35. The continuous music technique is described and evaluated in Eich (1995).

36. The well-known study of underwater divers, showing context-dependent memory, was done by Godden and Baddeley (1975).

37. Eich (1995) argues for mood as the key to state- and context-dependent memory.

38. The fact that research has not been productive in elucidating the exact nature of the link between memory and aroma has paradoxically fueled interest in the field even more. I do not want to leave readers with the mistaken assumption that investigations of this potential connection have been abandoned. Ample investigation continues to this day, but solid answers are still hard to find.

39. Research on emotional congruence in perception is led by Paula Niedenthal. One article reviewing her work is Niedenthal, Setterlund, and Jones (1994).

40. The quote is from page 401 of Niedenthal and Setterlund (1994).

41. Christianson and Safer (1996) provide evidence that negative emotions are more difficult to remember accurately than positive emotions.

42. Information on the MMPI's popularity is from Graham (1993) and Butcher (1990).

43. The topic of memory for emotion and physical pain is discussed in Christianson and Safer (1996).

44. The study showing pain congruence in memory was done by Eich et al. (1985).

45. Women's retrieval of autobiographical memories during menstrual pain was studied by Eich, Rachman, and Lopatka (1990).

46. The link between chronic pain and clinical depression is established in Fishbain et al. (1986).

47. The study describing psychoanalysts who were unable to recall plans for their own patients was done by von Benedek (1992).


## CHAPTER 7

1. The survey was conducted by Kassin, Ellsworth, and Smith (1989).

2. The quote from McGaugh (1992) is found on page 246.

3. Christianson's (1992) comment is published on page 288.

4. Shobe and Kihlstrom (1997) make their statement on page 74.

5. Terr's (1994) report appears on pages 10–11.

6. The laboratory simulation that showed subjects a film containing a violent or nonviolent clip regarding the bank robbery was conducted by Loftus and Burns (1982).

7. Similar classic studies, showing that violence impairs memory, include Clifford and Scott (1978) as well as Christianson and Nilsson (1984).

8. That incidents of rape leading to amnesia are almost always recalled within a few hours is reported by Christianson (1992).

9. Reports of Trevor Rees-Jones's memory of the August 1997 accident were published in Woods (1998).

10. General information on symptoms of psychogenic and organic amnesia is from Searleman and Herrman (1994).

11. The lifetime prevalence rate for fugue is from DSM-IV (First, 1994).

12. The lifetime prevalence rate for DID is from Ross (1991).

13. Lifetime prevalence rates for PTSD among American adults vary from 1 percent to 15 percent, with the most reliable estimates falling within 1 percent to 3 percent of the general population. These statistics are from Fullerton and Ursano (1997).

14. Much of the information concerning PTSD is from Krystal, Southwick, and Charney (1995).

15. The "higher neural thresholds" referred to are seen, in neuroscientific parlance, as a suppression of the P200 event-related potential. This potential appears to researchers as a spike in an averaged set of brain waves that usually appears about 200 milliseconds after a new stimulus has been presented. The spike is lower (weaker) among PTSD patients than others, indicating some suppression of the normal response to perceptual stimuli. The result is reported in Paige et al. (1990).

16. The study of holocaust memories was conducted by Wagenaar and Groeneweg (1990).

17. The study of eyewitnesses to a murder was done by Yuille and Cutshall (1986).

18. Terr's original study of the Chowchilla children, demonstrating memory enhancement with trauma, was published in 1981.

19. The study of the Chowchilla children's memories years later was published in Terr (1983).

20. Terr's theory, which suggests two types of traumatic memory, is presented in Terr (1994).

21. A critical analysis of the flaws in the study Terr uses to support her theory of traumatic memory is available in Shobe and Kihlstrom (1997).

22. Evidence that more intensely emotional memories are held with greater confidence is presented in Reisberg et al. (1988).

23. Research showing that traumatic memories are seldom susceptible to the misinformation effect is discussed in Christianson, Goodman, and Loftus (1992).

24. The finding that intense positive and negative memories are easily retrieved comes from Robinson (1980).

25. The diary investigation showing that upsetting memories became stronger with time was conducted by Larsen (1992).

26. The laboratory study showing greater accuracy among subjects who saw the emotional event of a woman's injury was conducted by Christianson and Loftus (1991).

27. The classic study using a simulated bank robbery was done by Loftus and Burns (1982).

28. The simulation in which a mother and son were seen on a walk was conducted by Christianson (1984).

29. Interviews of the witnesses to post office robberies are from Christianson and Hubinette (1993).

30. The study of four hundred individuals' most traumatic memories was carried out by Christianson and Loftus (1990).

31. Evidence that the memory of victims is sharper than that of bystanders can be found in Yuille and Cutshall (1986).

32. Christianson (1992) discusses the time of testing variable in greater detail.

33. The quote from Atwood is found on page 298 of her 1996 novel.

34. Information on the differences elicited by the use of recall and recognition tests is discussed in Christianson (1992).

35. Sven Christianson's comment concerning the relationship between information to be remembered and the traumatic experience itself is located on page 285 of his (1992) literature review.

36. Christianson argues for boosts in early perceptual processing and late conceptual processing in his 1992 review.

37. The report of the Human Capital Initiative Committee is presented in a special issue of the American Psychological Society's newsletter, *Observer*, February 1998.

38. Gold (1995) reviews evidence of neurotransmitters that can impair or enhance memory upon being secreted during stressful situations.

39. A persuasive argument against a separate memory system for traumatic events is presented in Shobe and Kihlstrom (1997).

40. Whitfield (1995) describes the supposed differences between ordinary and traumatic remembering in exactly this way on pages 39–47.

41. Davis et al. (1995) discuss the amygdala's operation in greater detail.

42. That damage to the amygdala causes impaired emotional expression and flat affect is provided in Damasio (1994).

43. LeDoux (1994) describes the two emotional memory pathways.

44. A good review of the action of stress hormones on memory is found in Gold (1995).

45. Information concerning the effects of administration time on hormonal effects is presented by McGaugh (1992).

46. Harmful effects of chronic, rather than acute, stress on the hippocampus are discussed in Moghaddam et al. (1994) and in Diamond et al. (1996). To provide a brief explanation in lay terms, the hippocampus contains more densely packed corticosterone receptors than does any other structure in the nervous system. Corticosterone is a natural hormone that is secreted under conditions of chronic stress, so its reception into the hippocampus implies a direct effect on both declarative and emotional memories. Too much of this hormone leads to neuron death as well as dendritic atrophy in the hippocampus.

47. My description of how epinephrine and glucose work to create traumatic memories is based on information provided by Gold (1995). Gold points out that direct injections of extra glucose cause the same memory effects as epinephrine does.

48. Research showing differential effects of various neurotransmitter systems is considered in Gold (1995).

49. The rapidity and permanence of fear conditioning is discussed in LeDoux (1994).

50. A good overview of recent thinking concerning the complex interaction of chemical and structural systems in the brain, related to memory, can be found in Gold (1995).

## CHAPTER 8

1. Historical information on the study of implicit memory through the ages is from Schacter (1987).

2. Freud presents his theory of repression in a 1915 essay.

3. Roediger (1990) makes the point that dictionaries define memory as explicit.

4. Early research showing that implicit memory occurs within the visual modality was done by Jacoby and Dallas (1981). That implicit memory by priming is obtained within the auditory modality is demonstrated by, among others, Schacter and Church (1992). Tactile priming produces implicit memory in Hamann (1996).

5. The story of Claparède is told in Schacter (1987).

6. Information about H. M. is found in Hilts (1995).

7. The quote providing examples of implicit abilities that amnesics have preserved is found on page 510 of Schacter (1987).

8. Several of Oliver Sacks's books are collections of case studies from patients he has treated for neurological deficits. These books are intelligent, entertaining, and analytical—the perfect combination for students in my cognitive science courses. To name only a few: *The Man Who Mistook His Wife for a Hat* (1970), *Awakenings* (1973), and *An Anthropologist on Mars* (1995).

9. Average rates of speed for speaking are provided in Tartter (1986). Average rates for reading are supplied in Carroll (1999).

10. Many experimenters have published studies in which some version of the priming paradigm presented here is used. Jacoby (1988) is one of the first to have developed it in the context of implicit memory.

11. So many important priming studies have been conducted on amnesics that it is difficult to know whose work to cite. The earliest studies were done by Warrington and Weiskrantz (1968), whose research did not receive the attention it deserved at the time. A representative study comparing amnesics and normal subjects, within the context of a developing subfield of implicit memory, was conducted by Graf, Squire, and Mandler (1984). They tested individuals whose amnesia resulted from three different types of injury or disease, thereby generalizing the effect across several neurological bases.

12. The fact that normal subjects do not strategize their implicit responses by pulling information from explicit stores, and that their results on implicit tests are statistically independent of their results on explicit tests, is explained by Schacter (1995).

13. Experimental differences between explicit and implicit memory are described in several articles: Schacter (1987), Roediger (1990), and Tulving and Schacter (1990).

14. The neurological system theory of implicit memory is presented in Schacter (1992).

15. Squire is also known for advocating a neurological system theory but believes the procedural system is adequate to the task. The idea that priming should be considered a part of the procedural (nondeclarative) system is espoused in Squire, Knowlton, and Musen (1993).

16. Schacter's characterization of priming as memory is quoted from page 818 of Schacter (1995).

17. An argument for priming as a perceptual system, rather than a form of memory, is found in Tulving and Schacter (1990). In his later review (1995), however, Schacter seems uncertain as to whether he now believes priming is a form of memory or a system of perception.

18. That amnesics can use new factual information and vocabulary on implicit tests is presented in Schacter (1987).

19. The double dissociation seen in patients with Alzheimer's and Huntington's is brought out in Schacter (1995).

20. The cognitive processing theory of implicit memory is explained in Roediger (1990).

21. Whitfield's (1995) words concerning the "scientific" study of body memories are on page 243.

22. The fact that concentration camp survivors report psychosomatic complaints is from Niederland (1981).

23. Reichian theory is described in West (1994).

24. Contemporary offshoots of Reichian therapy are described by Cranmer (1994).

25. Marcher describes Bodydynamics herself in an interview published by Bernhardt (1992). The two quotes are found on pages 281 and 286, respectively.

26. Conversion disorder's history dating back to 1900 B.C. is mentioned in Boffeli and Guze (1992).

27. Diagnostic criteria and symptoms of somatization disorder are located in DSM-IV (First, 1994).

28. The fact that DSM-IV does not require any memory problem for a diagnosis of somatization disorder is directly contradicted by van der Kolk et al. (1996). They state that "amnesia is one of the criteria for somatization disorder (DSM-IV)" (page 85). DSM-IV contains no such requirement, even though it says on page 449 that "dissociative symptoms such as amnesia" are possible.

29. Somatic symptoms in 75% of PTSD sufferers are discussed in Horowitz, Wilner, Kaltrieder, and Alvarez (1980).

30. The study showing that 42 percent of American adults have been misdiagnosed is presented in an editorial entitled "Medical Mistakes" in *American Medical News* (1997).

31. Comorbidity of conversion disorder is discussed in Boffeli and Guze (1992).

32. Comorbidity of somatization disorder with eating disorders is presented in Mehler and Weiner (1993).

33. Sports commentator Scott Hamilton said repeatedly during figure skater Caryn Kadavy's winning performance at the January 3, 1997, Ladies Professional Championship that because she had the flu and an inner ear infection, she had nothing else to rely on but muscle memory.

34. Schacter (1987) mentions some of these applications.

## CHAPTER 9

1. This quote is found on page 7 of Springer and Deutsch (1993).

2. Cognitive scientists use many synonymous terms for hemispheric differences. Readers who wish to conduct library research in this area may find a list of them helpful. Try cerebral or hemispheric lateralization, asymmetry, specialization, dominance, or differences.

3. A brief history of contributions from Dax and Broca is located in Springer and Deutsch (1993). Although its title is misleading, this book provides a fairly accurate, yet concise, explanation of contemporary research into hemispheric differences.

4. Pavlov's interest in hemispheric differences is discussed briefly in Hugdahl (1995).

5. Springer and Deutsch (1993) also discuss the historical contributions of Jackson and Sperry.

6. The first study of split-brain memory was done by Zaidel and Sperry (1974).

7. Evidence that verbal and visual forms of memory are mediated by left and right hemispheres, respectively, is plentiful in the asymmetry literature. An overview is presented in Springer and Deutsch (1993).

8. Research regarding hemispheric governance of music is explained in Springer and Deutsch (1993).

9. The right hemisphere's linguistic abilities are mentioned in many scientific journal articles and monographs, so it is difficult to select only one or two citations. The preeminent expert on right hemisphere language is Eran Zaidel. One of his general reviews on the topic is Zaidel (1985). Two references in which right hemisphere language is discussed in more recent years and from other points of view are Bottini et al. (1994) and Van Lancker (1991).

10. Evidence that right hemisphere processes may be scattered across larger areas of cerebral tissue is considered in Springer and Deutsch (1993).

11. Dahlia Zaidel (1995) reports that commisurotomy is very rare now that better drugs are available to treat severe epilepsy.

12. Carroll (1999) discusses the effects of hemispherectomy at different ages.

13. Springer and Deutsch (1993) consider the effects of sex and handedness on cerebral lateralization.

14. Lashley (1950) proposed the principle of equipotentiality. In frustration after twenty unsuccessful years of research attempting to find a specific area of memory storage, Lashley remarked, with a discouraged tongue in cheek, that "the necessary conclusion is that learning is just not possible" (page 477).

15. Penfield's research on the engram is described in Penfield and Perot (1963).

16. The quote about the ugly fact is from Huxley (1898).

17. Evidence regarding hippocampal tissue removal and memory ability is described in Jones-Gotman (1986).

18. Evidence that neural storage is linked to the locus of processing is found in Springer and Deutsch (1993).

19. The example of remembering a stranger's face is greatly simplified for the sake of clarity. Although both hemispheres are capable of processing normal faces, there is agreement in the literature that the right hemisphere is best at facial processing, especially of unfamiliar faces. However, it is also likely that the left hemisphere is better than the right at perceiving isolated facial features (such as nose, eyes). The everyday perception of a face is actually made possible by both hemispheres working in a more integrated fashion and at a level of finer detail than my example suggests. Likewise, certain aspects of a stranger's voice, even in so scant a sample as the word "hello," are probably perceived by one hemisphere while other aspects are perceived by the other.

20. The explanation of the medial temporal lobe system's binding together dispersed neurons to form a memory follows Squire and Zola-Morgan (1991).

21. Convergence zones are proposed by Damasio (1990).

22. Hemispheric differences that suggest the existence of two memory systems are described in Zaidel (1995).

23. A review of early reports on topographical memory loss is provided in Zangwill and Wyke (1990).

24. Evidence that the right hemisphere excels at memory for typical faces is abundant in the literature. A few of the many possible references are Cormier and Jackson (1995) and Schweinberger and Sommer (1991).

25. The experiment showing left hemisphere superiority for atypical visual recognition was done by Zaidel (1988).

26. The experiment using surrealistic paintings as stimuli was conducted by Zaidel and Kasher (1989).

27. Evidence of poor right hemisphere performance in recognizing disorganized faces was gathered by Zaidel (1991).

28. Gazzaniga uses the chicken/shovel case study as evidence for his left hemisphere interpreter theory in at least four books: Gazzaniga and LeDoux (1978), Gazzaniga (1985), Gazzaniga (1988), and Gazzaniga (1992).

29. The quote indicating an abundance of examples demonstrating left hemisphere interpretation is from page 13 of Gazzaniga (1988).

30. The experiment in which the left hemisphere inferred boiling from pan and water was done by Gazzaniga and Smylie (1984).

31. Right hemisphere superiority in correct recognition of pictures from a photographic scene was obtained by Phelps and Gazzaniga (1992).

32. Results of the split-brain patient whose right hemisphere is more veridical in recognizing forms, faces, and words are presented in Metcalfe, Funnell, and Gazzaniga (1995).

33. The strong critique of Metcalfe, Funnell, and Gazzaniga's (1995) study was published by Chiarello and Beeman (1997). Their quoted words are found on page 343.

34. The research showing that right hemisphere damage impairs autobiographical recollection of emotional episodes was done by Cimino et al. (1991).

35. The idea that right hemisphere emotion may be subcortical, while left hemisphere emotion is not, is explained fully in Gainotti, Caltagirone, and Zoccolotti (1993).

36. Autonomic responses mediated by the right hemisphere have been investigated by Hugdahl (1995).

37. Differences in incidental and intentional learning are offered in Luria and Simernitskaya (1977).

38. Conceptual priming along similar time courses occurs in both hemispheres according to Richards and Chiarello (1995).

39. Stem completion priming that was better in the right hemisphere than in the left was found by Marsolek, Kosslyn, and Squire (1992).

40. The flawed study suggesting right hemisphere dominance for traumatic memory recall was conducted by Schiffer, Teicher, and Papanicolaou (1995).

41. The idea that personal relevance is especially critical to right hemisphere memory is presented in Van Lancker (1991).

42. HERA is best explained in Nyberg, Cabeza, and Tulving (1996).

43. Ibid.

44. The quote concerning specific memory impairments among split-brain patients is found on page 215 of Zaidel (1995).

45. Robert Ornstein's views are described by Springer and Deutsch (1993) on page 6.

46. Springer and Deutsch (1993) refer to the "occupational hazard" of hemispheric differences research as "dichotomania" on page 7.

# CHAPTER 10

1. Estimates of alien abductions are considered by Newman and Baumeister (1996). According to their discussion, recent estimates range from 55,000 to 15 million.

2. A full explanation is in Bartlett (1932).

3. A brief review of the history behind false memory research, starting with Bartlett and working through classic investigations using various types of stimuli, is offered in Roediger and McDermott (1995).

4. The study showing false memory for a man hitting a girl at a pond was conducted by Haugaard et al. (1991).

5. That subjects will bet money on their false memories was determined in research described in Weingardt, Toland, and Loftus (1994).

6. The statistics concerning voting behavior are presented and discussed in Garry and Loftus (1994), but they were originally gathered by Abelson, Loftus, and Greenwald (1992).

7. The false word recall experiment that fueled false memory research in the late 1990s was done by Roediger and McDermott (1995).

8. The sample words related to "needle" are taken from the original study by Deese (1959), which Roediger and McDermott replicated.

9. These results are presented in Roediger and McDermott (1995).

10. McDermott (1996) offers information concerning several of the points in this list. The sixth item, that the effect persists despite the experimenter's warning, was discovered in research done by Payne et al. (1997).

11. Subjects who argued that associates were presented despite a tape recording were part of a study done by Payne et al. (1996).

12. Tulving (1985) deserves credit for formulating the remember/know test.

13. These results are presented in Roediger and McDermott (1995).

14. Research in which subjects claimed to remember which voice was used to present a nonexistent associate word was done by Payne et al. (1996).

15. Subjects' claims to "remember" whether a lure was presented visually or auditorily are described in Payne et al. (1997).

16. Explicit memory of the position of an unpresented lure in a list was investigated by Read (1996).

17. Evidence that justifying remember/know distinctions does not attenuate the false recall effect for associated words is presented in Payne et al. (1997).

18. The experiment in which misinformation was "remembered" from slides rather than a narrative was conducted by Roediger, Jacoby, and McDermott (1996).

19. The notion that repetition increases perceptions of truth has been verified by several experimenters. One recent demonstration is found in Begg, Anas, and Farinacci (1992). That repetition enhances subjects' preference for a stimulus was demonstrated in Zajonc (1968).

20. The burglary simulation in which repetition had strong effects on misinformation was done by Zaragoza and Mitchell (1996).

21. The effect of repeated testing and a two-day delay on false memory for unpresented word associates was done by McDermott (1996).

22. The study showing false memory for unpresented actions was done by Lampinen (1996) as part of an unpublished dissertation. It is described in Payne et al. (1997).

23. Described in Ceci (1995).

24. The boy's false description of the mousetrap event is found on page 103 of Ceci (1995).

25. The study in which 44 percent of preschool children remembered at least one false event in the very first interview was done by Ceci et al. (1994).

26. Ceci (1995) describes his research on the relationship between emotional valence and willingness to accept false stories as authentic memories.

27. The case study of the teenage boy, for which Loftus developed a standard method for false memory testing in adults, is reported in Loftus and Pickrell (1995).

28. Ibid.

29. On page 723, Loftus and Pickrell (1995) present this quote from the subject who remembered so vividly seeking her mother in a series of dressing rooms.

30. The false memory experiment that included being hospitalized, spilling punch, evacuating a store, or releasing the brake was conducted by Hyman, Husband, and Billings (1995).

31. A study by Hyman and Billings (1998) contains the quotes concerning the experimenter's suggestion (page 6) and the subject's recollection of spilling punch (page 10).

32. The study comparing false memories for being lost in a mall and receiving an enema was done by Pezdek, Finger, and Hodge (1997).

33. Anecdotes of false memory for traumatic events are presented in Garry and Loftus (1994).

34. Ibid.

35. Underwood (1965) coined the idea of implicit associative response to explain the false word recall obtained by Deese. Roediger and McDermott (1995) resurrected the notion and developed it to account for their recent findings of false memory for words.

36. The theory of spreading activation has a venerable history in cognitive psychology. It was developed by Collins and Loftus (1975).

37. The speculation that explicitly "remembered" associates are brought to conscious awareness during initial activation is provided in Roediger and McDermott (1995).

38. The theory of source or reality monitoring was first suggested by Johnson and Raye (1981). It is developed more fully in Johnson, Hashtroudi, and Lindsay (1993).

39. Garry and Loftus (1994) present the story of Reagan's error in misremembering the film clip as true history.

40. The relationship of alien abduction memories to sleep, long drives, and natural brain phenomena related to hypnagogic and hypnopompic hallucinations is discussed in Clark and Loftus (1996).

41. The quote comparing intracranial to extraterrestrial sources is from page 141 of Clark and Loftus (1996).

42. Neuropsychological evidence that the frontal lobes are involved in source monitoring is presented in Schacter and Curran (1995).

43. Subjects' classification of autobiographical memories as real or imagined on the basis of perceptual detail and inferential reasoning was obtained by Johnson et al. (1988).

44. Schacter and Curran (1995) present clinical evidence that source monitoring is at least partly dependent on the frontal lobes.

45. Nyberg, Cabeza, and Tulving (1996) describe the HERA model and analyze experiments that support it.

46. The effects of faulty metamemory on false remembering are considered in O'Sullivan and Howe (1995).

47. The study in which reports of early childhood memories climbed so steeply when subjects were given false information about metamemory was done by Malinoski and Lynn (in preparation) and is described in Loftus (1997).

48. Schematic reconstruction has been used to account for the misinformation effect in eyewitness testimony for many years (Loftus, 1979). Its application to false event memory is included in Hyman, Husband, and Billings (1995).

49. The study comparing false memories of various religious practices was conducted by Pezdek, Finger, and Hodge (1997).

50. The social demands of false memory studies are considered in some detail in Hyman, Husband, and Billings (1995).

51. Jones (1995) discusses social demand in laboratory settings, as do most other methodology texts.

52. Ceci (1995) reports on experts' inability to identify true memories.

53. PET scans showing no difference in brain activity during true and false recognition were conducted by Schacter et al. (1996).

54. The 1994 quote concerning inability to distinguish between true and false memories is from page 375 of Garry and Loftus (1994).

55. The recent quote concerning the inability to differentiate between true and false memories is from page 16 of Hyman and Billings (1998).

## CHAPTER 11

1. The survey showing that three-quarters of clinical psychologists report using memory recovery techniques was done by Poole et al. (1995).

2. Studies testing the efficacy of EMDR for processing existing memories of trauma are reviewed by a team of clinical practitioners in Tolin et al. (1995). Braun's (1988) BASK model is also used to process existing memories of past traumas according to behavioral, affective, sensory, and knowledge-based components of the recollection.

3. Janet's (1925) reports of false memory being intentionally implanted are discussed in Bowers and Farvolden (1996).

4. Incorrect assertions that detail, emotion, honesty, and disbelief (among others) are reliable indicators of a memory's authenticity are found on pages 166–73 of Fredrickson (1992). Incorrect reports that consistency, articulate speech, or willingness to confront (among others) are reliable indicators of a memory's authenticity are found on page 369 of Perlman (1993). Incredibly, he goes on to suggest that "we need proof to assert that something is a fantasy, and we should assume that it is reality when it comes to early memories" (page 370).

5. The quote is from page 282 of Lindsay and Read (1994).

6. That subjects use repression as a spontaneous explanation for the inability to remember an event that never happened is mentioned in Hyman and Pentland (1996).

7. Clients who commonly request hypnotism for memory enhancement are discussed in Fredrickson (1992). The quote is from page 148.

8. The practicing psychiatrist whose patients ask for amytal interviews is Piper (1993).

9. A discussion of the negative effects on metamemory of pleas to try harder in retrieval is found in O'Sullivan and Howe (1995).

10. Concerns about the television technique are raised in Laurence and Perry (1983). The quote is on page 524.

11. Evidence of confirmatory bias in psychotherapeutic assessment is provided in Lee et al. (1995).

12. Descriptive psycholinguistic rules of standard social conversation are discussed in Grice (1975).

13. The experiment in which children's errors on misleading questions was reduced by 26 percent through an explanation of socioemotional and sociolinguistic features of forensic discourse was done by Saywitz and Moan-Hardie (1994).

14. The theory of socioemotional effects on memory, used as a basis for Saywitz and Moan-Hardie's (1994) intervention, is described by Paris (1988).

15. Preliminary information on questioning is presented in Geiselman and Machlovitz (1987).

16. The superiority of free recall in open-ended questions is discussed in Hilgard and Loftus (1979).

17. Effects of subtle reinforcement are discussed in Fruzzetti et al. (1992) and also in Terr (1994).

18. Evidence that therapists' questions alter clients' memories of their own dreams is found in Belicki and Bowers (1982).

19. One of many researchers to encourage a second full recall is Smith (1983).

20. Watching oneself remember on videotape reduces overconfidence in memory according to Kassin (1985).

21. Allende's (1994) words are found on page 23.

22. Evidence that music cues memory in Alzheimer's patients is presented in Hanser and Clair (1995).

23. The use of battle sounds for retrieving war memories is discussed in Kolb (1988).

24. The continuous music technique is described and evaluated in Eich (1995).

25. The experiment in which subjects' accuracy increased from 40 percent to 60 percent after context reinstatement was done by Malpass and Devine (1980).

26. The most complete description of the cognitive interview and its rationale is provided in Fisher and Geiselman (1992). Most of the information on the cognitive interview presented in this chapter is from a review in Fisher, McCauley, and Geiselman (1994). This review also includes a full discussion of the empirical evidence that supports the efficacy of the procedure.

27. Matlin (1998) considers tip-of-the-tongue research in some detail.

28. Fisher, McCauley, and Geiselman (1994) discuss several forms of independent evidence that demonstrate the effectiveness of the cognitive interview.

29. Evidence that the DES and CIS correlate with false memory is provided by Hyman and Billings (1998). The obtained values were $r = .48$ for the DES and $r = .36$ for the CIS, both respectable correlations.

30. Two forms of the Gudjonsson Suggestibility Scale are described in Gudjonsson (1984) and Gudjonsson (1987).

31. The study that used the GSS to compare confabulation in depressive patients to normal controls is Sigurdsson et al. (1994).

32. That highly suggestible and hypnotizable individuals may be especially prone to both false memory and amnesia for real events is proposed in Baars and McGovern (1995).

33. Standard placebo effects of 55 percent to 60 percent are discussed in Shea (1991).

34. The obedience studies in which subjects delivered electric shock are reported in Milgram (1963).

35. Line length discrimination was affected by peer pressure in Asch (1958).

36. Studies in which teachers' expectations were manipulated are discussed in Rosenthal and Jacobson (1968).

37. Subjects' willingness to spend half days adding random numbers together for no earthly purpose is discussed in Orne (1962).

38. The true story of the woman who identified a man on television as her rapist is told in Lindsay and Read (1994).

39. The power of rapport, social proof, and public commitment to increase suggestibility is discussed in Cialdini (1993). The book also reviews traditional research in social psychology pertaining to suggestibility.

40. The study that obtained larger misinformation effects when leading questions were asked by people who are not seen as having a motive to mislead was done by Dodd and Bradshaw (1980).

41. The misinformation effect was reduced in one recent study when children, rather than adults, provided the misleading information. This study is described in Ceci, Ross, and Toglia (1987).

42. The study showing that 30 percent of adult questions were leading, even though the adults had been warned to remain objective and unbiased, was conducted by Pettit, Fegan, and Howie (1990), as cited by Lindsay and Read (1994).

43. Statistics on the current use of hypnosis as a retrieval enhancement technique are found in Lynn et al. (1997), who cite an in-press survey done by Lynn, Myers, and Malinoski.

44. The 32 percent figure is from Poole et al. (1995).

45. Yapko (1994) provides these statistics.

46. The power of hypnotic suggestion over morphine injection in blocking pain is demonstrated in Stern et al. (1977).

47. Reports of false memory dating to 1888 are cited by Laurence and Perry (1983). The original source, according to Laurence and Perry, is Bernheim (1888/1973).

48. The facts that hypnosis increases inaccuracy, confidence, and misinformation are documented in hundreds of scientific journal articles. A few of the best reviews of this literature include Smith (1983), Erdelyi (1994), and Lynn et al. (1997).

49. Hypnotically enhanced imagery is also demonstrated in a number of scientific articles. Reviews of this literature include Erdelyi (1994) and Lynn et al. (1997).

50. The study in which merely asking a question about noises caused false memories was done by Laurence and Perry (1983).

51. Social factors relevant to the hypnotically induced memory are considered in Krass, Kinoshita, and McConkey (1989).

52. Hypnotized subjects' willingness to guess was tested by Buckhout et al. (1981).

53. The study of hypnotic recall using woodworking accidents was done by Zelig and Beidleman (1981).

54. The quote, based on a review of existing literature, is from page 82 of Lynn et al. (1997).

55. The quote is found on page 44 of Calof (1993), as cited in Lindsay and Read (1994).

56. Professional hypnosis societies that advocate against hypnosis for retrieval enhancement are mentioned in Clark and Loftus (1996).

57. Use of the Frye rule (*Frye v. United States*, 1923) is discussed in Smith (1983).

58. The research in which hypnotized and nonhypnotized subjects underwent age regression and subsequently reported infant memories was done by Spanos (1996).

59. The review of amytal interviews was done by Piper (1993); the quote is from page 465.

60. Piper (1993) mentions these effects of amytal interviewing on page 455.

61. Research teams who have argued that the imagery technique produces temporary dissociation include Lindsay and Read (1994) and Bowers and Farvolden (1996).

62. The study comparing guided imagery and control conditions in memory for bogus events was done by Hyman and Pentland (1996).

## CHAPTER 12

1. It wasn't until 1996, when a collection of articles from both practitioners and scientists was published on the topic of repressed memories (Pezdek & Banks, 1996), that several people on both sides began to suggest genuine collaboration in an effort to gain greater knowledge about memory. Even then, many of the suggestions were riddled with bitter commentary. Most of the concerns about recovered memory voiced between 1990 and 1996 took the form of vehement accusations that served only to further alienate each side from the other.

2. The use of crystal balls and automatic handwriting as common methods of psychical research in the late 1800s is discussed in Schacter (1987).

3. Attention to psychic studies in the late 1800s is discussed in most history of psychology textbooks. One that provides a concise treatment is Schultz and Schultz (1996).

4. A discussion of whether early psychology was to be purely scientific or partly applied is provided in Hergenhahn (1997).

5. Hergenhahn (1997) and Hothersall (1995) both offer information about Lightner Witmer and his establishment of clinical psychology.

6. The response to Freud's lectures at Clark University is discussed in Hornstein (1992). The quotes from Woodworth and Ladd-Franklin concerning psychoanalysis are presented on pages 255 and 256 of Hornstein (1992). Watson's pronouncement of psychoanalysis as "voodooism" is from Schultz and Schultz (1996), page 393.

7. Cattell's response to Freudian theory is described in Hornstein (1992).

8. The quote regarding society's pressure to produce a second type of psychology is from page 639 of Cook (1958).

9. The list of psychiatric privileges that clinical psychologists have won since World War II is from Hergenhahn (1997).

10. Continuing hostility between the American Psychological Association and the American Psychiatric Association is mentioned in Leahey (1991).

11. The APA's intent to emphasize scientific training over professional service in developing the scientist/practitioner model is described in Leahey (1991).

12. The quote that characterizes the scientist/practitioner model as a rhetorical device is from page 995 of Stricker and Trierweiler (1995). The quote claiming that the scientist/practitioner model remains unrealized is found on page 145 of Borkovec (1997).

13. More information on the rationale and history of the Psy.D. is offered in Hergenhahn (1997).

14. The APA's goal "to promote psychology as a science" is stated on page 545 of Hergenhahn (1997).

15. The APA's goal "to advance psychology as a science, as a profession, and a means of promoting human welfare" is presented on page 546 of Hergenhahn (1997).

16. A thorough discussion of the APA's history of capitulating to practitioners is found in Hilgard (1987).

17. Hergenhahn (1997) reports that only 33 percent of all APA members worked in academia by 1985. A small portion of that 33 percent worked as clinical psychologists in both academia and clinical practice.

18. The APS membership in 1999 numbers about 16,000.

19. Average percentages of growth per year, for psychology as a whole and divided into separate areas, are provided in Leahey (1991).

20. The history textbook in which mechanisms of integration are identified is Hilgard (1987).

21. The book on psychology's future is good within its disciplinary limitations: Solso and Massaro (1995). The quoted words are found on the book's dust jacket.

22. The quote from a clinician who argues that we need general information rather than stories of specific case successes is found on page 262 of Erwin (1985). Italics are in the original.

23. McFall, Treat, and Viken (1997) ask the question "Who can count the apples in a seed?" (page 175) in reference to this issue.

24. A more thorough discussion of science and coverage of common flaws in interpreting scientific research can be found in Jones (1995).

25. This quote is on page 326 of Alpert (1996).

26. A general description of the master learner program, in which professors enroll in their colleagues' courses as students, is provided in Jones (1998).

27. Onken (1997) presents literature from the first of several planned collaborative workshops for the National Institute of Drug Abuse.

28. Pennsylvania's efforts to integrate clinical and experimental work is described in Borkovec (1997).

29. The quote is on page 146 of Borkovec (1997).

30. The review of EMDR studies that points out many of the errors I have mentioned was done by four clinicians: Tolin, Montgomery, Kleinknecht, and Lohr (1995).

31. The study was done by Silver, Brooks, and Obenchain (1995).

32. That EMDR holds some promise by virtue of its grounding in the operations of working memory is described fully in Andrade, Kavanagh, and Baddeley (1997). The research described in this article is an outstanding example of collaboration between clinical and experimental sides of psychology that will lead to the development of effective scientific psychotherapies.

33. Some readers might balk at my use of hunting and fishing as examples of licensure. Although a fishing license signifies little more than that one has paid for the privilege of throwing a line in a stream, hunting licenses in some states do require completion of gun safety courses that verify basic knowledge.

34. The exchange between Miller and Koch is described in Leahey (1991). Leahey presents Koch's quote on page 392.

# Glossary

*active memory*—conscious awareness of thoughts or events occurring in the immediate present; also called *short-term memory, immediate memory,* or *working memory.*

*agnosia*—perceptual disorder caused by brain damage in which common objects can be seen and described but are not recognized or identified.

*amygdala*—part of the limbic system that mediates emotionally conditioned learning.

*amytal interview*—a technique in which sodium amytal is injected into the bloodstream while the patient attempts to answer questions about past experiences.

*anamnesis*—a therapeutic strategy of memory instruction for retaining autobiographical events and increasing specificity in encoding.

*anterograde amnesia*—loss of memory for events occurring after brain injury.

*aphasia*—language disturbance.

*aphasic arrest*—temporary inability to speak.

*associative cortex*—outer areas of the brain containing synaptic connections that represent various forms of experience.

*autobiographical memory*—knowledge of one's own life experiences.

*autonoetic awareness*—conscious awareness of feeling as if an event in episodic memory is being reexperienced.

*autonomic*—pertaining to the nervous system that regulates breathing, blood flow, and rapid hormonal changes in response to the environment.

*axon*—the long portion of each neuron that conveys an electrical charge toward the connecting dendrite of the next neuron.

*basal ganglia*—a part of the brain that helps coordinate movement and is linked to procedural memory.

*behaviorism*—the school of thought, common in the United States from 1920 to 1960, in which outward behavior but not mental processes were studied by psychologists.

255

*body memories*—unsupported idea that the muscles, tendons, joints, and organs of the human body are literally capable of remembering information.

*bottom-up processing*—type of unconscious cognitive processing in which direct information from the stimulus itself is given priority, with little aid from conceptual knowledge.

*brain stem*—core structure in the deep center of the brain that regulates life support systems.

*Capgras syndrome*—the belief, caused by brain damage, that one's own family or friends are imposters.

*central fissure*—primary crease in the brain's outer surface that separates the parietal lobe from the frontal lobe.

*cerebellum*—the lower posterior portion of the brain that coordinates physical movement.

*cerebral laterality*—the notion that separate cognitive functions are governed by independent hemispheres.

*childhood amnesia*—the normal inability of adults to retrieve accurate memories of very early childhood events; sometimes called *infantile amnesia*.

*cognitive interview*—an interview process that uses specific techniques to enhance retrieval of episodic memories.

*cognitive science*—the interdisciplinary study of the human mind and brain, comprised of the disciplines of neurology, anthropology, philosophy, computer science, linguistics, and cognitive psychology.

*commisurotomy*—surgical separation of the left and right hemispheres by severing the band of fibers that connects the hemispheres.

*confabulation*—unconscious development and recounting of long bizarre stories about events that never occurred.

*confirmatory bias*—normal tendency to inspect most carefully those pieces of evidence that will confirm one's assumptions.

*confounding variables*—factors that are linked to variables of scientific interest in a way that precludes accurate interpretation of results.

*consolidation*—the neurological process of creating a permanent memory.

*context dependence*—the fact that recall is best when attempted in the same context as encoding.

*context reinstatement*—creation of the mental and physical context in which a previous experience transpired.

*continuous music technique*—a method by which desired moods can be temporarily instated for the purpose of retrieval enhancement.

*conversion*—a rare mental disorder that causes physical symptoms of ill health to occur with no known physiological basis.

*cortex*—large outer regions of the brain containing gray matter.

*decay*—common cause of forgetting as the strength of a stored trace naturally weakens with time.

*declarative memory*—knowledge of factual information; also called *semantic memory*.

*dendrites*—tree-like branches that reach toward other neurons and accept synaptic transmissions.

*diencephalon*—brain structure that is thought to play a significant role in consolidating new memories.

*dissociative disorders*—a set of mental disorders characterized by a separation of identity, personality, and/or cognitive processing.

*dissociative identity disorder*—psychological division into two or more selves, each of whom holds memories separate from the others; formerly called *multiple personality disorder.*

*distributed practice*—the fact that memory is best for material learned gradually over time.

*distributed storage*—method of representing information in neurons that are scattered throughout large regions of cortex.

*ecological validity*—the extent to which a research study investigates typical behavior in everyday life.

*electroencephelograph (EEG)*—measurement of electrical activity in the brain.

*electromyelograph (EMG)*—measurement of electrical activity in the muscles.

*emotion network model*—the idea that each emotion is represented in the mind by a separate organizing feature that pulls emotionally related information together into an individual category.

*empirical*—based on observable evidence, not theory.

*encoding*—the process of directing new information into long-term memory.

*encoding specificity*—the fact that items are best recalled when the conditions of encoding and retrieval are similar.

*engram*—hypothesized pattern of neural connections that represents a past experience; also called *trace.*

*epinephrine*—stress hormone produced by the human body as part of the sympathetic nervous system's "fight-or-flight" response.

*episodic memory*—knowledge of specific past events.

*event-related potential (ERP)*—comparison of electrical activity in specific neuroanatomical regions while the subject performs different tasks.

*experimental psychology*—very broadly, the scientific study of the human mind and behavior including developmental, social, physiological, cognitive, organizational, comparative, health, and sport psychologies. Makes use of a wide variety of experimental and nonexperimental research techniques. Sometimes used to refer to any part of psychology that is not directly concerned with the diagnosis and treatment of mental disorders.

*explicit memory*—conscious awareness of remembering material that has been retrieved.

*eye movement desensitization and reprocessing (EMDR)*—a therapeutic technique that helps people learn to cope with distressing memories.

*flashbulb memory*—a vivid visual memory of a significant event.

*frontal lobe*—the area of cortex located toward the front and top of the head, which is involved in higher mental activities of thinking, planning, and organizing.

*fugue*—very rare mental disorder, preceded by extreme stress, in which individuals suddenly forget their personal identities.

*functional magnetic resonance imaging (f MRI)*—scanning technique that shows the structure and active functioning of the brain.

*glucose*—the brain's primary source of fuel.

*hemispherectomy*—surgical removal of one cerebral hemisphere.

*hemispheric encoding/retrieval asymmetry (HERA)*—a theory that the right prefrontal cortex retrieves episodic memories, while the left prefrontal cortex retrieves semantic memories and encodes episodic memories.

*hippocampus*—part of the medial temporal lobe within the brain that is especially important for consolidating and storing new memories.

*hypothalamus*—inner part of the brain that controls food intake, endocrine levels, water balance, sexual rhythms, and the autonomic nervous system.

*iconic memory*—recall or recognition in the form of a visual image that lasts only a few seconds after stimulus presentation.

*immediate memory*—conscious awareness of thoughts or events occurring in the immediate present; also called *working memory*, *short term memory*, or *active memory*.

*implicit memory*—unconscious knowledge of the past, based on previous experience.

*incidental learning*—remembering without intending to remember.

*infantile amnesia*—the normal inability of adults to retrieve accurate memories of events that took place during infancy or very early childhood; sometimes called *childhood amnesia*.

*intentional learning*—approaching an event or body of information with the purposeful intent of remembering it.

*interference*—common cause of forgetting as newly learned material interferes with the stored traces of existing material.

*lexical knowledge*—information regarding pronunciation, spelling, and the appropriate usage of words.

*lexicon*—mental vocabulary.

*limbic system*—part of the brain that controls motivation and emotion and plays a significant role in remembering. The hippocampus and amygdala are located in the limbic system.

*lobectomy*—surgical removal of one lobe of the brain.

*long term memory*—all knowledge of facts, events, skills, and procedures held in the mind for more than a few seconds.

*long term potentiation*—an electro-chemical process that causes freshly linked neurons to enjoy a boost in excitatory potential, allowing a temporary period during which the new memory can be activated with ease.

*massed practice*—ineffective process in which we attempt to learn a body of information all at one time.

*medial temporal lobe*—area of the brain that allows us to create new memories, comprised of hippocampus and adjacent areas.

*metamemory*—awareness of our own memory performance.

*misinformation effect*—the fact that subtly misleading information, often in the form of a single word, leads subjects to create inaccurate memories.

*mnemonic*—pertaining to memory.

*mnemonic interlock*—retrieval efforts that continually occur at shallow levels, and can go no deeper, so that rumination of the same general idea repeats itself.

*Mnemosyne*—the Greek goddess of memory; pronounced NEM-uh-zyne.

*mood congruence*—the normal tendency to remember material that closely matches our moods at the time of encoding, so that sad stimuli are best remembered when we feel sad, happy stimuli when we feel happy.

*mood dependence*—the fact that retrieval is best when mood at the time of encoding is similar to mood at the time of retrieval.

*multiple personality disorder*—psychological division into two or more selves, each of whom holds memories separate from the others; now called *dissociative identity disorder*.

*myelin*—a fatty sheath that covers the axons, allowing for rapid transmission of nerve impulses.

*neural networks*—bundles of neurons that can be activated simultaneously despite dispersed locations.

*neuroblasts*—baby brain cells that are destined by DNA to become neurons.

*neurology*—the study of the anatomy and physiology of the human brain and nervous system, along with medical treatment of dysfunction.

*neuron*—the basic cell of the brain.

*neuropsychology*—the study of psychological processes and disorders as they are related to the anatomy and physiology of the brain.

*neurotransmitters*—chemicals released when a neuron is stimulated by electrical activity.

*nonsense syllable*—three-letter nonword syllable (like "zud") originally created by Ebbinghaus to study normal forgetting.

*nucleus*—the center of control for each cell.

*olfactory nerve*—bundle of axons that mediate the sense of smell.

*organic amnesia*—memory loss attributed to physical cause.

*overgenerality bias*—failure to provide specific memories, often observed in people who suffer from depression.

*pain congruence*—the fact that current level of pain alters memories of chronic pain that was experienced in the past.

*parietal lobe*—the area of cortex, located beneath the top of the head, that governs sensory activity.

*placebo effect*—a common type of bias in which the mere belief that a treatment will have an effect actually causes the effect to occur.

*plasticity*—the brain's ability to change automatically in response to its environment.

*positron emission tomography (PET)*—scanning technique that displays the functional operations of the brain.

*post traumatic stress disorder (PTSD)*—a mental ailment marked by the inability to forget traumatic memories that are so vivid they seem alive.

*primacy*—ability to best remember that which comes first.

*priming*—unconscious activation of neurons that represent certain details of a memory.

*proactive interference*—the fact that experiences occurring before an event alter the memory of it.

*procedural memory*—knowledge of skills and procedures.

*prosopagnosia*—very rare inability to recognize familiar faces, caused by brain damage.

*pruning*—the normal process of neuronal death that improves brain organization so that greater resources can be devoted to surviving neurons.

*psychogenic amnesia*—loss of memory following the occurrence of a psychologically traumatic event.

*psycholingustics*—the study of psychological processes used to produce or comprehend language.

*psychotherapist*—broadly, anyone who provides psychological therapy, including psychiatrists (M.D.), clinical psychologists (Ph.D.), counseling psychologists (Ph.D. or M.A.), social workers (M.S.W.), or others having no formal education in a psychological field.

*reality monitoring*—unconscious process by which our minds determine whether an experience really occurred or was part of a dream or thought.

*recall*—ability to remember past information without cues.

*recency*—ability to best remember that which comes last.

*recognition*—ability to remember past information that has been presented again.

*reduplicative paramnesia*—the belief, caused by brain damage, that one exists in two physical locations at the same time.

*reminiscence bump*—the normal increase of recall for memories of events that occurred between fifteen and thirty years of age.

*repisodic memory*—generic recall or recognition for similar events that occur repeatedly, omitting or confusing the details of each instance.

*reticular activating system*—collection of neurons within the brain stem that maintain physical alertness and arousal.

*retroactive interference*—the fact that experiences occurring after an event alter the memory of it.

*retrograde amnesia*—loss of memory for events that occurred prior to brain injury.

*rote repetition*—the act of memorizing by repeating a stimulus over and over again.

*schema*—knowledge of the typical sequence of events that is likely to occur in a highly generalized experience.

*semantic memory*—knowledge of factual information; also called *declarative memory*.

*sensory cortex*—area of the parietal lobe that mediates physical sensations in the body.

*serial position curve*—data produced when short term memory is tested. Stimuli in first and last positions tend to be remembered best.

*short term memory*—conscious awareness of thoughts or events occurring in the immediate present; also called *working memory, immediate memory,* or *active memory*.

*social desirability bias*—normal human tendency to attempt to please others, often a serious problem in psychological research.

*somatization*—psychological conflict that manifests itself in physical symptoms of the human body.

*source amnesia*—common aspect of memory in which the experience of an event or fact is retained but information as to its original source is lost.

*source monitoring*—unconscious process by which our minds decide the most likely source of a piece of remembered information.

*spreading activation theory*—theory proposing that neurons connected by experience sometimes share physical activation.

*state dependence*—the fact that information is recalled best when an individual recreates the same physical state as occurred during encoding.

*Sternberg paradigm*—an experimental technique that shows reaction times increasing in linear proportion to the number of stimuli in short-term memory.

*subcortical transfer*—secondary connecting points between the two hemispheres that are still intact even in the surgically split brain.

*suggestibility*—normal human susceptibility to accept very subtle external suggestions.

*Sylvian fissure*—primary crease in the brain's outer surface, which separates the temporal lobe from the frontal lobe.

*synapses*—tiny gaps between neurons that allow communication.

*temporal lobe*—area of cortex near the side of the head that governs hearing.

*thalamus*—the part of the brain through which all senses except smell must pass, used for perceptual coordination.

*top-down processing*—unconscious procedure in which greater attention is given to background experience and context than to the stimulus itself.

*topographical memory*—ability to remember physical locations.

*Wada test*—injection of an anesthetic that temporarily numbs one hemisphere of the brain.

*weapon focus*—common finding in eyewitness testimony research in which people remember a weapon but not the person who used it.

*working memory*—conscious awareness of thoughts or events occurring in the immediate present; also called *immediate memory, short term memory,* or *active memory.*

# References

Abelson, R. P., Loftus, E. F., & Greenwald, A. G. (1992). Attempts to improve the accuracy of self-reports of voting. In J. M. Tanur (Ed.), *Questions about survey questions: Meaning, memory, expression, and social interactions in surveys* (pp. 138–153). New York: Russell Sage.

Allende, I. (1994). *Paula.* New York: HarperCollins.

Alpert, J. L. (1996). Professional practice, psychological science, and the recovered memory debate. In K. Pezdek & W. P. Banks (Eds.), *The recovered memory/false memory debate* (pp. 325–340). San Diego: Academic Press.

Andrade, J., Kavanagh, D., & Baddeley, A. (1997). Eye-movements and visual imagery: A working memory approach to the treatment of post-traumatic stress disorder. *British Journal of Clinical Psychology, 36,* 209–223.

Aristotle. (1952a). De anima. In R. M. Hutchins (Ed.), *Great books of the Western world* (Vol. 8, pp. 631–668). Chicago: Encyclopaedia Britannica.

Aristotle. (1952b). On memory and reminiscence. In R. M. Hutchins (Ed.), *Great books of the Western world* (Vol. 8, pp. 690–695). Chicago: Encyclopaedia Britannica.

Arnold, S. E., & Trojanowski, J. Q. (1996). Human fetal hippocampal development: I. Cytoarchitecture, myeloarchitecture, and neuronal morphologic features, *Journal of Comparative Neurology, 367,* 274–292.

Arnold, S. E., & Trojanowski, J. Q. (1996). Human fetal hippocampal development: II. The neuronal cytoskeleton. *The Journal of Comparative Neurology, 367,* 293–307.

Asch, S. E. (1956). Studies of independence and conformity: I. A minority of one against a unanimous majority. *Psychological Monographs, 70.*

Asch, S. E. (1958). Effects of group pressure upon modification and distortion of judgments. In E. E. Maccoby, T. M. Newcomb, & E. L. Hartley (Eds.), *Readings in social psychology.* New York: Holt, Rinehart, & Winston.

Atkinson, R. L., Atkinson, R. C., Smith, E. E., & Bem, D. J. (1990). *Introduction to psychology.* New York: Harcourt Brace Jovanovich.

Atwood, M. (1996). *Alias Grace.* New York: Doubleday.

Baars, B. J. (1986). *The cognitive revolution in psychology.* New York: Guilford Press.

Baars, B. J., & McGovern, K. (1995). Steps toward healing: False memories and traumagenic amnesia may coexist in vulnerable populations. *Consciousness and Cognition, 4,* 68–74.

Bahrick, H. P., Hall, L. K., & Berger, S. A. (1996). Accuracy and distortion in memory for high school grades. *Psychological Science, 7*, 265–271.

Baker, B. (1994, January/February). The changing face of social work. *Common Boundaries*, 32–37.

Banaji, M. R., & Crowder, R. G. (1989). The bankruptcy of everyday memory. *American Psychologist, 44(9)*, 1185–1193.

Barclay, C. R., & Wellman, H. M. (1986). Accuracies and inaccuracies in autobiographical memories. *Journal of Memory and Language, 25*, 93–103.

Bartlett, F. C. (1932). *Remembering.* Cambridge, MA: Cambridge University Press.

Begg, I. M., Anas, A., & Farinacci, S. (1992). Dissociation of processes in belief: Source recollection, statement familiarity, and the illusion of truth. *Journal of Experimental Psychology: General, 121*, 446–458.

Belicki, K., & Bowers, P. (1982). The role of demand characteristics and hypnotic ability in dream change following a presleep instruction. *Journal of Abnormal Psychology, 91*, 426–432.

Belli, R. F., & Loftus, E. F. (1996). The pliability of autobiographical memory: Misinformation and the false memory problem. In D. C. Rubin (Ed.), *Remembering our past: Studies in autobiographical memory* (pp. 157–179). New York: Cambridge University Press.

Belli, R. F., Windschitl, P. D., McCarthy, T. T., & Winfrey, S. E. (1992). Detecting memory impairment with a modified test procedure: Manipulating retention interval with centrally presented event items. *Journal of Experimental Psychology: Learning, Memory, and Cognition, 18*, 356–367.

Bernhardt, P. (1992). Individuation, mutual connection, and the body's resources: an interview with Lisbeth Marcher. *Pre- and Peri-Natal Psychology Journal, 6*, 281–293.

Bernheim, H. (1888/1973). *Hypnosis and suggestion in psychotherapy.* New York: Aronson.

Bikel, O. (Producer). (1995, April 4). Divided memories, Part I. *Frontline.* Alexandria, VA: Public Broadcasting System.

Black, J. (1997). Common symptoms: Abuse related illnesses. [On-line.] Available: http://wchat.on.ca/web/asarc/illness.html.

Boffeli, T. J., & Guze, S. B. (1992). The simulation of neurologic disease. *Psychiatric Clinics of North America, 15*, 301–310.

Borkovec, T. D. (1997). On the need for a basic science approach to psychotherapy research. *Psychological Science, 8(3)*, 145–147.

Bothwell, R. K., Deffenbacher, K. A., & Brigham, J. C. (1987). Correlation of eyewitness accuracy and confidence: Optimality hypothesis revisited. *Journal of Applied Psychology, 72*, 691–695.

Bottini, G., Corcoran, R., Sterzi, R., Paulesu, E., Schenone, P., Scarpa, P., Frackowiak, R. S. J., & Frith, C. D. (1994). The role of the right hemisphere in the interpretation of figurative aspects of language: A positron emission tomography activation study. *Brain, 117*, 1241–1253.

Bower, G. H. (1981). Mood and memory. *American Psychologist, 36*, 129–148.

Bower, G. H., Monteiro, K. P., & Gilligan, S. G. (1978). Emotional mood as a context for learning and recall. *Journal of Verbal Learning and Verbal Behavior, 17*, 573–578.

Bowers, K. S., & Farvolden, P. (1996). Revisiting a century-old Freudian slip—from suggestion disavowed to the truth repressed. *Psychological Bulletin, 119*, 355–380.

Braun, B. G. (1988). The BASK (behavior, affect, sensation, knowledge) model of dissociation. *Dissociation, 1(1)*, 4–23.

Broad, W. J. (1986, January 29). The shuttle explodes. *The New York Times*, pp. A1, A10.

Buckhout, R., Eugenio, P., Licitra, T., Oliver, L., & Kramer, T. H. (1981). Memory, hypnosis, and evidence: Research on eyewitnesses. *Social Action and the Law, 7*, 67–72.

Butcher, J. N. (1990). *The MMPI–2 in psychological treatment*. New York: Oxford University Press.

Calof, D. (1993, September/October). Facing the truth about false memory. *Networker*, 39–45.

Carroll, D. W. (1999). *Psychology of language*. Pacific Grove, CA: Brooks/Cole.

Ceci, S. J. (1995). False beliefs: Some developmental and clinical considerations. In D. L. Schacter (Ed.), *Memory distortion: How minds, brains, and societies reconstruct the past* (pp. 91–125). Cambridge, MA: Harvard University Press.

Ceci, S. J., & Bruck, M. (1993). Suggestibility of the child witness: A historical review and synthesis. *Psychological Bulletin, 113*, 403–439.

Ceci, S. J., Loftus, E. F., Leichtman, M. D., & Bruck, M. (1994). The possible role of source misattributions in the creation of false beliefs among preschoolers. *International Journal of Clinical and Experimental Hypnosis, 42*, 304–320.

Ceci, S. J., Ross, D., & Toglia, M. (1987). Age differences in suggestibility: Narrowing the uncertainties. In S. Ceci, M. Toglia, & D. Ross (Eds.), *Children's eyewitness memory* (pp. 79–91). New York: Springer-Verlag.

Chiarello, C., & Beeman, M. (1997). Toward a veridical interpretation of right-hemisphere processing and storage. *Psychological Science, 8*, 343–344.

Chomsky, N. (1959). Review of Skinner's *Verbal behavior. Language, 35*, 26–58.

Christianson, S. A. (1984). The relationship between induced emotional arousal and amnesia. *Scandinavian Journal of Psychology, 25*, 147–160.

Christianson, S. A. (1992). Emotional stress and eyewitness memory: A critical review. *Psychological Bulletin, 112*, 284–309.

Christianson, S. A. (Ed.). (1992). *The handbook of emotion and memory: Research and theory*. Hillsdale, NJ: Erlbaum.

Christianson, S. A., Goodman, J., & Loftus, E. F. (1992). Eyewitness memory for stressful events: Methodological quandaries and ethical dilemmas. In S. Christianson (Ed.), *The handbook of emotion and memory: Research and theory* (pp. 217–241). Hillsdale, NJ: Erlbaum.

Christianson, S. A., & Hubinette, B. (1993). Hands up! A study of witnesses' emotional reactions and memories associated with bank robberies. *Applied Cognitive Psychology, 7(5)*, 365–380.

Christianson, S. A., & Loftus, E. F. (1990). Some characteristics of people's traumatic memories. *Bulletin of the Psychonomic Society, 28*, 195–198.

Christianson, S. A., & Loftus, E. F. (1991). Remembering emotional events: The fate of detailed information. *Cognition & Emotion, 5,* 81–108.

Christianson, S. A., & Nilsson, L. G. (1984). Functional amnesia as induced by a psychological trauma. *Memory & Cognition, 12,* 142–155.

Christianson, S. A., & Safer, M. A. (1996). Emotional events and emotions in autobiographical memories. In D. C. Rubin (Ed.), *Remembering our past: Studies in autobiographical memory* (pp. 218–243). New York: Cambridge University Press.

Cialdini, R. B. (1993). *Influence: The psychology of persuasion.* New York: William Morrow.

Cimino, C. R., Verfaellie, M., Bowers, D., & Heilman, K. M. (1991). Autobiographical memory: Influence of right hemisphere damage on emotionality and specificity. *Brain and Cognition, 15,* 106–118.

Clark, D. M., & Teasdale, J. D. (1982). Diurnal variation in clinical depression and accessibility of positive and negative experiences. *Journal of Abnormal Psychology, 91,* 87–95.

Clark, S. E., & Loftus, E. F. (1996). The construction of space alien abduction memories. *Psychological Inquiry, 7(2),* 140–143.

Clifford, B. R., & Scott, J. (1978). Individual and situational factors in eyewitness testimony. *Journal of Applied Psychology, 63,* 352–359.

Coleman, P. G. (1986). *Aging and reminiscence process: Social and clinical implications* (pp. 154–155). Chichester, England: John Wiley & Sons.

Collins, A. M., & Loftus, E. F. (1975). A spreading-activation theory of semantic processing. *Psychological Review, 82,* 407–428.

Connor, S. (1989). *Postmodernist culture: An introduction to theories of the contemporary.* Oxford: Blackwell.

Conway, M. A. (1995). Autobiographical knowledge and autobiographical memories. In D. C. Rubin (Ed.), *Remembering our past* (pp. 67–93). New York: Cambridge University Press.

Cook, S. W. (1958). The psychologist of the future: Scientist, professional, or both. *American Psychologist, 13,* 635–644.

Cormier, P., & Jackson, T. (1995). Effects of instruction on a divided visual-field task of face processing. *Perceptual and Motor Skills, 80,* 923–927.

Cotman, C. W., & Nieto-Sampredo, M. (1982). Brain function, synapse renewal, and plasticity. *Annual Review of Psychology, 33,* 371–401.

Cowan, N. (Ed.). (1997). *The development of memory in childhood.* Hove East Sussex, England: Psychology Press.

Craik, F. I. M, & Tulving, E. (1975). Depth of processing and the retention of words in episodic memory. *Journal of Experimental Psychology: General, 104(3),* 268–294.

Cranmer, D. (1994). Core energetics. In D. Jones (Ed.), *Innovative therapy: A handbook* (pp. 117–130). Buckingham, England: Open University Press.

Culbertson, R. (1995). Embodied memory, transcendence, and telling: Recounted trauma, re-establishing the self. *New Literary History, 26,* 169–195.

Damasio, A. R. (1990). Category-related recognition defects as a clue to the neural substrates of knowledge. *Trends in Neuroscience, 13,* 95–98.

Damasio, A. R. (1994). *Descartes' error: Emotion, reason, and the human brain.* New York: Grosset/Putnam.

Davis, M., Campeau, S., Kim, M., & Falls, W. A. (1995). Neural systems of emotion: The amygdala's role in fear and anxiety. In J. L. McGaugh, N. M. Weinberger, & G. Lynch (Eds.), *Brain and memory: Modulation and mediation of neuroplasticity* (pp. 3–40). New York: Oxford University Press.

DeCasper, A. J., & Spence, M. J. (1986). Prenatal maternal speech influences newborns' perception of speech sounds. *Infant Behavior and Development, 9,* 133–150.

Deese, J. (1959). On the prediction of occurrence of particular verbal intrusions in immediate recall. *Journal of Experimental Psychology, 58,* 17–22.

Deregowski, J. B. (1980). *Illusions, patterns, and pictures: A cross-cultural perspective.* New York: Academic Press.

Diamond, D. M., Ingersoll, N., Fleshner, M., & Rose, G. M. (1996). Psychological stress impairs spatial working memory: Relevance to electrophysiological studies of hippocampal function. *Behavioral Neuroscience, 110,* 661–672.

Dillard, A. (1982). *Living by fiction.* New York: Harper & Row.

Dodd, D. H., & Bradshaw, J. M. (1980). Leading questions and memory: Pragmatic constraints. *Journal of Verbal Learning and Verbal Behavior, 19,* 695–704.

Dudycha, G. J. & Dudycha, M. M. (1941). Childhood memories: A review of the literature. *Psychological Bulletin, 38,* 668–682.

Easterbrook, J. A. (1959). The effect of emotion on cue utilization and the organization of behavior. *Psychological Review, 66,* 183–201.

Eich, E. (1995). Mood as a mediator of place dependent memory. *Journal of Experimental Psychology: General, 124,* 293–308.

Eich, E. (1995). Searching for mood dependent memory. *Psychological Science, 6,* 67–75.

Eich, E., Rachman, S., & Lopatka, C. (1990). Affect, pain, and autobiographical memory. *Journal of Abnormal Psychology, 99,* 174–178.

Eich, E., Reeves, J. L., Jaeger, B., & Graf-Radford, S. B. (1985). Memory for pain: Relation between past and present pain intensity. *Pain, 23,* 375–379.

Erdelyi, M. (1994). Hypnotic hypermnesia: The empty set of hypermnesia. *International Journal of Clinical and Experimental Hypnosis, 42,* 379–390.

Erwin, E. (1985). Holistic psychotherapies: What works? In D. Stalken & C. Glymour (Eds.), *Examining holistic medicine* (pp. 245–272). Buffalo: Prometheus Books.

Fagan, J. F. (1990). The paired-comparison paradigm and infant intelligence. In A. Diamond (Ed.), *The development and neural bases of higher cognitive functions* (pp. 337–364). New York: New York Academy of Science.

First, M. B. (Ed.). (1994). *Diagnostic and statistical manual of mental disorders (IV).* Washington, DC: American Psychiatric Association.

Fishbain, D. A., Goldberg, M., Meagher, B. R., & Rosomoff, H. (1986). Male and female chronic pain patients categorized by *DSM-III* psychiatric diagnostic criteria. *Pain, 26,* 181–198.

Fisher, R. P., & Geiselman, R. E. (1992). *Memory-enhancing techniques for investigative interviewing.* Springfield, IL: Charles C. Thomas.

Fisher, R. P., Mccauley, M. R., & Geiselman, R. E. (1994). Improving eyewitness testimony with the cognitive interview. In D. F. Ross, J. D. Read, & M. P. Toglia (Eds.), *Adult eyewitness testimony: Current trends and developments* (pp. 245–269). New York: Cambridge University Press.

Fivush, R., & Hammond, N. R. (1990). Autobiographical memory across the preschool years: Toward reconceptualizing childhood amnesia. In R. Fivush & J. A. Hudson (Eds.), *Knowing and remembering in young children* (pp. 223–248). New York: Cambridge University Press.

Fowler, R. D. (Ed.). (1991). Responses to Banaji and Crowder. [Special section.] *American Psychologist, 46*, 16–48.

Fredrickson, R. (1992). *Repressed memories: A journey to recovery from sexual abuse.* New York: Simon & Schuster.

Freeman, M. (1993). *Rewriting the self.* London: Routledge.

Freud, S. (1899/1962). Screen memories. In *the complete psychological works of Sigmund Freud, Volume 3, 1893–1899* (pp. 301–322). London: The Hogarth Press and the Institute of Psycho-Analysis.

Freud, S. (1915). Repression. In R. M. Hutchins (Ed.), *Great books of the Western world* (Vol. 54, pp. 422–427). Chicago: Encyclopaedia Britannica.

Fruzzetti, A. E., Toland, K., Teller, S. A., & Loftus, E. F. (1992). Memory and eyewitness testimony. In M. Gruneberg & P. Morris (Eds.), *Aspects of memory: Vol. 1. The practical aspects* (pp. 18–50). London: Routledge.

Fullerton, C. S., & Ursano, R. J. (1997). The other side of chaos: Understanding the patterns of posttraumatic responses. In C. S. Fullerton & R. J. Ursano (Eds.), *Posttraumatic stress disorder* (pp. 3–20). Washington, DC: American Psychiatric Press.

Gainotti, G., Caltagirone, C., & Zoccolotti, P. (1993). Left/right and cortical/subcortical dichotomies in the neuropsychological study of human emotions. *Cognition and Emotion, 7*, 71–93.

García Márquez, G. (1970). *One hundred years of solitude.* New York: Harper & Row.

Gardner, H. (1985). *The mind's new science.* New York: Basic Books.

Garry, M., & Loftus, E. F. (1994). Pseudomemories without hypnosis. *International Journal of Clinical and Experimental Hypnosis, 42*, 363–378.

Gazzaniga, M. S. (1985). *The social brain.* New York: Basic Books.

Gazzaniga, M. S. (1988). *Mind matters.* Boston: Houghton Mifflin.

Gazzaniga, M. S. (1992). *Nature's mind.* New York: Basic Books.

Gazzaniga, M. S., & LeDoux, J. E. (1978). *The integrated mind.* New York: Plenum Press.

Gazzaniga, M. S., & Smylie, C. S. (1984). Dissociation of language and cognition. *Brain, 107*, 145–153.

Geiselman, R. E., & Machlovitz, H. (1987). Hypnosis memory recall: Implications for forensic use. *American Journal of Forensic Psychology, 1:87*, 37–47.

Gentry, M., & Herrmann, D. J. (1990). Memory contrivances in everyday life. *Personality and Social Psychology Bulletin, 16(2)*, 241–253.

Ginsburg, H., & Opper, S. (1979). *Piaget's theory of intellectual development.* Englewood Cliffs, NJ: Prentice-Hall.

Godden, D. R., & Baddeley, A. D. (1975). Context-dependent memory in two natural environments: On land and underwater. *British Journal of Psychology, 66,* 325–331.

Gold, P. E. (1995). Modulation of emotional and nonemotional memories: Same pharmacological systems, different neuroanatomical systems. In J. L. McGaugh, N. M. Weinberger, & G. Lynch (Eds.), *Brain and memory: Modulation and mediation of neuroplasticity* (pp. 41–74). New York: Oxford University Press.

Graf, P., Squire, L. R., & Mandler, G. (1984). The information that amnesic patients do not forget. *Journal of Experimental Psychology: Learning, Memory, and Cognition, 10,* 164–178.

Graham, J.R. (1993). *MMPI–2: Assessing personality and psychopathology.* New York: Oxford University Press.

Gray, J. A. (1990). Brain systems that mediate both emotion and cognition. *Cognition and Emotion, 4,* 269–288.

Greenwald, A. G., & Banaji, M. R. (1989). The self as a memory system: Powerful, but ordinary. *Journal of Personality and Social Psychology, 57,* 41–54.

Grice, H. (1975). Logic and conversation. In P. Cole & J. Morgan (Eds.), *Speech acts: Syntax and semantics: Vol. 3* (pp. 41–58). New York: Academic Press.

Gruneberg, M., & Morris, P. (Eds.). (1992). *Aspects of memory: Vol. I: The practical aspects.* London: Routledge.

Gudjonsson, G. H. (1984). A new scale of interrogative suggestibility. *Personality and Individual Differences, 5,* 303–314.

Gudjonsson, G. H. (1987). A parallel form of the Gudjonnson suggestibility scale. *British Journal of Clinical Psychology, 26,* 215–221.

Hacking, I. (1995). *Rewriting the soul: Multiple personality and the sciences of memory.* Princeton, NJ: Princeton University Press.

Hamann, S. B. (1996). Implicit memory in the tactile modality: Evidence from Braille stem completion in the blind. *Psychological Science, 7,* 284–288.

Hamilton, A. (1995). A new look at personal identity. *Philosophical Quarterly, 45 (180),* 332–349.

Hanser, S. B., & Clair, A. A. (1995). Retrieving the losses of Alzheimer's disease for patients and care-givers with the aid of music. In T. Wigian, B. Saperston, & R. West (Eds.), *The art and science of music therapy: A handbook* (pp. 342–360). New York: Harwood Academic Publishers.

Harris, R. J. (1973). Answering questions containing marked and unmarked adjectives and adverbs. *Journal of Experimental Psychology, 97,* 399–401.

Haugaard, J. J., Reppucci, N. D., Laurd, J., & Nauful, T. (1991). Children's definitions of the truth and their competency as witnesses in legal proceedings. *Law and Human Behavior, 15,* 253–272.

Hergenhahn, B. R. (1997). *An introduction to the history of psychology.* Pacific Grove, CA: Brooks/Cole.

Heuer, F., & Reisberg, D. (1992). Emotion, arousal, and memory for detail. In S. Christianson (Ed.), *The handbook of emotion and memory: Research and theory* (pp. 151–180). Hillsdale, NJ: Erlbaum.

Hilgard, E. R. (1987). *Psychology in America: A historical survey.* New York: Harcourt Brace.

Hilgard, E. R., & Loftus, E. (1979). Effective interrogation of the eyewitness. *International Journal of Clinical and Experimental Hypnosis, 27,* 342–357.

Hilts, P. (1995). *Memory's ghost.* New York: Simon & Schuster.

Hook, J. C., Davis, J. L., & Beiser, D. G. (Eds.). (1994). *Models of information processing in the basal ganglia.* Cambridge, MA: Bradford Books.

Hornstein, G. A. (1992). The return of the repressed: Psychology's problematic relations with psychoanalysis, 1909–1960. *American Psychologist, 47,* 254–263.

Horowitz, M. J., Wilner, N. Kaltreider, N., & Alvarez, M. A. (1980). Signs and symptoms of posttraumatic stress disorder. *Archives of General Psychiatry, 37,* 85–92.

Hothersall, D. (1995). *History of psychology.* New York: McGraw-Hill.

Howe, M. L., & Courage, M. L. (1993). On resolving the enigma of infantile amnesia. *Psychological Bulletin, 113,* 305–326.

Hugdahl, K. (1995). Classical conditioning and implicit learning: The right hemisphere hypothesis. In R. J. Davidson & K. Hugdahl (Eds.), *Brain Asymmetry* (pp. 235–267). Cambridge, MA: MIT Press.

Human Capital Initiative Committee. (1998, February). Basic research in psychological science: A human capital initiative report. [Special issue.] *Observer,* 1–39.

Huxley, T. H. (1898). Biogenesis and abiogenesis. *Collected Essays* (Vol. 8). New York: Appleton.

Hyman, I. E., Jr., & Billings, F. J. (1998). Individual differences and the creation of false childhood memories. *Memory, 6,* 1–20.

Hyman, I. E., Jr., & Pentland, J. (1996). The role of mental imagery in the creation of false childhood memories. *Journal of Memory and Language, 35,* 101–117.

Hyman, I. E., Jr., Husband, T. H., & Billings, F. J. (1995). False memories of childhood experiences. *Applied Cognitive Psychology, 9,* 181–197.

Jacoby, L. L. (1988). Memory observed and memory unobserved. In U. Neisser & E. Winograd (Eds.), *Remembering reconsidered: Ecological and traditional approaches to the study of memory* (pp. 145–177). Cambridge, England: Cambridge University Press.

Jacoby, L. L., & Dallas, M. (1981). On the relationship between autobiographical memory and perceptual learning. *Journal of Experimental Psychology: General, 110,* 306–340.

Johnson, G. (1991). *In the palaces of memory.* New York: Vintage Books.

Johnson, M. K., & Raye, C. L. (1981). Reality monitoring. *Psychological Review, 88,* 67–85.

Johnson, M. K., Hashtroudi, S., & Lindsay, D. S. (1993). Source monitoring. *Psychological Bulletin, 114,* 3–28.

Johnson, M. K., Suengas, A. G., Foley, M. A., & Raye, C. L. (1988). Phenomenal characteristics of memories for perceived and imagined autobiographical events. *Journal of Experimental Psychology: General, 117,* 371–376.

Jones, J. L. (1995). *Understanding psychological science.* New York: HarperCollins.

Jones, J. L. (1998). Master learners: Faculty development and the enhancement of undergraduate education. *Liberal Education, 84*, 42–47.

Jones-Gotman, M. (1986). Memory for designs: The hippocampal contribution. *Neuropsychologia, 24*, 193–203.

Kalat, J. W. (1992). *Biological psychology.* Belmont, CA: Wadsworth Publishing Company.

Kassin, S. M. (1985). Eyewitness identification: Retrospective self-awareness and the accuracy-confidence correlation. *Journal of Personality and Social Psychology, 49*, 878–893.

Kassin, S. M., Ellsworth, P. C., & Smith, V. L. (1989). The "general acceptance" of psychological research on eyewitness testimony. *American Psychologist, 44(8)*, 1089–1098.

Kihlstrom, J. F., & Harackiewicz, J. M. (1982). The earliest recollection: A new survey. *Journal of Personality, 50*, 134–147.

Koch, S. (1980). Psychology and its human clientele: Beneficiaries or victims? In R. A. Kasschau & F. S. Kessel (Eds.), *Psychology and society: In search of symbiosis.* New York: Holt, Rinehart & Winston.

Kolb, L. C. (1988). Recovery of memory and repressed fantasy in combat-induced post-traumatic stress disorder of Vietnam veterans. In H. M. Pettinati (Ed.), *Hypnosis and memory* (pp. 265–274). New York: Guilford Press.

Kotre, J. (1995). *White gloves: How we create ourselves through memory.* New York: Free Press.

Krass, J., Kinoshita, S., & McConkey, K. M. (1989). Hypnotic memory and confident reporting. *Applied Cognitive Psychology, 3*, 35–51.

Krystal, J. H., Southwick, S. M., & Charney, D. S. (1995). Post traumatic stress disorder: Psychobiological mechanisms of traumatic remembrance. In D. L. Schacter (Ed.), *Memory distortion: How minds, brains, and societies reconstruct the past* (pp. 150–172). Cambridge, MA: Harvard University Press.

Larsen, S. F. (1992). Potential flashbulbs: Memories of ordinary news as a baseline. In E. Winograd & U. Neisser (Eds.), *Affect and accuracy in recall: The problem of "flashbulb" memories* (pp. 32–64). Cambridge: Cambridge University Press.

Larsen, S. F., Thompson, C. P., & Hansen, T. (1996). Time in autobiographical memory. In D. C. Rubin (Ed.), *Remembering our past: Studies in autobiographical memory* (pp. 129–156). New York: Cambridge University Press.

Lashley, K. S. (1950). In search of the engram. In *Symposium of the society for experimental biology: Vol. 4.* New York: Cambridge University Press.

Laurence, J. R., & Perry, C. (1983). Hypnotically created memory among highly hypnotizable subjects. *Science, 222*, 523–524.

Leahey, T. H. (1991). *A history of modern psychology.* Englewood Cliffs, NJ: Prentice-Hall.

LeDoux, J. (1994). Emotion, memory, and the brain. *Scientific American, 270*, 50–57.

Lee, D. Y, Barak, A., Uhlemann, M. R., & Patsula, P. (1995). Effects of preinterview suggestion on counselor memory, clinical impression, and confidence in judgments. *Journal of Clinical Psychology, 51*, 666–675.

Lindsay, D. S. (1993). Eyewitness suggestibility. *Current Directions in Psychological Science, 2,* 86–89.

Lindsay, D. S., & Read, J. D. (1994). Psychotherapy and memories of childhood sexual abuse: A cognitive perspective. *Applied Cognitive Psychology, 8,* 281–338.

Lipton, J. P. (1977). On the psychology of eyewitness testimony. *Journal of Applied Psychology, 62,* 90–93.

Loftus, E. F. (1979). *Eyewitness testimony.* Cambridge, MA: Harvard University Press.

Loftus, E. F. (1997). Memory for a past that never was. *Current Directions in Psychological Science, 6,* 60–65.

Loftus, E. L., & Burns, T. E. (1982). Mental shock can produce retrograde amnesia. *Memory & Cognition, 10,* 318–323.

Loftus, E. F., Donders, K., Hoffman, H. G., & Schooler, J. W. (1989). Creating new memories that are quickly accessed and confidently held. *Memory & Cognition, 17,* 607–616.

Loftus, E. F., Levidow, B., & Duensing, S. (1992). Who remembers best? Individual differences in memory for events that occurred in a science museum. *Applied Cognitive Psychology, 6,* 93–107.

Loftus, E. F., & Loftus, G. R. (1980). On the permanence of stored information in the human brain. *American Psychologist, 35,* 409–420.

Loftus, E. F., & Palmer, J. C. (1974). Reconstruction of automobile destruction: An example of the interaction between language and memory. *Journal of Verbal Learning and Verbal Behavior, 13,* 585–589.

Loftus, E. F., & Pickrell, J. E. (1995). The formation of false memories. *Psychiatric Annals, 25,* 720–725.

Loftus, E. F., Schooler, J. W., Boone, S. M., & Kline, D. (1987). Time went by so slowly: Overestimation of event duration by males and females. *Applied Cognitive Psychology, 1,* 3–13.

Lorimer, L. T. (Ed.). (1995). Minerva. In *The encyclopedia Americana* (Vol. 19, p. 161). Danbury, CT: Grolier.

Lorimer, L. T. (Ed.). (1995). Thoth. In *The encyclopedia Americana* (Vol. 26, pp. 701–702). Danbury, CT: Grolier.

Lowenthal, R. I., & Marrazzo, R. A. (1990). Milestoning: Evoking memories for resocialization through group reminiscence. *The Gerontologist, 30(2),* 269–272.

Luria, A. R., & Simernitskaya, E. G. (1977). Interhemispheric relations and the functions of the minor hemisphere. *Neuropsychologia, 15,* 175–177.

Luus, C. A. E., & Wells, G. L. (1994). Eyewitness identification confidence. In D. F. Ross, J. D. Read, & M. P. Toglia (Eds.), *Adult eyewitness testimony: Current trends and developments.* New York: Cambridge University Press.

Lynn, S. J., & Payne, D. G. (1997). Memory as the theater of the past. *Current Directions in Psychological Science, 6(3),* 55–83. (special issue, Cambridge University Press.)

Lynn, S. J., Lock, T. G., Myers, B., & Payne, D. G. (1997). Recalling the unrecallable: Should hypnosis be used to recover memories in psychotherapy? *Current Directions in Psychological Science, 6,* 79–83.

Lynn, S.J., & Payne, D.G. (1997). Memory as the theater of the past: The psychology of false memories. *Current Directions in Psychological Science, 6*, 55.

MacLean, P. D. (1990). *The triune brain in evolution: Role in paleocerebral functions.* New York: Plenum Press.

Malpass, R. S., & Devine, P. G. (1980). Guided memory in eyewitness identification. *Journal of Applied Psychology, 66*, 343–350.

Markowitsch, H. J. (1995). Anatomical basis of memory disorders. In M. S. Gazzaniga (Ed.), *The cognitive neurosciences* (pp. 765–779). Cambridge, MA: MIT Press.

Marsolek, C. J., Kosslyn, S. M., & Squire, L. R. (1992). Form-specific visual priming in the right cerebral hemisphere. *Journal of Experimental Psychology: Learning, Memory, and Cognition, 18*, 492–508.

Matlin, M. W. (1998). *Cognition.* New York: Harcourt Brace.

Matlin, M. W., & Foley, H. J. (1992). *Sensation and perception.* Needham Heights, MA: Allyn and Bacon.

Matt, G. E., Vazquez, C., & Campbell, W. K. (1992). Mood-congruent recall of affectively toned stimuli: A meta-analytic review. *Clinical Psychology Review, 12*, 227–255.

McCloskey, M., & Zaragoza, M. (1985). Misleading postevent information and memory for events: Arguments and evidence against memory impairment hypotheses. *Journal of Experimental Psychology: General, 114*, 1–16.

McDermott, K. B. (1996). The persistence of false memories in list recall. *Journal of Memory and Language, 35*, 212–230.

McFall, R. M., Treat, T. A., & Viken, R. J. (1997). Contributions of cognitive theory to new behavioral treatments. *Psychological Science, 8(3)*, 174–176.

McGaugh, J. L. (1992). Affect, neuromodulatory systems, and memory storage. In S. A. Christianson (Ed.), *The handbook of emotion and memory: Research and theory* (pp. 245–268). Hillsdale, NJ: Erlbaum.

McHenry, R. (Ed.). (1993). Mnemosyne. In *The New Encylopaedia Britannica* (Vol. 8, p. 206). Chicago: Encyclopaedia Britannica.

Medical mistakes. (1997). *American Medical News, 40(40)*, 2.

Mehler, P. S., & Weiner, K. L. (1993). Medical presentations of covert sexual abuse in eating disorder patients. *Eating Disorders, 1*, 259–263.

Meltzoff, A. N. (1995). What infant memory tells us about infantile amnesia: Long-term recall and deferred imitation. *Journal of Experimental Child Psychology, 59*, 497–515.

Metcalfe, J., Funnell, M., & Gazzaniga, M. S. (1995). Right-hemisphere memory superiority: Studies of a split-brain patient. *Psychological Science, 6*, 157–164.

Middleton, H. (1993). *Rivers of memory.* Boulder, CO: Pruett Publishing Co.

Milgram, S. (1963). Behavioral study of obedience. *Journal of Abnormal Social Psychology, 67*, 371–378.

Moghaddam, B., Bolinao, M. L., Stein-Behrens, B., & Sapolsky, R. (1994). Glucocorticoids mediate the stress-induced extracellular accumulation of glutamate. *Brain Research, 655*, 251–254.

Molyneaux, C. V., & Larsen, J. D. (1992). Acceptance of misleading information by children and adults. *Psychological Reports, 71*, 267–274.

Morrison, T. (1987). *Beloved*. New York: Plume.

Münsterberg, H. (1908). *On the witness stand: Essays on psychology and crime*. New York: Clark, Boardman, Doubleday.

Neisser, U. (1967). *Cognitive psychology*. New York: Appleton-Century-Crofts.

Neisser, U. (1976). *Cognition and reality*. San Francisco: W. H. Freeman.

Neisser, U. (1981). John Dean's memory: A case study. *Cognition, 9*, 1–22.

Neisser, U. (1982). *Memory observed: Remembering in natural contexts*. San Francisco: W. H. Freeman.

Neisser, U., & Harsch, N. (1992). Phantom flashbulbs: False recollections of hearing the news about *Challenger*. In E. Winograd & U. Neisser (Eds.), *Affect and accuracy in recall*. Cambridge: Cambridge University Press.

Newman, L. S., & Baumeister, R. F. (1996). Toward an explanation of the UFO abduction phenomenon: Hypnotic elaboration, extraterrestrial sadomasochism, and spurious memories. *Psychological Inquiry, 7(2)*, 99–126.

Niederland, W. G. (1981). The survivor syndrome: Further observations and dimensions. *Journal of the American Psychoanalytic Association, 29*, 413–425.

Niedenthal, P. M., Setterlund, M. B., & Jones, D. E. (1994). Emotional organization of perceptual memory. In P. M. Niedenthal & S. Kitayama (Eds.), *The heart's eye: Emotional influences in perception and attention* (pp. 87–113). San Diego: Academic Press.

Niedenthal, P., & Setterlund, M. B. (1994). Emotion congruence in perception. *Personality and Social Psychology Bulletin, 20*, 401–411.

Nigro, G., & Neisser, U. (1983). Point of view in personal memories. *Cognitive Psychology, 15*, 467–482.

Nurius, P. S. (1994). Assessing and changing self-concept: Guidelines from the memory system. *Social Work, 39*, 221–229.

Nyberg, L., Cabeza, R., & Tulving, E. (1996). PET studies of encoding and retrieval: The HERA model. I. *Psychonomic Bulletin & Review, 2*, 134–147.

Nyberg, L., Cabeza, R., & Tulving, E. (1996). PET studies of encoding and retrieval: The HERA model. II. *Psychonomic Bulletin & Review, 3*, 135–148.

Onken, L. S. (1997). Behavioral therapy development and psychological science. [Special section.] *Psychological Science, 8(3)*, 143–197.

O'Sullivan, J. T., & Howe, M. L. (1995). Metamemory and memory construction. *Consciousness and Cognition, 4*, 104–110.

Orne, M. T. (1962). On the social psychology of the psychological experiment: With particular reference to demand characteristics and their implications. *American Psychologist, 17*, 776–783.

Paige, S. T., Reid, G. M., Allen, M. G., & Newton, J. E. O. (1990). Psychophysiological correlated posttraumatic stress disorder in Vietnam veterans. *Biological Psychiatry, 27*, 419–430.

Paine, A.B. (1912). *Mark Twain: A biography, Vol. IV*. New York: Harper and Brothers.

Paris, S. (1988). Motivated remembering. In F. Weinert & M. Perlmutter (Eds.), *Memory development: Universal changes and individual differences* (pp. 221–242). Hillsdale, NJ: Erlbaum.

Parrott, W. G. (1993). Beyond hedonism: Motives for inhibiting good moods and for maintaining bad moods. In D. M. Wegner & J. W. Pennebaker (Eds.), *Handbook of mental control* (pp. 278–305). Englewood Cliffs, NJ: Prentice Hall.

Parrott, W. G., & Sabini, J. (1990). Mood and memory under natural conditions: Evidence for mood incongruent recall. *Journal of Personality and Social Psychology, 59,* 321–336.

Payne, D. G., Elie, C. J., Blackwell, J. M., & Neuschatz, J. S. (1996). Memory illusions: Recalling, recognizing, and recollecting events that never occurred. *Journal of Memory and Language, 35,* 261–285.

Payne, D. G., Neuschatz, J. S., Lampinen, J. M., & Lynn, S. J. (1997). Compelling memory illusions: The qualitative characteristics of false memories. *Current Directions in Psychological Science, 6,* 56–60.

Pederson, D. M., & Wheeler, J. (1993). The Muller-Lyer illusion among Navajos. *Journal of Social Psychology, 121,* 3–6.

Penfield, W., & Perot, P. (1963). The brain's record of auditory and visual experience. *Brain, 86(4),* 595–696.

Perlman, S. D. (1993). Unlocking incest memories: Preoedipal transference, countertransference, and the body. *Journal of the American Academy of Psychoanalysis, 21(3),* 363–386.

Pezdek, K., & Banks, W. P. (Eds.). (1996). *The recovered memory/false memory debate.* San Diego: Academic Press.

Pezdek, K., Finger, K., & Hodge, D. (1997). Planting false childhood memories: The role of event plausibility. *Psychological Science, 8,* 437–441.

Phelps, E. A., & Gazzaniga, M. S. (1992). Hemispheric differences in mnemonic processing: The effects of left hemisphere interpretation. *Neuropsychologia, 30,* 293–297.

Pillemer, D. B., & White, S. H. (1989). Childhood events recalled by children and adults. In H. W. Reese (Ed.), *Advances in child development and behavior* (Vol. 21, pp. 297–340). New York: Academic Press.

Piper, A., Jr. (1993, Winter). "Truth serum" and "recovered memories" of sexual abuse: A review of the evidence. *Journal of Psychiatry & Law,* 447–471.

Plato. (1952a). Meno. In R. M. Hutchins (Ed.), *Great books of the Western world* (Vol. 7, pp. 174–190). Chicago: Encyclopaedia Britannica.

Plato. (1952b). Theaetetus. In R. M. Hutchins (Ed.), *Great books of the Western world* (Vol. 7, pp. 512–550). Chicago: Encyclopaedia Britannica.

Poole, D. A., Lindsay, D. S., Memon, A., & Bull, R. (1995). Psychotherapy and the recovery of memories of childhood sexual abuse: U.S. and British practitioners' opinions, practices, and experiences. *Journal of Consulting and Clinical Psychology, 63(3),* 426–437.

Proust, M. (1981). *Remembrance of things past.* New York: Random House.

Radin, E. D. (1964). *The innocents.* New York: William Morrow.

Read, J. D. (1996). From a passing thought to a false memory in two minutes: Confusing real and illusory events. *Psychonomic Bulletin & Review, 3,* 105–111.

Reisberg, D., & Heuer, F. (1995). Emotion's multiple effects on memory. In J. L. McGaugh, N. M. Weinberger, & G. Lynch (Eds.), *Brain and memory: Modulation and mediation of neuroplasticity* (pp. 84–92). New York: Oxford University Press.

Reisberg, D., Heuer, F., McLean, J., & O'Shaughnessy, M. (1988). The quantity, not the quality, of affect predicts memory vividness. *Bulletin of the Psychonomic Society, 26,* 100–103.

Richards, L., & Chiarello, C. (1995). Depth of associated activation in the cerebral hemispheres: Mediated versus direct priming. *Neuropsychologia, 33,* 171–179.

Robinson, J. A. (1980). Affect and retrieval of personal memories. *Motivation and Emotion, 4,* 149–174.

Robinson, J. A., & Swanson, K. L. (1993). Field and observer modes of remembering. *Memory, 1(3),* 169–184.

Roediger, H. L., III. (Ed.). (1985). Ebbinghaus Symposium. [Special section.] *Journal of Experimental Psychology: Learning, Memory, and Cognition, 11(3),* 413–500.

Roediger, H. L., III. (1990). Implicit memory: Retention without remembering. *American Psychologist, 45,* 1043–1056.

Roediger, H. L., III, Jacoby, D., & McDermott, K. B. (1996). Misinformation effects in recall: Creating false memories through repeated retrieval. *Journal of Memory and Language, 35,* 300–318.

Roediger, H. L., III, & McDermott, K. B. (1995). Creating false memories: Remembering words not presented in lists. *Journal of Experimental Psychology: Learning, Memory, and Cognition, 21,* 803–814.

Rosen, H., & Kuehlwein, K. T. (Eds.). (1996). *Constructing realities: Meaning-making perspectives for psychotherapists.* San Francisco: Jossey-Bass.

Rosenthal, R., & Jacobson, L. (1968). *Pygmalion in the classroom.* New York: Winston.

Ross, C. A. (1991). Epidemiology of multiple personality disorder and dissociation. *Psychiatric Clinics of North America, 14,* 596–600.

Roth, M. (1994, November, December). We are what we remember (and forget). *Tikkun, 9(6),* pp. 41–42, 91.

Rovee-Collier, C., & Shyi, G. (1992). A functional and cognitive analysis of infant long-term retention. In M. L. Howe, C. J. Brainerd, & V. F. Reyna (Eds.), *Development of long-term retention* (pp. 3–55). New York: Springer-Verlag.

Rubin, D. C. (Ed.). (1996). *Remembering our past: Studies in autobiographical memory.* New York: Cambridge University Press.

Rumelhart, D. E., McClelland, J. L., & the PDP research group. (1986). *Parallel distributed processing: Explorations in the microstructure of cognition. Volume 1: Foundations.* Cambridge, MA: MIT Press.

Sacks, O. (1970). *The man who mistook his wife for a hat.* New York: HarperCollins.

Sacks, O. (1973). *Awakenings.* New York: HarperCollins.

Sacks, O. (1995). *An anthropologist on Mars.* New York: Alfred A. Knopf.

Salaman, E. (1970). *A collection of moments.* New York: St. Martin's Press.

Saywitz , K. J., & Moan-Hardie, S. (1994). Reducing the potential for distortion of childhood memories. *Consciousness and Cognition, 3,* 408–425.

Schacter, D. L. (1987). Implicit memory: History and current status. *Journal of Experimental Psychology: Learning, Memory, and Cognition, 13,* 501–518.

Schacter, D. L. (1992). Understanding implicit memory: A cognitive neuroscience approach. *American Psychologist, 47,* 559–569.

Schacter, D. L. (1995). Implicit memory: A new frontier for cognitive neuroscience. In M. S. Gazzaniga (Ed.), *The cognitive neurosciences* (pp. 815–824). Cambridge, MA: MIT Press.

Schacter, D. L. (1995). Memory distortion: history and current status. In D. L. Schacter (Ed.), *Memory distortion: How minds, brains, and societies reconstruct the past.* Cambridge, MA: Harvard University Press.

Schacter, D. L. (Ed.). (1995). *Memory distortion: How minds, brains, and societies reconstruct the past.* Cambridge, MA: Harvard University Press.

Schacter, D. L. (1996). *Searching for memory: The brain, the mind, and the past.* New York: Basic Books.

Schacter, D. L., & Church, B. (1992). Auditory priming: Implicit and explicit memory for words and voices. *Journal of Experimental Psychology: Learning, Memory, and Cognition, 18,* 915–930.

Schacter, D. L., & Curran, T. (1995). The cognitive neuroscience of false memories. *Psychiatric Annals, 25,* 726–730.

Schacter, D. L., Reiman, E., Curran, T., Yun, L. S., Bandy, D., McDermott, K. B., & Roediger, H. L., III. (1996). Neuroanatomical correlates of veridical and illusory recognition memory: Evidence from positron emission tomography. *Neuron, 17,* 267–274.

Schiffer, F., Teicher, M. H., & Papanicolaou, A. C. (1995). Evoked potential evidence for right brain activity during the recall of traumatic memories. *Journal of Neuropsychiatry and Clinical Neurosciences, 7,* 169–175.

Schneider, S. L., & Laurion, S. K. (1993). Do we know what we've learned from listening to the news? *Memory & Cognition, 21,* 198–209.

Schooler, J. W., Clark, C. A., & Loftus, E. F. (1988). Knowing when memory is real. In M. Gruneberg, P. Morris, & R. Sykes (Eds.), *Practical aspects of memory: Current research and issues, Volume 1* (pp. 83–88). New York: Wiley.

Schulkind, J. (Ed.). (1976). *Moments of being.* New York: Harcourt Brace Jovanovich.

Schultz, D. P., & Schultz, S. E. (1996). *A history of modern psychology.* New York: Harcourt Brace.

Schweinberger, S. R., & Sommer, W. (1991). Contributions of stimulus encoding and memory search to right hemisphere superiority in face recognition: Behavioral and electrophysiological evidence. *Neuropsychologia, 29,* 389–413.

Searleman, A., & Carter, H. (1988). The effectiveness of different types of pragmatic implications found in commercials to mislead subjects. *Applied Cognitive Psychology, 2,* 265–272.

Searleman, A., & Herrmann, D. (1994). *Memory from a broader perspective.* New York: McGraw-Hill.

Semon, R. (1904/1921). *The mneme.* London: George Allen and Unwin.

Semon, R. (1909/1923). *Mnemic psychology.* London: George Allen and Unwin.

Shea, J. D. (1991). Suggestion, placebo, and expectation: Immune effects and other bodily change. In J. F. Schumaker (Ed.), *Human suggestibility: Advances in theory, research, and application* (pp. 253–276). New York: Routledge.

Sheingold, K., & Tenney, Y. J. (1982). Memory for a salient childhood event. In U. Neisser (Ed.), *Memory observed: Remembering in natural contexts* (pp. 201–212). San Francisco: Freeman.

Shepard, G., & Koch, C. (1990). Introduction to synaptic circuits. In G. Shepard (Ed.), *The synaptic organization of the brain.* New York: Oxford University Press.

Sherry, D. F. & Schacter, D. L. (1987). The evolution of multiple memory systems. *Psychological Review, 94,* 439–454.

Shields, C. (1993). *The Stone diaries.* New York: Penguin.

Shobe, K. K., & Kihlstrom, J. F. (1997). Is traumatic memory special? *Current Directions in Psychological Science, 6,* 70–74.

Sigurdsson, E., Gudjonsson, G. H., Kolbeinsson, H., & Petursson, H. (1994). The effects of electroconvulsive therapy and depression on confabulation, memory processing, and suggestibility. *Nordic Journal of Psychiatry, 48,* 443–451.

Silver, S. M., Brooks, A., & Obenchain, J. (1995). Treatment of Vietnam war veterans with PTSD: A comparison of eye movement desensitization and reprocessing, biofeedback, and relaxation training. *Journal of Traumatic Stress, 8,* 337–342.

Skinner, B. F. (1957). *Verbal behavior.* New York: Appleton-Century-Crofts.

Smith, J. A. (1994). Reconstructing selves: An analysis of discrepancies between women's contemporaneous and retrospective accounts of the transition to motherhood. *British Journal of Psychology, 85,* 371–392.

Smith, M. C. (1983). Hypnotic memory enhancement of witnesses: Does it work? *Psychological Bulletin, 94,* 387–407.

Smith, V. L., & Ellsworth, P. C. (1987). The social psychology of eyewitness accuracy: Misleading questions and communicator expertise. *Journal of Applied Psychology, 72,* 294–300.

Solso, R. L., & Massaro, D. W. (1995). *The science of the mind: 2001 and beyond.* New York: Oxford University Press.

Spanos, N. P. (1996). *Multiple identities and false memories.* Washington, DC: American Psychological Association.

Springer, S. P., & Deutsch, G. (1993). *Left brain, right brain.* New York: W. H. Freeman.

Squire, L. R., & Knowlton, B. J. (1995). Memory, hippocampus, and brain systems. In M. S. Gazzaniga (Ed.), *The cognitive neurosciences* (pp. 825–837). Cambridge, MA: MIT Press.

Squire, L. R., Knowlton, B. & Musen, G. (1993). The structure and organization of memory. *Annual Review of Psychology, 44,* 453–495.

Squire, L. R., & Zola-Morgan, S. (1991). The medial temporal lobe memory system. *Science, 253,* 1380–1386.

Stern, J. R., Brown, M., Ulett, G. A., & Sletten, I. A. (1977). A comparison of hypnosis, acupuncture, morphine, Valium, aspirin, and placebo in the management of experimentally induced pain. *Annals of the New York Academy of Sciences, 296,* 175–193.

Stern, L. B., & Dunning, D. (1994). Distinguishing accurate from inaccurate eyewitness identifications: A reality monitoring approach. In D. F. Ross, J. D. Read, & M. P. Toglia (Eds.), *Adult eyewitness testimony: Current trends and developments* (pp. 273–299). New York: Cambridge University Press.

Stevens, W. (1954). *Collected poems of Wallace Stevens.* New York: Knopf.

Stricker, G., & Trierweiler, S. J. (1995). The local clinical scientist. *American Psychologist, 50,* 995–1002.

Swain, R. A., Armstrong, K. E., Comery, T. A., Humphreys, A. G., Jones, T. A., Kleim, J. A., & Greenough, W. T. (1995). Speculations on the fidelity of memories stored in synaptic connections. In D. L. Schacter (Ed.), *Memory distortion: How minds, brains, and societies reconstruct the past* (pp. 274–297). Cambridge, MA: Harvard University Press.

Takehiko, O. (1997). Mastery and the mind. In I. Bloom & J. A. Fogel (Eds.), *Meeting of minds: Intellectual and religious interaction in East Asian traditions of thought* (pp. 297–340). New York: Columbia University Press.

Tan, A. (1991). Ten thousand things. *Lear's, 4(4),* 64–93.

Tartter, V. C. (1986). *Language processes.* New York: Holt, Rinehart, and Winston.

Taylor, S. E. (1983). Adjustment to threatening events: A theory of cognitive adaptation. *American Psychologist, 38,* 1161–1173.

Terr, L. (1981). Psychic trauma in children: Observations following the Chowchilla school-bus kidnapping. *American Journal of Psychiatry, 138,* 14–19.

Terr, L. (1983). Chowchilla revisited: The effects of psychic trauma four years after a school-bus kidnapping. *American Journal of Psychiatry, 140,* 1543–1550.

Terr, L. (1994). *Unchained memories.* New York: Basic Books.

Tolin, D. F., Montgomery, R. W., Kleinknecht, R. A., & Lohr, J. M. (1995). An evaluation of eye movement desensitization and reprocessing (EMDR). In L. Vandercreek, S. Knapp, & T. L. Jackson (Eds.), *Innovations in clinical practice: A source book* (pp. 423–437). Sarasota, FL: Professional Resource Press.

Tulving, E. (1972). Episodic and semantic memory. In E. Tulving & W. Donaldson (Eds.), *Organization of memory.* New York: Academic Press.

Tulving, E. (1983). *Elements of episodic memory.* Oxford: Clarendon Press.

Tulving, E. (1985). Memory and consciousness. *Canadian Psychologist, 26,* 1–12.

Tulving, E. (1991). Memory research is not a zero-sum game. *American Psychologist, 46,* 41–45.

Tulving, E. (1993). What is episodic memory? *Current Directions in Psychological Science, 2(3),* 67–70.

Tulving, E. (1995). Introduction. In M. Gazzaniga (Ed.), *The cognitive neurosciences* (p. 751). Cambridge, MA: MIT Press.

Tulving, E., & Donaldson, W. (Eds.). (1972). *Organization of memory.* New York: Academic Press.

Tulving, E., & Schacter, D. L. (1990). Priming and human memory systems. *Science, 247,* 301–306.

Tversky, B., & Tuchin, M. (1989). A reconciliation of the evidence on eyewitness testimony: Comments on McCloskey & Zaragoza (1985). *Journal of Experimental Psychology: General, 118,* 86–91.

Underwood, B. J. (1965). False recognition produced by implicit verbal responses. *Journal of Experimental Psychology, 70,* 122–129.

van der Kolk, B. A. (1994). The body keeps the score: Memory and the evolving psychobiology of posttraumatic stress. *Harvard Review of Psychiatry, 1,* 253–265.

van der Kolk, B. A., Pelcovitz, D., Roth, S., Mandel, F. S., McFarlane, A., & Herman, J. L. (1996). Dissociation, somatization, and affect dysregulation: The complexity of adaptation to trauma. *American Journal of Psychiatry, 153,* 83–93.

Van Lancker, D. (1991). Personal relevance and the human right hemisphere. *Brain and Cognition, 17,* 64–92.

Vargha-Khadem, F., Gadian, D.G., Watkins, K.E., Connelly, A., Van Paesschen, W., & Mishkin, M. (1997). Differential effects of early hippocampal pathology on episodic and semantic memory. *Science, 277,* 376–380.

Von Benedek, L. (1992). The mental activity of the psychoanalyst. *Psychotherapy Research, 2,* 63–72.

Wagenaar, W. A. (1986). My memory: A study of autobiographical memory over six years. *Cognitive Psychology, 18,* 225–252.

Wagenaar, W. A., & Groeneweg, J. (1990). The memory of concentration camp survivors. *Applied Cognitive Psychology, 4,* 77–87.

Warrington, E. K., & Weiskrantz, L. (1968). New method of testing long-term retention with special reference to amnesic patients. *Nature, 217,* 972–974.

Weaver, C. A., III. (1993). Do you need a "flash" to form a flashbulb memory? *Journal of Experimental Psychology: General, 122,* 39–46.

Weingardt, K. R., Toland, H. K., & Loftus, E. F. (1994). Reports of suggested memories: Do people truly believe them? In D. F. Ross, J. D. Read, & M. P. Toglia (Eds.), *Adult eyewitness testimony: Current trends and developments* (pp. 3–26). New York: Cambridge University Press.

Weingartner, H., Miller, H., & Murphy, D. L. (1977). Mood-state-dependent retrieval of verbal associations. *Journal of Abnormal Psychology, 86,* 276–284.

West, W. (1994). Post-Reichian therapy. In D. Jones (Ed.), *Innovative therapy: A handbook* (pp. 131–145). Buckingham, England: Open University Press.

Whitfield, C. L. (1995). *Memory and abuse.* Deerfield Beach, FL: Health Communications, Inc.

Whymper, E. (1871/1996). *Scrambles amongst the Alps.* New York: Dover.

Williams, J. M. G. (1992). Autobiographical memory and emotional disorders. In S. Christianson (Ed.), *The handbook of emotion and memory: Research and theory* (pp. 451–477). Hillsdale, NJ: Erlbaum.

Williams, J. M. G. (1996). Depression and the specificity of autobiographical memory. In D. C. Rubin (Ed.), *Remembering our past: Studies in autobiographical memory* (pp. 244–267). New York: Cambridge University Press.

Williams, J. M. G., & Broadbent, K. (1986). Autobiographical memory in attempted suicide patients. *Journal of Abnormal Psychology, 95,* 144–149.

Williams, J. M. G., & Scott, J. (1988). Autobiographical memory in depression. *Psychological Medicine, 18*, 689–695.

Winson, J. (1985). *Brain and psyche: The biology of the unconscious.* New York: Doubleday/Anchor Press.

Woods, A. (1998, March 3). Bodyguard remembers Princess Diana's voice after crash. *The Durango Herald,* p. 3B.

Woolf, V. (1940). A sketch of the past. In J. Schulkind (1976). *Moments of being.* New York: Harcourt Brace Jovanovich.

Yapko, M. (1994). *Suggestions of abuse.* New York: Simon & Schuster.

Yuille, J. C., & Cutshall, J. L. (1986). A case study of eyewitness memory of a crime. *Journal of Applied Psychology, 71*, 291–301.

Zaidel, D. (1995). Separated hemispheres, separated memories. Lessons on long-term memory from split-brain patients. In R. Campbell & M. A. Conway (Eds.), *Broken memories: Case studies in memory impairment* (pp. 213–224). Cambridge, England: Blackwell.

Zaidel, D. W. (1988). Hemi-field asymmetries in memory for incongruous scenes. *Cortex, 24*, 231–244.

Zaidel, D. W. (1991). Effects of violations of a face schema in the left and right hemispheres of split-brain patients and normal subjects. *Society for Neuroscience Abstracts, 17*, 867.

Zaidel, D. W., & Kasher, A. (1989). Hemispheric memory for surrealistic versus realistic paintings. *Cortex, 25*, 617–641.

Zaidel, D., & Sperry, R. W. (1974). Memory impairment after commissurotomy in man. *Brain, 97*, 263–272.

Zaidel, E. (1985). Language in the right hemisphere. In D. F. Benson & E. Zaidel (Eds.), *The dual brain: Hemispheric specialization in humans* (pp. 205–231). New York: Guilford Press.

Zajonc, R. B. (1968). Attitudinal effects of mere exposure. *Journal of Personality and Social Psychology Monograph Supplement, 9*, 1–27.

Zangwill, O. L., & Wyke, M. A. (1990). Hughlings Jackson on the recognition of places, persons, and objects. In C. Trevarthen (Ed.), *Brain circuits and functions of the mind: Essays in honor of Roger W. Sperry* (pp. 281–292). Cambridge, England: Cambridge University Press.

Zaragoza, M. S., & Mitchell, K. J. (1996). Repeated exposure to suggestion and the creation of false memories. *Psychological Science, 7*, 294–300.

Zelig, M., & Beidleman, W. B. (1981). The investigative use of hypnosis: A word of caution. *International Journal of Clinical and Experimental Hypnosis, 29(4)*, 401–412.

Zola-Morgan, S., & Squire, L. R. (1993). Neuroanatomy of memory. *Annual Review of Neuroscience, 16*, 547–563.

# Acknowledgments

Students in three of the memory courses that I taught during 1995 and 1996 urged me to write this book. Upon starting the project, I enlisted the aid of four undergraduates: Hillary Bish, Debbie Moore, and Messina Salazar gathered preliminary research materials, while JoAnn Herkenhoff served as my assistant for two years, conducting specific library research, reading chapter drafts, and typing in some of my revisions. Members of the Fort Lewis College library offered advice on obscure sources and secured hundreds of interlibrary loan requests. The academic administration of Fort Lewis College supplied a one-term sabbatical from teaching, which helped me to complete the project, and my colleagues campuswide provided encouragement. I also wish to thank the memory researchers who have devoted their energies to discovering the disciplinary knowledge that is described in this book. Many of my friends and relatives demonstrated a genuine and lasting interest in the manuscript, helping to buoy my efforts on slow days. I appreciate their kind words and expressions of support more than they will ever know. Most of all, I am grateful to Gerry Jones and Alan Krajecki for their unwavering faith in my abilities.

# About the Author

Janet L. Jones is a cognitive scientist who specializes in studying the processes that occur in the human mind and brain during perception, language use, memory, and thought. Originally from Arizona, she studied psychology and Chinese language at Pomona College in Claremont, California. A bachelor's degree from that institution was followed by her M.A. and Ph.D. in cognitive psychology from the University of California at Los Angeles. She is presently an associate professor of psychology at Fort Lewis College in Durango, Colorado. Since 1985, Dr. Jones has enjoyed teaching a wide variety of college courses in experimental psychology and cognitive science. Her own research and scholarship has also garnered several awards. She is an active member of the American Psychological Society, the American Psychological Association, the Western Psychological Association, the UCLA Psychological Alumni Association, the International Alliance of Teacher Scholars, the Association of American Colleges and Universities, Sigma Xi's International Scientific Research Society, and Phi Beta Kappa. Dr. Jones has published poetry, newspaper pieces, magazine essays, and scientific journal articles. This is her third book.

# Index

Abduction memories, 156, 169–170
Absentmindedness, 19. *See also* Forgetting, normal
Accuracy, 45–60
  autobiographical memory, 56–57
  correlation with confidence level, 55, 56
  emotional memory, 81–82
  equated with detail recall, 77, 82
  eyewitness memory, 49–52, 59
  flashbulb memory, 47–48
  high school grades recall, 48–49, 52
  traumatic memory, 104, 110
  *See also* Distortion, memory
Acetylcholine, 113
Active memory, 22
Agnosia, 140, 146, 152
Alcohol consumption, 80, 90, 121, 125
Alzheimer's disease, 20–21, 126, 143, 187, 218–219
American Association of Clinical Psychologists, 210
American Medical Association, 197
American Medical Society, 132
American Psychiatric Association, 208
American Psychological Association
  education/training criteria, 209
  ethics guidelines, 99
  eyewitness testimony survey, 98
  funding for collaboration, 221
  historic background, 207, 209–211
  practitioner licensing, 204–205
  traumatic memory studies, 110
American Psychological Society (APS), 211, 221
*American Psychologist* (journal), 19
American Society of Clinical Hypnosis, 197
Amnesia
  clinical, 117
  combat, psychosomatic symptoms, 130
  deficit localization, 140
  drug-related, skills retained, 121

frontal, overgeneral recall, 85
high-risk patients, 191
historic background, 11, 14
neurological, skills retained, 118
organic, 38, 102, 120–121, 126, 143
psychogenic, 101–102, 106, 121, 195, 218
source, 19, 76–78, 83, 169–170, 192
*See also* Childhood amnesia; Infantile amnesia
Amnesics
  implicit memory retention, 37, 120–121, 123–127
  procedural skill retention, 23, 36, 37, 121
Amphetamines, 90–91
Amygdala, 110, 111–114, 151
Amytal interviews, 181, 197–198
Anamnesis strategy, 86
*Annual Review of Neuroscience*, 212
*Annual Review of Psychology*, 212
Anxiety disorders, 85, 104
Aphasia, 14, 136, 139, 140, 152
Aristotle, 12–13, 45, 133
Aroma, 40, 91, 187
Arousal
  chemical link with memory, 104
  correlation with mood, 89–90
  physiological, 81, 82, 83
  terminology confusion, 100
Associative cortex, 39, 114, 126
Authority figures, confidence reinforcement, 77
Autism, 18
Autobiographical memory, 19
  altered by perspective, 30–31
  categories of knowledge, 71–72
  characteristics, 24–25, 128
  early childhood, 35, 39, 41, 162–163, 203
  false memory construction, 30, 58, 156, 162–167, 172
  integration with identity, 152
  post-traumatic shutdown, 101–103

retrieval to cues, 40, 57, 58, 70, 75, 150
retrieval to music, 187
source monitoring, 170, 172
*See also* Emotional memory; Ordinary
    memory; Traumatic memory
"Autonoetic" awareness, 23, 25, 38, 42

Barbiturates, 91, 198
Bartlett, Frederic, 77, 157
Basal ganglia, 23, 39, 114, 126
Behavioral therapies, 16–19, 80, 221
Bias, unconscious, 63
Binet, Alfred, 49
Bodily states, 80, 90–92. *See also* Alcohol
    consumption
"Body memories," 128–133
Bodywork therapy, 130–131
Bottom-up processing, 127
Brain assymetry. *See* Hemispheres, cerebral
Brain structure development, 32–34, 36–40
Brain structures
    consolidation sites, 72, 144
    distributed storage sites, 39
    episodic memory servers, 22, 38–39, 73,
        142, 153
    explicit memory creation, 125
    immature, 37–39, 42, 112, 203
    interactions between, 114, 139, 140
    language production sites, 22
    motor skills locus, 23, 126
    paleomammalian layer, 39
    priming function, 126
    rational thought mediators, 73, 80
    semantic memory servers, 22, 153
    sensory mediator, 32, 73, 111
    source monitoring, 170
    trauma memory systems, 110, 111–114, 151
    *See also* Hemispheres; Hippocampus
Brain surgeries, 33, 136, 138, 141
Broca, Paul, 14, 15, 17, 136

California Psychological Inventory (CPI), 92
Calvin, William, 225
Capgras syndrome, 152
Categorization, 62, 87, 89
Ceci, Stephen, 162, 163, 174
Cerebellum, 39, 114
Cerebral laterality. *See* Hemispheres, cerebral
Certification
    enforcement of, 210
    licensure, 4, 204, 223–224
    state, 208
*Challenger* explosion, 46–48, 81
Charcot, Jean, 13

Chemicals, natural, 113
Childhood amnesia, 19, 34, 36–37, 39, 41–43.
    *See also* Childhood trauma
Childhood memories, 36
    earliest reported, 28–31, 171, 203
    forgotten, 4, 19, 28, 34–36, 41, 42
    implanted, 175
    social effect, 165–166, 173, 175
    *See also* Infant memories
Childhood trauma, 29, 31, 98, 105, 118–119
Children
    declarative memory development, 35–40
    language acquisition theory, 17
    linguistic immaturity, 35, 37, 40–41, 42
    misinformation research, 49, 52
    overgenerality in recall, 85
    physical immaturity, 37, 112, 163, 171, 192,
        203
    retention of school lessons, 19, 67
    suggestibility, 51, 162–163, 167, 199
    toddler memory retention, 36, 41
Chomsky, Noam, 17
Chowchilla school bus incident (CA), 98, 105
Christianson, Swen, 98, 109
Claparède, Edouard, 120
Clinical psychology
    historic background, 15–16, 207–212
    *See also* Practitioners; Psychology;
        Research events
*Cognition and Emotion* (journal), 80
Cognitive interview, 188–190, 200
Cognitive processing
    automatic neuron activation, 168
    bottom-up, implicit, 127
    categorization, 62, 87, 89
    top-down, explicit, 127, 146, 157
*Cognitive Psychology* (Neisser), 17
Cognitive psychology, 17–20, 119, 188
Cognitive science, 20–21, 213
    assymetry studies, 38, 137
    false memory research, 191
    infantile amnesia research, 36
    interdisciplinary approach, 11, 20, 204, 205
    knowledge of brain/memory, 7, 11
    public opinion of, 20
    traumatic memory research, 114
Cognitive skills, 118, 120–121
Collective memory, nationistic, 78
Commisurotomy, 136, 138
Compartmentalization, memory, 103
Conceptual processing, 109
Confabulation, 170, 186, 188, 191, 198, 199
Confidence, rememberer, 54–57
    childhood rememberances, 29–30

correlation with accuracy, 55, 56
false memory recall, 158–162, 170, 174
flashbulb memory accuracy, 48
information source recall, 77
misinformation research on, 77, 157, 160–161
normal recall, 49
personal recollections, 182
recall under hypnosis, 195–196, 197
"remembering" versus "knowing," 160–162, 164, 168–169
traumatic memory recall, 105
Consolidation
  brain structures involved, 72, 144, 172
  chemical mediation, 112
  complete, 72
  post-traumatic, 108, 112
  unconscious biases, 63
Consolidation enhancement
  active learning exercises, 67
  sleep period, 72
Construction, unconscious, 157–158
  autobiographical memory, 25, 58
  compliance with internal goals, 75
  effect of prior knowledge, 77
  gap-filling, 69, 75, 82, 84, 169, 203
  *See also* False memories
Constructive memory theories, 77–78, 155–156
Context
  internal, 91
  retrieval conditions, 73, 90–92
  social, 183–184
Context-dependent memory, 80, 90–92
Context restatement, 187–188, 189, 200
Contextual memory, 82–83, 95, 107–108
Conversion disorder, 130, 131, 132
Corpus callosum, 136, 139, 140
Corticosterone, 112
Courage, Mary, 41
Creative Imagination Scale (CIS), 190

Damasio, Antonio, 80
Dax, Marc, 136
Decade of the Brain (1990s), 32
Declarative memory system, 35–39, 40–41, 112, 114
Deese, James, 158, 167
Depression
  clinical, 84, 93, 191
  comorbidity, 132
  cyclical, 84
  mood dependence, 88
  overgenerality in recall, 85–86

DES (Dissociative Experiences Scale), 190
Descartes, René, 118, 213
Detail recollection
  constructive, 157, 162–165, 171, 174
  emotional material, 82
  equated with accuracy, 54, 77, 82
  traumatic material, 104
*Diagnostic and Statistical Manual* (DSM-IV), 93, 131, 132
DID. *See* Dissociative identity disorder
Diencephalon, 22, 32, 125
Discourse analysis, 188
Dissociability, 191
Dissociated memories, 100, 130
Dissociative disorders, 14, 104
Dissociative identity disorder (DID)
  occurrance rate, 103
  post-traumatic, 101, 103, 104
  procedural memory retention, 121
The Dissociative Experiences Scale (DES), 190
Distortion, memory, 61–78
  during retrieval, 72–76
  during storage, 70–72
  emotions/mood, 74, 184, 187, 203–204
  expectations, 31
  inferences, 31, 62, 69
  normal inaccuracy, 58
  purpose/function, 62
  situational anxiety, 185
  social context, 183–184
  sodium amytal, 198
Dream interpretation, 5
Drug abuse treatment, 221
DSM-IV (*Diagnostic and Statistical Manual*), 93, 131, 132

Easterbrook hypothesis, 82, 107
Eating disorders, 132
Ebbinghaus, Hermann
  explicit word studies, 122
  fatigue studies, 16
  memory studies, 15
  mood dependence studies, 88
  nonsense syllable studies, 14, 71, 118
  theories of forgetting, 14, 71, 106
Education/training, 209, 212
  cognitive interview technique, 190
  memory components, 3–4, 7–8
  recommendations, 218–224
Eich, Eric, 89–90, 93
Eidetic memory, 19
Electrical stimulation, 113, 138–139, 143

Electroencephelograph (EEG), 138, 151
Electromyelograph (EMG), 151
Emotional memory, 79–94
    accuracy, 81–82
    central detail recall, 82, 95, 107, 108
    consistency, 83
    neurological basis, 111–113, 150–152
    versus "nonemotional" memory, 94
    vividness, 81–82
    *See also* Traumatic memory
Emotions
    anxiety, and amygdala, 111
    and emotional recall, 74, 92–93
    interwoven with cognition, 79–80, 92
    James-Lange theory, 79
    in memory categorization, 89
    motive mediation, 83, 88
    role in autobiographical memory, 25
    *See also* Arousal; Fear; Mood
Encoding process, 66–70
Encoding specificity, 188
Endorphins, 113
Engrams
    developed over time, 182
    petrified/impoverished, 76, 196
    research on, 77
    *See also* Traces, memory
Environment, physical, 80, 90–92. *See also*
    Context *entries*; Event schemata
Epilepsy, 37, 61, 236
Epinephrine, 112–113
Episodic memory
    "autonoetic" awareness, 23, 25, 38, 42
    characteristics, 22–25, 39, 50, 128, 203
    false memory construction, 156
    neural structures of, 38, 42, 110, 112,
      125
    research on, 35
    retrieval from, 73, 152–154, 188
    *See also* Events; Repisodic memory
Episodic memory loss, 101–102, 142, 143
Estrogen, 69, 143
Event-related potentials (ERPs), 138, 141, 151,
    152
Events
    date/time errors, 57–58
    generic event memory, 25
    neutral, detail recall, 82, 95, 107–108
    normal processing, 63, 104
    novel, and synapse creation, 68
    past event memory system, 22–24
    terminology confusion, 100
    *See also* Stressful events
Event schemata, 162, 167, 171–173

Event-specific knowledge, 71, 77
Expectations
    cultural, 63, 77, 157
    internal, 63–64
    of practitioner, 182, 194
    social, 173, 183–184, 192
    violation of, 146
Experimental psychology, 7
    historic background, 15–16, 206–212
    public opinion of, 18, 19, 20, 50
    research focus, 7, 204, 205, 215, 216–217
    *See also* Psychology; Research events
Expert witnesses, 51, 98, 208
Explicit memory, 24
    compared to implicit memory, 117–19,
      124–125, 127, 203
    top-down processing, 127, 146, 157
    *See also* Nonsense syllable studies; Priming
      studies
Eye movement desensitization and
    reprocessing (EMDR), 178, 222–223
Eyewitness memory, 49–52, 163
    accuracy rate, 59
    context dependence, 91
    effect of stress/violence, 51, 98, 104–107
    effect of weapons, 51, 80, 82–83
    false, 166–167, 192
    false conviction rate, 50
    misinformation effect, 52–54, 76, 106, 157,
      160, 169, 173, 194
    research methodology, 50
    survey of experts, 98
    *See also* Misinformation effect

False memories, 155–175
    aided by repetition, 160–161, 168, 193
    autobiographical, 25, 30, 58–59, 156–158,
      162–167, 171–172
    creation of, 167–173, 200
    detail construction, 54, 157, 162–165, 170,
      171, 174
    diagnosing, 173–175, 179, 181, 190–191
    false recall effect, 158–161
    false recognition, 158–160, 167, 174, 192
    implanted, 173, 175, 178, 217–218
    implicit associations, 158–161, 167–168,
      203
    normal inaccuracy, 58–60
    occurrance rates, 163, 165, 174–175, 199
    schematic reconstruction, 162, 171–173
    social effect, 158, 165–166, 173, 175,
      192–193, 200
    source amnesia, 169–171
    under hypnosis, 195–196

*See also* Construction, unconscious;
   Misinformation effect
Family photographs, 5
Fear, 79–80, 111, 113–114, 150
Fechner, Gustav, 14, 15
Field memory, 74
"Fight or flight" response, 112
Fisher, Ron, 188
Flashbulb memory, 19, 46–49
Flavor, 40, 91, 92
Forensic interviews, 184, 188–190
Forgetting, inhibited, 83, 104, 106
Forgetting, normal
   causing normal inaccuracy, 58, 62
   event repetition effect, 105
   measurement of rate, 14, 71
   memory decay, 16, 71, 125
   short-term memory, 21–22, 66–67
   theory formulation, 14
Foucaultian thought, 15
Freud, Sigmund
   memory research, 13–14, 15, 77, 119, 130
   psychoanalytic theory, 2, 28, 207–208
Frontal lobes, 14, 22, 38, 170
Fruzzetti, Alan, 51
Frye rule, 197
Fugue, 14, 101, 102–103, 106, 121

Gamma aminobutyric acid (GABA), 113
Gardner, Howard, 225
Gazzaniga, Michael, 147–150
Geiselman, Ed, 188
Gender differences, 141–142
General-event knowledge, 71–72, 77
Generalization, 69, 75
Glucose, 113, 138
Glutamate, 113
Gollin figure test, 120
Groups, self-help, 200
Gudjonsson Suggestibility Scale (GSS), 190
Guided imagery, 199
Gulf War (1991), 130

H. M., hippocampus loss, 37, 112, 120–121
Hall, G. Stanley, 206
Hallucination, 169, 182
Harsch, Nicole, 46–47
Hemisphere, left
   analytical/sequential processing, 137, 145
   damaged, and language, 136
   episodic memory encoding, 38
   intentional learning, 151
   interpretation, 147–150
   logical experience, 144

right hand control, 140
   speech abilities, 137, 142
   verbel memory, 136, 144
Hemisphere, right, 145–147
   damaged, overgeneral recall, 85
   emotional memory, 150–152
   episodic memory retrieval, 38–39
   holistic experience, 65, 144
   incidental learning, 151
   left hand control, 140
   linguistic capacities, 137, 140
   top-down processing, 146–147
   visual memory, 136, 142–146, 148–149
Hemispherectomy, 33, 138, 141
Hemispheres, cerebral, 135–154
   encoding/retrieval, 152–154
   handedness studies, 141–142
   music processing, 64–65, 137
   perceptual processing, 144
   subcortical transfer, 139
   veridicality, 147–150
   *See also* Hemisphere, left; Hemisphere,
      right; Split-brain studies
Hemispheric Encoding/Retrieval Assymetry
      model (HERA), 153, 170
Hemispheric expression, 199
HERA. *See* Hemispheric Encoding/Retrieval
      Assymetry model
Hippocampus, 114
   architectural evolution, 32–33, 68
   bypassed in trauma, 111–112
   and declarative memory, 112
   explicit memory formation, 37–39
   neuron potentiation, 68, 151
   role in recall, 73, 143, 144, 172
Hormonal mediation, 33, 69
Hormone imbalances, 143–144
Hormones, 69, 73, 112–113, 151
Howe, Mark, 41
Hull, Clark, 118
Human Capital Initiative Committee, 110
Huntington's disease, 126
Hypnosis, 194–197
   age regression, 197
   in memory recovery, 5, 178, 181, 182
   mood inducing, 88
   television technique in, 182, 196
Hypnotizability, 190, 191, 195
Hysteria, 11, 14

Identity
   creation/preservation, 2, 152
   post-traumatic dissociation, 103
   *See also* Autobiographical memory

Illusory memory, 158–162
Image scans, 18
Imagination, 169–170, 190, 191, 199
Implicit memory, 117–133
    among amnesics, 37, 120–121, 123–127
    bottom-up processing, 127
    compared to explicit memory, 24, 124–125,
        127, 203
    historic background, 118–119
    measurement methods, 121–124
    neurological process, 124, 125–127
    *See also* Priming studies
Infantile amnesia, 28–29, 31, 34, 38
    linguistic theory, 35, 37, 40–41, 42
Infant memories, 171
    age regression experience, 197
    birth memories, 195
    celebrity narratives, 27
    prenatal memories, 27–28, 31, 33
    retrieval misinformation, 5, 6
    stored/retrievable, 28, 156
    unsubstantiated speculation, 181
    *See also* Childhood memories
Infants
    "deferred imitation," 35–36
    motor responses, 34–35
    neurological development, 32–34, 36–40
    perceptual recognition, 34–35
    *See also* Children
Inference, 62, 75, 170
Intelligence testing, 49, 192, 207, 210
Interference, 62
    explicit versus implicit memory, 105
    eyewitness memory accuracy, 51
    and normal forgetting, 16, 62, 71
    and normal inaccuracy, 58
    proactive/retroactive, 181
    repisodic memory, 105
Interference studies, 223
Intermediate memory, 22
International Society of Hypnosis, 197

Jackson, Hughlings, 136, 145, 146
James-Lange theory of emotions, 79
Janet, Pierre, 13, 119, 130, 178

K. C., amnesic, 23, 38
Kihlstrom, John, 98
Koch, Sigmund, 224
Kraepelin, Emil, 16

Laboratory studies, 50, 215

Language disorder. *See* Aphasia
Lashley, Karl, 143
Learning
    consolidation techniques, 67
    emotional effects, 80
    foreign language study, 19
    intentional versus incidental, 151
    relearning previous knowledge, 118
Learning disorders, 207, 210
LeDoux, Joseph, 111
*Left Brain, Right Brain* (Springer; Deutsch),
    154
Lexical memory, 25, 50, 120, 121–122, 143
Licensure. *See* Certification
Lifetime-period knowledge, 72, 77
Limbic system, 125
Lobectomy, 138
Loftus, Elizabeth, 52–53, 163–164
Long-term memory, 18, 21–22, 71

Magnetic resonance imaging, functional
    (fMRI), 138
Marcher, Lisbeth, 131
McDermott, Kathleen, 158, 159–160
McDougall, William, 118
McGaugh, James, 98
Media, popular
    memory fallacies, 11, 27–28, 61–62
    as misinformation source, 6, 204, 224,
        225
    and sensationalism, 100, 106
    split brain reports, 135
    "truth serum" reports, 198
Medial temporal lobe system, 22, 37, 72, 73,
    144
Meltzoff, Andrew, 35–36
Memorization, 12, 13, 19. *See also* Nonsense
    syllable studies
Memory
    constructivist viewpoint, 77–78, 155–156
    mood-dependence, 79–95
    neural network model, 72
    normal inaccuracy, 58–60
    normal processes of, 62–63
    and self, 1–10, 15
        *See also* Autobiographical memory;
        Episodic memory; Metamemory;
        Procedural memory; Semantic memory
Memory focus
    central detail, 82, 95, 107–108
    peripheral details, 82–83, 95, 107–108
    weapon focus, 51, 80, 82–83

Memory improvement, 67, 109, 160–161, 168.
  *See also* Retrieval enhancement
Memory metaphors
  black box, 16, 19
  computer, 4, 19, 45–46
  internal photographer, 82
  video camera, 45–46, 78, 102, 155, 171, 174,
    180
*Meno* (Plato), 12
Metamemory, 180–183
  collective, 174
  faulty, 167, 171
  overconfidence in, 55–56
  patient knowledge of, 180–182, 188, 200
Methodological issues
  converging evidence, 142–143, 153
  ecological validity, 50
  ethical constraints, 50, 99, 167, 215
  flawed studies, 99–100, 105, 107–108, 148,
    152, 166, 222–223
  limits of technology, 141
  merit of memory studies, 14
Miller, George, 17, 224
Minnesota Multiphasic Personality Inventory
  (MMPI), 92
Misinformation effect, 52–54, 76, 106, 157,
    160, 169, 173, 194
Mnemonic interlock, 85
Mnemosyne, identified, 2, 12
Mood, 79–84
  congruence with memory, 87–90
  reinstating with music, 187–188
Mood dependent memory, 88–90
Mood disorders, 84–87
Motor skills, 34–35, 36, 118, 120, 126, 153
Muller-Lyer illusion, 65(figure), 66
Multiple personality disorder, 11, 14, 218–219
Munsterberg, Hugo, 49, 206
Music, 64–65, 137, 187

Narrative memory, 19, 25
National Institute on Drug Abuse, 221
National Science Foundation, 110
Naturalistic studies, 104–106, 108, 196
Neisser, Ulric, 17, 19, 46–48, 49, 58
Neural impulses, rate of travel, 113
Neural network activation
  internal spreading, 167–168, 171, 172
  source monitoring, 170, 172
Neural network model of memory, 72
Neurological development, 32–34, 36–40
Neurological plasticity, 33–34, 38, 68

Neurological systems theory, 125–126
Neurology, 15, 204, 206
Neuron potentiation, 68, 151
Neurons
  activation theories, 68, 72–73, 144, 167
  automatic activation, 89, 168, 170, 172
  death of, pruning, 34, 37, 38
  memory trace processing, 132–133, 143
  structure/function, 32, 38, 68
Neurotransmitters, 32, 73, 113–114, 203
Nobel Prize, 135, 136
Nonsense syllable studies, 14, 16, 49, 71, 118,
    157

Observer memory, 74
Ordinary memory, 109–111, 113, 127–128
Ornstein, Robert, 154
Overgeneral recall, 84–86

Pain, physical, 93, 195
Palmer, John, 52–53
Paranormal phenomena, 15–16, 118, 206
Parenting practices, 18, 86
Penfield, Wilder, 61–62, 138, 143
Perception, 63–66
  context dependence, 65–66, 91–92
  event, 63, 109
  mediated by inference, 69
  psychological, 14, 63
  sensory, 12, 25, 63–64, 91–92
Perceptual disorder. *See* Agnosia
Perceptual memory, 18, 25
Peripheral detail recall, 82–83, 95, 107–108
Permanent memory fallacy, 61–62, 66–67
PET scans
  described, 138, 141
  false memory studies, 174
  memory retrieval studies, 73, 153
  prefrontal cortex development, 38, 42
Phobia therapy, 18
Phonagnosia, 152
"Photographic" memory, 19
Piaget, Jean, 40, 167
Pinker, Steven, 225
Placebo effect, 191–192, 198
Poetzl, O., 118
Poole, Debra, 5–6
Popular psychology, 128, 204, 213, 224–225
Positron emission tomography. *See* PET scans
Postmodern era, 26
Post-traumatic stress disorder (PTSD)
  clinical studies, 103–104, 105, 106

occurrance rate, 104
overgenerality in recall, 85
somatic symptoms, 132
suppression of new events, 104
Practitioners
authority figure status, 54, 77, 184
expertise, 174, 214–215
licensure/certification, 4, 204, 208
memory knowledge deficit, 3–6
need for usable science, 8, 97, 100,
    216–217
orientation for new clients, 183–185
professional knowledge updates, 204,
    212
therapeutic use of recall, 58–59, 76, 90
Prefrontal cortex, 37–39, 42, 73, 114, 142, 153
Priming, emotional, 84
Priming studies, 120, 122–124, 125, 126, 151,
    215
Procedural memory
amnesic retention, 23, 36, 37, 121
characteristics, 23–24, 25, 128, 203
infantile, 35–36, 39
knowledge included in, 126
neural structures involved, 110, 126
retained for split-brain patients, 153
Progesterone, 69
Prosopagnosia, 146, 152
Psycholinguistics
foreign language learning, 19
language acquisition, 17, 37, 40–41, 42, 62
social conversation, 183–185
word retrieval, 117, 121–22, 158–159
*See also* Priming studies
Psychological shift, 36–37, 39
Psychological tests, 92–93, 190—191, 200
Psychology
acceptance as science, 15–16
clinical/experimental fissure, 7–8, 10, 205,
    218
cognitive, 17–20, 119, 188, 213
epistomology, 213–217
health/sport, 18
historic background, 11, 13–20,
    206–212
need for collaboration, 8, 114–115, 205–206,
    218, 220–223, 226
options for change, 217–226
popular, 128, 204, 213, 224–225
social, 173
*See also* Research events
The Psychonomic Society, 211

Psychosomatic illness, 130–132
Psychotherapy
Freudian influence, 28
historic background, 207–213
public opinion of, 18
*See also* Practitioners
PTSD. *See* Post-traumatic stress disorder

Questioning techniques, 200
cognitive interview, 188–189
distancing and pacing, 186–187
open-ended questions, 73, 185
police interrogation, 82

Rape recall, 101, 102, 166–167, 192
Reality monitoring, 169, 170, 191, 193
Recognition memory, 109, 146–147, 158–160,
    167, 174
Reconstruction, 58, 63, 162, 171–173
Recovered memory
ongoing debate, 156, 216, 217
post-traumatic, 101–103, 143
*See also* Repressed memory
Recovered memory movement, 11
Reduplicative paramnesia, 152
Rees-Jones, Trevor, 102
Rehearsal, 81, 109
Reich, Wilhelm, 130–131
Reincarnation memories, 156
*Remembrance of Things Past* (Proust), 91
"Reminiscence bump," 29, 39, 76
Repisodic memory, 25, 58, 105
Repressed memory
debates regarding, 204, 211, 212
as defense mechanism, 4
Freudian, 119
public knowledge of, 181
versus normal forgetting, 218
Research events
high school grades recall, 49
"lost in mall" memories, 164–165, 167
mousetrap accident, 162–163, 174
neighbor's pond incident, 157
reaction to violent visuals, 101, 106,
    107–108, 151
response to advertising, 69
simulated crime scenes, 51–52, 56, 160
spilled wedding punch, 165, 172
teacher's markers event, 184
traffic accident event, 53
voice change studies, 73
voting behavior, 157–158

"War of the Ghosts" study, 77–78
woodworking accidents, 196
word list studies, 157, 158–160, 167–168
Research issues
    conceptual confusion, 100
    false memory testing, 158, 163–165
    premature presentation, 100, 106
    terminology confusion, 21, 100, 212, 219
    *See also* Methodological issues
Restak, Richard, 225
Retrieval, memory
    authenticity determination, 173–175, 179,
        181, 190–191
    automatic associations, 73, 89, 159,
        167–168
    convergence zones, 144
    distortion process, 72–76
    enhanced for intense events, 83, 106
    hemispheric lateralization, 153
    language-based, 40–41
    mediated by inference, 69
    mood dependence, 88–90
    obstacles to, 191
    recall tests, 90, 109, 158–160, 167
    recognition tests, 109, 158–160, 167, 192
    successive recall in, 72, 73, 74–75
    *See also* Hypnosis; Questioning techniques
Retrieval enhancement, 177–201
    alternate modes of expression, 41, 186,
        189, 199
    context restatement, 187–188, 189, 200
    context similarity, 75, 90, 93
    mental health environment, 183–185
    metamemory education, 180–183
    mood induction, 89–90
    *See also* Memory improvement
Roediger, Henry, 126–127, 158, 159–160
Rubin, David, 25

Sacks, Oliver, 121, 225
Schacter, Daniel, 59–60, 72, 118, 121, 125–127
Self-concept, 1–10
    development of, 25, 41–43
    education/training for, 219
    experiential memory, 23
    personal history, 24, 26, 57
    present versus possible self, 70, 75
    shaped by memory, 2, 49, 67, 84, 87, 155
    *See also* Autobiographical memory
Self-help books, 204, 224
Self motivation, 88
Self-referential pronouns, 42

Semantic memory
    characteristics, 22–24, 25, 39, 128, 203
    false memory construction, 156
    long-term, 145
    lost to Alzheimer's disease, 143
    neural structures involved, 110, 125, 153
    post-traumatic shutdown, 102
    research on, 35
Semon, Richard, 77
Sensory cortex, 111, 112, 114
Seven, "magic number," 17
Sexual abuse memories, 181
Shobe, Katharine, 98
Short-term memory, 18, 37, 66
    terminology confusion, 21–22, 219
Skinner, B. F., 16, 17
Social desirability bias, 158, 165–166, 167,
    173, 175
Society for Clinical and Experimental
    Hypnosis, 197
Sodium amytal, 198
Somatic memory, 128–133, 188
Soul, 15
Source amnesia, 19, 76–78, 83, 169–170, 192
Source monitoring, 167, 169, 170–172
Speech impediments, 207
Sperry, Roger, 135, 136, 154
Split-brain studies
    deficits in patients, 153–154
    early assymmetry research, 136, 138
    emotional memory, 150
    facial recognition, 146–147
    interpretative left brain, 147
    lateralized stimulus presentation, 139–140,
        143, 145–149
Stanford-Binet IQ test, 49
Startle pathway, 113
Storage, memory
    distributed, 39, 70, 143–144, 145
    heightened emotion effect, 80, 98
    mediated by inference, 69
    unconscious biases, 63
    *See also* Consolidation; Encoding
Stressful events
    effect on court testimony, 98
    enhanced memory of, 98
    overgenerality in recall, 85–86
    *See also* Trauma; Traumatic memory
Suggestibility, 191–194
    in children, 162–163
    clinical environment, 76
    increased by rapport, 193

measuring, 190
reduced in trauma memory, 105–106
risk factor for memory flaws, 191
Suggestion
hypnotic, 182, 195, 197
memory implantation technique, 178
unintended, 179, 192–194, 197
Suicidal patients, 85
Surveys, 4–5, 45, 94, 98
Survivors memories
combat soldiers, 130
concentration camp, 130
Nazi holocaust, 104
Sylvian fissure, 14
Sympathetic nervous system, 104, 112
Synaptic connections, 32, 34, 38, 68, 74, 77

Terminology confusion, 21, 100, 212, 219
Terr, Lenore, 98, 105, 215
Testosterone, 69
Thalamus, 32, 73, 111
Therapists. *See* Practitioners
Thorndike, Edward Ivan, 16
Thorndike, L., 118
Thyroid, 143
Time passage
effect on memory accuracy, 56–57,
104–105, 109, 161, 192
rate of forgetting, 14
Titchener, Edward B., 15, 206
Top-down processing, 127, 146, 157
Topographical memory, 145
Tower of Hanoi puzzle, 120
Traces, memory
components of, 128
cued retrieval technique, 188
distributed storage, 39, 68, 70, 143–144,
145
neural manipulation, 132–133
*See also* Engrams
Trauma
associated disorders, 101–106
childhood, 29, 98, 105, 118, 119
physical, 102
repeated exposure, Type II, 104, 105, 215
sungle event, Type I, 105, 215
terminology confusion, 100
Traumatic memory, 97–115
characteristics, 107, 109–111, 127–128
enhanced, evidence for, 103–107
false, 166–167
impaired, evidence for, 100–103, 105,
106–107

implicit "body memory," 128–129, 132
neurological basis, 111–115, 151–152,
203
radical loss, 101–102
retention of, 98, 100, 104–106, 108,
118–119
retrieval techniques, 178, 187, 195
*See also* Amygdala; Emotional memory
"Truth serum," 198
Tulving, Endel
"autonoetic" awareness, 23, 25
hemispheric assymetry, 153, 170
multiple memory systems, 19–20, 22–23,
125–126

Van Lancker, Diana, 152
Vasopressin, 112
Verbal memory, 136
Verbal narrative
for memory retrieval, 25, 40–41, 58–59,
186, 189
self-concept creation, 25, 42
Veterans Administration, 208, 209
Violence, 51, 98, 104–105
Visual cortex, 63
Visual illusions, 64(figure), 65(figure), 66
Visual memory, 136

Wada test, hemisphere function, 139
Watson, John, 16
Weapons, 51, 80, 82–83
Williams, Mark, 84–85, 86
Witmer, Lightner, 16, 207
Word list research, 49–50
association studies, 16, 160
explicit word studies, 122
false memory studies, 157, 158–160,
167–168
word retrieval, 90, 117, 121–122,
158–159
*See also* Nonsense syllable studies
Working memory, 17, 22, 37, 67
World War II, 208, 210
Written memories
daily event diaries, 56, 87
of emotional events, 46–48, 104
journaling, 5, 198–199
police reports, 104
Wundt, Wilhelm, 14, 15, 206–207, 208

Yapko, Michael, 4, 5, 45

Zaidel, Dahlia, 145, 146, 154